Rethinking Asylum

Each year, hundreds of thousands of people apply for asylum in Europe, North America, and Australia. Some fear political persecution and genocide; some are escaping civil war or environmental catastrophe; others flee poverty, crime, or domestic violence. Who should qualify for asylum? Traditionally, asylum has been reserved for the targets of government persecution, but many believe that its scope should be widened to protect others exposed to serious harm. Matthew Price argues for retaining asylum's focus on persecution – even as other types of refugee aid are expanded – and offers a framework for deciding what constitutes persecution. Asylum, he argues, not only protects refugees but also expresses political values by condemning states for mistreating those refugees. Price's argument explains not only why asylum remains politically relevant and valuable, but also why states should dismantle many of the barriers that they have erected against asylum seekers over the last fifteen years.

MATTHEW E. PRICE holds a Ph.D. in Political Science from Harvard University and a J.D. from Harvard Law School.

Rethinking Asylum: History, Purpose, and Limits

MATTHEW E. PRICE

CAMBRIDGE
UNIVERSITY PRESS

CAMBRIDGE UNIVERSITY PRESS
Cambridge, New York, Melbourne, Madrid, Cape Town, Singapore, São Paulo, Delhi

Cambridge University Press
The Edinburgh Building, Cambridge CB2 8RU, UK

Published in the United States of America by Cambridge University Press, New York

www.cambridge.org
Information on this title: www.cambridge.org/9780521707473

First published 2009

Printed in the United Kingdom at the University Press, Cambridge

A catalogue record for this publication is available from the British Library

Library of Congress Cataloging in Publication Data
Price, Matthew E., 1975–
Rethinking asylum : history, purpose, and limits / Matthew E. Price.
    p.   cm.
ISBN 978-0-521-88116-6 (hardback) – ISBN 978-0-521-70747-3 (paperback)
1. Asylum, Right of.   I. Title.
K3268.3.P75   2009
342.08′3–dc22

                                                              2009004694

ISBN 978-0-521-88116-6 hardback
ISBN 978-0-521-70747-3 paperback

For Becky

Contents

Acknowledgments

I am grateful to a large number of people for their insight, generosity of spirit, and encouragement over the years. This project began in 2001 as a doctoral dissertation in Harvard University's Department of Government. The chair of my dissertation committee, Dennis Thompson, has been unflagging in his support ever since I stumbled into his office as a sophomore in college. I owe him a deep debt of gratitude for his guidance and mentorship, and for his patient willingness to comment on countless drafts of my writing over the years. Nancy Rosenblum has been a model advisor: her unfailingly wise counsel and warm encouragement have made all the difference to me. Glyn Morgan, with whom I first explored my interest in what we owe to those abroad, has always pushed me to have the courage of my convictions.

Matt Stephenson's insights were critical in initially giving shape to this project and in helping me to crystallize its argument, and Dan Markel offered very helpful last-minute suggestions that markedly improved the manuscript. The writing process would have been much less enjoyable without their friendship and intellectual companionship. Martha Minow generously read the entire manuscript and offered extremely useful suggestions. I am grateful for her sage advice, practical wisdom, and mentorship. The anonymous referees for Cambridge University Press similarly alerted me to holes in my argument and offered helpful suggestions on how to plug them. Judge Michael Boudin taught me to temper abstract theory with sensitivity to practical consequences. His approach to legal problem solving shaped my thinking in profound ways. A number of other teachers, friends, and colleagues generously offered me their comments on parts of the manuscript or engaged in discussion of its themes, including Debbie Anker, Arthur Applbaum, Sandra Badin, Noah Dauber, Christine Desan, Rosalind Dixon, Dan Ernst, Ben Friedman, Bryan Garsten, Yvonne Gastelum, Ryan Goodman, Andreas Kalyvas, Josh Kaul, Meg Mott, Andrea

Sangiovanni, Martin Sandbu, Richard Tuck, Kenneth Winston, Abby Wright, and the 2001–2002 fellows at Harvard's Center for Ethics and the Professions.

For funding and office space, I owe thanks to Harvard's Center for Ethics and the Professions, Center for International Development, and Center for European Studies, and to the Harvard Graduate Student Council.

An earlier version of Chapter 1 appeared as "Politics or Humanitarianism? Recovering the Political Roots of Asylum," in the *Georgetown Immigration Law Journal*, 19 (2005), pp. 277–311 and is reprinted with permission of the publisher, Georgetown Immigration Law Journal, © 2005. An earlier version of Chapter 4 appeared as "Unwilling or Unable: Asylum and Non-State Agents of Persecution," in *Passing Lines: Sexuality and Immigration*, edited by Brad Epps, Keja Valens and Bill Johnson González, published by Harvard University, David Rockefeller Center for Latin American Studies, 2005, pp. 341–64. An earlier version of Chapter 5 appeared as "Persecution Complex: Justifying Asylum Law's Preference for Persecuted People," in the *Harvard International Law Journal*, 47 (2006), pp. 413–67, © 2006 by the President and Fellows of Harvard College and the Harvard International Law Journal, www.law.harvard.edu/students/orgs/ilj. I am grateful for permission to reprint portions of those articles.

To my parents, who were proud instead of worried when I told them that I wanted to study political philosophy, my appreciation is unending.

Lastly, my friends tell me that it is no coincidence that I finally settled on a topic and began to write shortly after meeting Becky Anhang. Without her intellect, support, and patience, this book might never have been written. More importantly, with her partnership, my life while writing could not have been happier.

Introduction

In December 1994, Angela's 13-year-old daughter was killed by a gang member in the Tivoli Gardens area of West Kingston, Jamaica, where Angela lived. She reported the killing to the police and gave them the name of the gang member who had pulled the trigger. Three weeks later, her 21-year-old son was also shot and killed after he publicly vowed that his sister's killer would go to prison. The same week, gang members threatened Angela as well, accusing her of informing to the police. In search of safety, Angela moved to other parts of the island in 1996 and 1997, but in each place, she was subjected to sexual abuse by men who threatened to expose her identity. During that time, her brother was shot by the same gang, as was her boyfriend's eldest daughter. Finally, in 1998, she fled to the United Kingdom and claimed asylum.[1]

Alain Baptiste, a Haitian, noticed in 2003 that he had begun to lose weight and that he generally felt unwell. Concerned, he went to the doctor and tested positive for HIV.[2] Despondent, Alain decided he could not remain in Haiti. He feared that he would be ostracized once others found out about his HIV-positive status – which they surely would, given his deteriorating health. He was also likely to lose his job. Even more importantly, he would have no access to adequate medical care. In short, staying in Haiti would be tantamount to a death sentence. He left for the United States and sought asylum there.

Rodi Alvarado Peña's husband, Francisco Osorio, began to threaten and assault her soon after they were married in Guatemala. Once, when her period was fifteen days late, he broke her jaw. When he misplaced something, he would grab her head and strike furniture with it. As the marriage progressed, his violence became more frequent and increasingly severe. When Rodi complained that he was hurting her, he would reply, "You're my woman, you do what I say." On several occasions she fled to her relatives, but Osorio found her and dragged her home, beating her until she was unconscious. Rodi called the police for help on a number of occasions: three times her husband ignored police summons and no further action was taken; twice the police ignored her calls. Osorio had served in the military, and he told Rodi that calling the police was therefore useless. Once she appeared before a judge who said that he would not intervene in a domestic affair. Ultimately, Rodi left for the United States to seek asylum. Her sister subsequently told her that Osorio had left word that he would "hunt her down and kill her if she [came] back to Guatemala."[3]

Should Angela, Alain, and Rodi be permitted to remain in their countries of refuge? The ordinary avenues of immigration are closed to them: they have neither relatives there nor employable skills. They hope to be granted asylum, an exception to the usual restrictions on immigration. Each year in Western Europe, North America, and Australia, over 500,000 people apply for asylum – many (though not all) with stories as deserving of sympathy as those of Angela, Alain, and Rodi. Sadly, stories of human tragedy are seemingly infinite in their variety. What criteria should determine whether these asylum seekers receive a reprieve from deportation?

Some would respond to this question by challenging its premise: states should open their borders to all who seek to enter. Immigration restrictions, the argument goes, are the modern-day equivalent of feudalism, dividing the world into haves and have-nots based upon the utterly arbitrary fact of where one happens to be born. Justice requires that one's life chances should not be dependent on such arbitrary facts, and so the freedom to move across borders should be regarded as a basic right.[4] As a matter of theory, much can be said for this position. As a practical matter, it is a political non-starter. Immigration quotas might be increased, but they will not be abandoned altogether; and, for the foreseeable future, ordinary immigration is likely to remain available only to those who have something to offer: job skills; resources to invest; a family connection to citizens or permanent legal residents; or (in some places) a shared ethnicity.

Others might respond by challenging the premise from the opposite direction: why should states *ever* offer a reprieve from immigration controls when closed borders advance the national interest? Our obligation to help others, the argument goes, is limited to those who are already members of our society. It stems from a shared national identity, or alternatively, from a tacit social contract among compatriots.[5] While we may allow outsiders to become members of our society when it serves our collective interest to do so, why should we ever be obligated to admit them?

One answer to this challenge appeals to what is known as the duty of "mutual aid": when a person urgently needs one's assistance to avoid serious harm, and one can provide that assistance at minimal cost or risk to oneself, one has a moral duty to do so.[6] For example, if a person were to pass a child drowning in a shallow pond, he would have a moral duty to assist, even if he might get his pants dirty in the process. The danger faced by the child is extreme and urgent, and the cost and risk of assistance negligible. This duty follows from our recognition of others' humanity: other people deserve our moral concern because of their capacity for suffering in the way that we suffer. Refugees, like children drowning in shallow ponds, urgently need assistance, and states can provide refuge at very low cost – at least when the number seeking refuge is small. Opinions can differ about when that threshold is passed – are 10,000 refugees too many to absorb easily? Perhaps 50,000 or 500,000? – but that is a question of implementation, not of principle.*

Further, as a practical matter, asylum is deeply rooted in the traditions and political narratives of Western states. Arguments persist about whether it should be broader or narrower in scope, but few campaign for its elimination altogether. Indeed, it is striking that over the past fifteen years – a period in which states have adopted a variety of measures designed to make it more difficult to file an asylum claim – no state has moved to abandon asylum altogether, or even to narrow substantially the substantive grounds for eligibility.

***

So the question remains: who should be eligible for asylum? Who should benefit from this loophole in otherwise restrictive immigration

---

* When a state is directly responsible for making a foreigner's homeland uninhabitable, it may have more demanding obligations toward those foreigners. In such a case, restorative justice demands that the state rectify conditions of insecurity that it has directly caused. The paradigmatic historical example is the American acceptance of tens of thousands of Vietnamese refugees in the late 1970s. See Michael Walzer, *Spheres of Justice* (New York: Basic Books, 1983), p. 49. A similar obligation arguably exists today for the resettlement by the United States of some of those displaced by the Iraqi war – especially for those whose lives are endangered because of the help they provided to the coalition forces.

Some may be tempted to argue further that states are responsible for refugee flows, and are thereby specially obligated to refugees, merely because they offered diplomatic or political support to a persecutory regime or imposed destabilizing structural adjustment programs on developing economies through the IMF or World Bank. That, however, stretches the concept of special obligation, created by direct responsibility, too far.

policies? The traditional answer holds that asylum is meant to protect those who have a "well-founded fear of being persecuted for reasons of race, religion, nationality, membership of a particular social group, or political opinion." This standard – which I call "the persecution requirement" – reflects the definition of "refugee" in the 1951 UN Convention Relating to the Status of Refugees and the corresponding 1967 Protocol, and it is found in the laws of virtually every Western state.[7] Jews in Nazi Germany and dissidents in the Soviet Union are the classic examples of persecuted people, targeted by the state for harm on account of an immutable characteristic or political beliefs.

The persecution requirement seemed natural in a Cold War world in which those who sought refuge in the West typically fled from strong, oppressive states. Today, many of those who seek asylum – such as Angela and Rodi – flee violence committed by groups as varied as guerrilla armies, death squads, criminal gangs, family members, and clans, as well as government security forces. Many are not themselves targets, but rather are simply victims – people caught in the cross-fire of anarchic violence. Others flee grinding poverty, famine, natural disaster, or – like Alain – seek access to life-saving medical treatment. These realities have put pressure on the traditional focus of asylum. Limiting asylum to persecuted people may seem too narrow: those fleeing from the violence that accompanies state breakdown and civil war, or from famine or extreme poverty, need protection from harm just as much as do persecuted people.

Accordingly, asylum is now discussed by academics, refugee advocates, and increasingly by courts, in *humanitarian* terms: as a kind of escape valve to otherwise restrictive immigration policies, intended to provide protection for foreigners who face serious threats of any kind to their security. A humanitarian theory of asylum suggests that eligibility ought to be widened beyond the persecuted. Scholars Aristide Zolberg, Astri Suhrke, and Sergio Aguayo suggest that "[a]n optimal policy would start from the explicit premise of moral equivalence" among targets of persecution and other victims of violence:

Whether the individuals are activists or passive bystanders simply caught in [a] conflict is immaterial from the point of view of their immediate security. Their need clearly could be the same regardless of the cause ... It follows that in a ... normative sense, the three types of refugees are equally deserving. The activist, the target, and the victim have an equally valid claim to protection from the international community.[8]

From a humanitarian perspective, a foreigner's *need for protection* – regardless of whether that need results from persecution, civil war, famine, extreme poverty, or some other cause – grounds a claim for asylum.[9] The more serious and urgent is the need for protection, the stronger is that claim.

This humanitarian view of asylum's purpose enjoys widespread support among scholars and refugee advocates.[10] It is not hard to see why: urgency of need for protection provides a morally appealing yardstick for the strength of one's asylum claim because it adopts the victim's viewpoint. Drawing a distinction between various causes of insecurity – for example, persecution on the one hand, and civil war on the other – intuitively seems morally dubious. Why should our duty to assist people depend on the *reason* they are in distress? Isn't it the *fact* of distress that should matter? It is certainly what matters to victims: it makes no difference to people dodging bullets whether or not they are the intended target.

The humanitarian view is increasingly reflected in international law and practice. At the regional level, as early as 1969, the Organization of African Unity extended its definition of the "refugee" to cover not only persecuted people, but also those forced to flee abroad "owing to external aggression, occupation, foreign domination or events seriously disturbing public order."[11] In 1984, Latin American states issued the non-binding Cartagena Declaration on Refugees which "enlarg[ed] the concept of a refugee" to include those who flee due to "generalized violence, foreign aggression, internal conflicts, massive violation of human rights, or other circumstances which have seriously disturbed the public order."[12]

The United Nations High Commissioner on Refugees (UNHCR) has followed suit. In 1994, it noted that individuals' "need for international protection" – a category broader than "fear of persecution," since a need for protection can arise due to many causes other than persecution – "most clearly distinguishes refugees from other aliens."[13] More recently, the UNHCR has explicitly endorsed the protection of "human security" as its guiding principle, suggesting that aid should be directed not only at those who flee their countries because of persecution, but also at those whose basic security and subsistence needs are unmet.[14] As one observer has noted, this position marks an important shift for the UNHCR: "It is no longer the quality of 'refugee,' however defined, that entitles one to protection. It is the need for protection that entitles one to treatment as a refugee"[15] – that is, to eligibility for asylum.

While the persecution requirement remains on the law books in virtually every Western state, over the last fifteen years courts in Australia, Canada, Britain, New Zealand, the United States, and elsewhere have broadened their interpretation of "persecution" in order to make asylum available to many groups traditionally excluded, including battered women and people fleeing ethnic conflicts.[16] Commonwealth courts in particular have linked refugee law to human rights law, interpreting "persecution" as "the sustained or systemic violation of human rights demonstrative of a failure of state protection."[17] This approach, much celebrated by refugee advocates, has significantly broadened eligibility for asylum to include claimants who have been victimized by private parties (as opposed to government agents).

Moreover, the United Kingdom and Canada have effectively amended the persecution requirement by granting the same legal status to certain non-persecuted refugees as they do to those who are persecuted. In the UK, "humanitarian protection" is available under the rubric of asylum to those who face a "real risk" of torture, inhuman or degrading punishment, the death penalty, unlawful killing, or a "serious and individual threat to a civilian's life or person by reason of indiscriminate violence in situations of international or internal armed conflict."[18] In Canada, asylum is available not only to persecuted people, but also to those who face a substantial risk of torture or an individualized risk to their lives against which the state is unable or unwilling to provide protection, unless caused by the inability of that state to provide adequate medical care.[19]

The end of the Cold War has affected public thinking about asylum in another respect as well. During the Cold War, asylum was viewed in *political* terms: intertwined with foreign policy, asylum was a vehicle for expressing Western political values. Asylum seekers were seen as "ballots for freedom,"[20] symbols of liberal democracy's ideological superiority over Communism. By labeling those who fled the Eastern Bloc as "persecuted" – a word that reflects a value judgment – the West expressed its condemnation of Communist regimes. One unfortunate consequence of investing asylum with an ideological valence was that states were often unwilling to shelter refugees who fled from friendly authoritarian regimes (for example, those who fled from El Salvador to the United States during the 1980s).

In a post-Cold War world, one less defined by grand ideological struggle, a political conception of asylum – according to which asylum expresses political values and communicates condemnation of persecuting regimes – is in disfavor. The same impulse driving humanitarianism also suggests that asylum should be politically neutral. What matters from the humanitarian point of view is whether asylum seekers need protection. From that perspective, identifying and calling to task the party responsible for an asylum seeker's insecurity is not only beside the point, but can interfere with the purpose of asylum to protect. This position was reflected as early as 1967 in the UN General Assembly Resolution on Territorial Asylum: "The grant of asylum by a State is a peaceful and humanitarian act and … as such, it cannot be regarded as unfriendly by any state."[21] Similar sentiments have been repeated in other international conventions,[22] and have been widely endorsed in the academic literature.[23] From a humanitarian standpoint, asylum has a "palliative" purpose.[24]

In sum, the last fifteen years have seen a marked shift away from what I call a "political" conception of asylum, one focused on helping persecuted people, expressive of value judgments about the conduct of persecuting states, and connected to a broader political program to reform those states. There has been instead a move toward a politically neutral "humanitarian" view, focused on helping people exposed to harm regardless whether that harm stems from persecution or some other cause.

***

The last fifteen years have also been a period of crisis for asylum policy. The number of asylum applications in industrialized countries has soared from only 13,000 per year in the 1970s to about 200,000 in 1985, reaching a peak in 1992 at over 857,000 due to an influx of refugees from the former Yugoslavia, largely to Germany (which received 438,191 asylum seekers that year). After dipping slightly in the mid-1990s, the number of applications climbed again, from about 375,000 in 1997 to over 625,000 in 2002 (see Figure I.1, below).[25]

The surge in asylum seekers was followed by an intensifying public backlash. Asylum seekers were decried as "economic migrants" in search of jobs who used asylum to circumvent otherwise restrictive immigration controls, and as "bogus" applicants who were drawn to the West by the promise of welfare benefits. Many also saw asylum seekers as a cultural threat whose presence in large numbers could undermine the liberal and secular values of their host countries.

Critics pointed not only to the historically unprecedented levels of new asylum applicants, but also to states' utter ineffectiveness at removing hundreds of thousands of asylum seekers whose claims had been rejected.

Suspicion of asylum seekers has been exacerbated by fears of terrorism. Such concerns were present even before September 11, 2001. Following the 1993 World Trade Center bombing, carried out in part by Ramzi Yousef, who had entered the US as an asylum seeker, the US Congress enacted legislation substantially curtailing asylum seekers' procedural rights.[26] After 9/11, the disclosures that one of the hijackers had gained residence in Germany by filing for asylum and that Ahmed Ressam, who plotted to blow up Los Angeles International Airport, had gained entry to Canada as an asylum seeker, reinforced fears that al-Qaeda operatives could use the asylum system to evade immigration controls.[27] Moreover, law enforcement authorities have expressed concern that transnational human smuggling and trafficking gangs, which themselves may have ties to terrorists, receive significant income from smuggling asylum seekers across borders.[28]

In response to public hostility toward asylum seekers, states have adopted a broad array of measures to reduce the number of applicants. These include barriers to entry that prevent asylum seekers from arriving in the first place, such as visa requirements and the interception of asylum seekers on the high seas; onerous procedural requirements, such as filing deadlines, that make it more difficult for an asylum claim to be heard on its merits; reductions in the public benefits available to asylum seekers while their applications are pending; detention of asylum seekers pending determination of their status, often in facilities housing criminals; and expedited proceedings, with minimal judicial review, designed to remove failed asylum seekers quickly. These policies are blunt instruments, largely failing to distinguish between those who seek asylum in bad faith and those who are genuinely eligible. Efforts to crack down on asylum seekers led to a sharp reduction in applications filed in industrialized countries between 2003 and 2006, from 625,000 in 2002 to barely 300,000 in 2006 (see Figure I.1, below). The number of applications filed in 2006 in Germany was the lowest since 1983; in Australia, the lowest since at least 1989; in Belgium, the lowest since 1995.[29]

In the past fifteen years, states have also begun offering less to those applicants who actually receive asylum. While traditionally recipients of asylum have received permanent residence and citizenship in the state

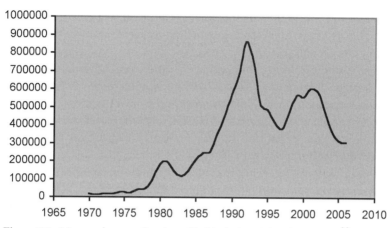

Figure I.1. New asylum applications filed in industrialized countries[30]

of refuge fairly quickly after being granted asylum, increasingly states have given asylum recipients only "temporary protection." After a predetermined period of time, usually somewhere between one and five years, recipients are required to re-prove their need for continuing protection or face deportation.[31] Temporary protection is attractive to states for several reasons. First, it "prevent[s] the permanent integration of foreigners" and, therefore, advances states' "objective to control migration."[32] Second, temporary protection can be used by states to justify cutting back the rights and benefits they offer to recipients of asylum: when shelter is presumed to be temporary, states have less reason to invest in refugees' integration. Indeed, temporary protection reflects a trend toward giving refugees the bare minimum consistent with states' international law obligation of non-refoulement – that is, the duty not to expel or return refugees to territories where their lives or freedom would be threatened on account of race, religion, nationality, membership of a particular social group, or political opinion.[33]

In the last seven years, asylum has grabbed the headlines more in Britain than anywhere else, where the number of new applicants surged from about 32,000 in 1996 to over 103,000 in 2002. After the introduction of stern measures designed to deter such applications, the number of new applicants in Britain was down sharply in 2003 and continued to fall through 2006, to 27,850 – the lowest number of applications in that country since 1989.[34] Nonetheless, public opinion remains hostile to asylum seekers. In a 2004 poll, 82 percent of Britons thought that the government could "do more" to "to ensure Britain is not seen as a soft touch for bogus asylum seekers." In 2003, 67 percent thought a "small minority" – less than a quarter – of asylum seekers were "genuinely fleeing persecution."[35] And in a 2002 poll, 43 percent of Britons thought that asylum seekers sought refuge in Britain for economic reasons or to look for work, up from 11 percent in 1997.[36] Asylum seekers are regularly attacked in the tabloids as leeches on Britain's welfare state, and the government is assailed for having lost control of its borders.

Public support for restrictive measures may be connected in three ways with the shift from a political to a humanitarian view of asylum. First, the humanitarian view decouples asylum from foreign policy and thereby diminishes its ideological significance. When asylum is no longer seen as intertwined with foreign policy, the public may be less supportive of it. Along these lines, refugee scholar Andrew Shacknove has written:

During the Cold War the refugee regime, reconstituted under the aegis of the United Nations, served the new ideological purposes of the [Western] States ... Many policy innovations in the affluent States reflect a basic doubt about whether asylum any longer serves their interests ... In a period when communism has ceased to be a serious ideological force and asylum States are experiencing low economic growth and heightened demand for entry, concern with domestic tranquility exceeds any possible ideological benefit derived from granting asylum.[37]

One should not be surprised at Western states' waning enthusiasm for asylum when the only motivation for granting it is humanitarian compassion.

Second, the humanitarian view pushes toward expanding eligibility for asylum beyond the persecuted. But, as immigration expert David Martin has argued, political realities make asylum a "scarce resource." Western publics support asylum as a way to help people who truly need assistance, but only if they feel assured that their obligations are limited and that border controls are being maintained. If the public perceives that the asylum system is being used as a loophole by "ordinary" immigrants, and that "resettlement rights are not being reserved only for those who show the kind of special threat that clearly justifies an exception from the usual rigours of the immigration law,"[38] resistance toward asylum will increase. When courts widen eligibility for asylum – by treating more types of harm as "special threats" justifying an exception from border controls – they may stoke the public's fear of opening the floodgates, and thereby cement support for restrictive measures that prevent asylum claims from ever being made.

Third, a humanitarian approach to asylum is intertwined with the trend toward temporary protection, with fewer rights and benefits, and away from permanent resettlement. If the purpose of asylum is solely to address the refugee's immediate need for protection, it is hard to see why refuge continues to be needed once that immediate threat has passed. Thus, the humanitarian approach implies that protection should be only temporary. And when asylum recipients are seen as temporary sojourners admitted for humanitarian purposes, rather than putative members admitted to effectuate the asylum state's own ideological commitments, states more readily "contest[ ]" the "boundaries of ... humane treatment"[39] and offer less in the way of benefits and social services.

Asylum policy over the last fifteen years has thus been marked by two trends. One trend is in the direction of liberalization, through court decisions granting asylum to previously excluded applicants. The other is in the direction of restriction, stimulated by public resistance to rising numbers of applicants. The grounds for eligibility are thus broader today than two decades ago, but various restrictive measures make it much harder for refugees to get their claims heard. Both trends are linked to a shift from a "political" view of asylum, focused on assisting persecuted people and thus expressive of political values, to a politically neutral "humanitarian" view aimed more broadly at assisting anyone in need of protection, whether persecuted or not. The humanitarian approach pushes toward expanding eligibility for asylum beyond persecution; but it also empties asylum of ideological significance, leaving skeptical publics to wonder whether asylum isn't merely a welfare program for the rest of the world.

***

At such a time, a reassessment and articulation of asylum's theoretical underpinnings is especially important. Whom is asylum supposed to benefit? What purpose does it serve? What is lost when states close their doors to those seeking refuge? This book offers a theory of asylum that explains and justifies asylum's traditional focus on persecuted people, as well as the importance of its continuing vitality.

The argument for reserving asylum for persecuted people is premised on the fact that asylum is just one of many ways to help refugees. For example, states also distribute relief and development aid to refugees who remain in their countries or regions of origin. Indeed, many in refugee policy circles say that more resources should be devoted to solving the root causes of refugee flows rather than treating the symptoms.[40] Asylum is also just one of several ways in which states admit refugees to their territory. States also offer "humanitarian protection," often on a temporary basis, to some refugees who do not qualify for asylum but who are nonetheless in need of protection; and some states have overseas refugee resettlement programs, under which a limited number of refugees are selected abroad, often by the UNHCR, and resettled in host states.

A persuasive theory of asylum should begin by asking what is distinctive about it. What does it accomplish that other modes of assistance cannot? What value does asylum add to the "refugee policy toolkit"? The humanitarian approach to asylum cannot offer a compelling answer to this question. Asylum, after all, is a very inefficient medium for humanitarian assistance. There are over 9 million refugees recognized by the UNHCR in the world today. Only a small fraction of these people receive asylum in Western states; the vast majority are unable to make their way to Europe or North America where they would be able to apply. Asylum, therefore, neglects those refugees who arguably need protection the most: those who lack the resources and mobility to remove themselves from the zone of danger.

Moreover, the cost of administering asylum programs is high because an individualized determination of eligibility is usually required; drawn-out proceedings create an incentive to file applications in bad faith, since asylum seekers are generally shielded from deportation until their applications are reviewed; and in the EU and Canada, states must foot the bill for social services like housing and health care while applications are pending. In 2003, for example, Britain spent more than $1.5 billion to support 93,000 asylum seekers.[41] Meanwhile, the entire UNHCR budget, meant to provide relief for over 20 million refugees and internally displaced persons, amounted to $1.17 billion in that year, of which the UK donated about $47 million.[42]

From a humanitarian perspective, it is hard to see why one should prefer asylum to other, less costly ways of helping refugees. Thus, the refugee scholars and advocates James Hathaway and Alexander Neve and law professor Peter Schuck have argued for a shift from permanent asylum in industrialized countries to temporary protection programs located in refugees' regions of origin. Such an approach would recognize the interest of the industrialized states in controlling unwanted migration and "free up substantial sums of money ... presently wasted on the processing of non-genuine claims in the North," while at the same time ensuring that those in need of protection will still receive it.[43] These scholars are right that asylum should not be regarded as the main solution to the predicament of the world's refugees, but their approach presumes that asylum is merely one more humanitarian program for refugee relief that can be readily replaced by other such programs, like temporary protection.

According to the political view of asylum, the humanitarian approach is bottomed on a conceptual error: it treats persecution as simply another kind of harm, and asylum as one of several more or less interchangeable forms of relief. But persecuted people face a distinctive kind of harm that sets them apart from other people who need protection abroad. They do not merely experience insecurity; they are targeted for harm in a manner that repudiates their claim to political membership. They are thus not only refugees, but also exiles – people who have been expelled from their own political communities. Asylum responds to that distinctive kind of harm by providing a distinctive remedy. It communicates condemnation of the persecutory regime responsible for the persecuted refugee's plight, and, in recognition of the unique harm that persecuted people have suffered, offers them surrogate political membership (not merely protection) in the state of refuge. By contrast, the humanitarian approach is directed toward the asylum seeker's welfare and communicates nothing to their state of origin. It is palliative: it is concerned exclusively with providing asylum seekers with the protection that, for the moment, they lack.

Thus, according to the political conception, even if refugee policy on the whole should be more oriented toward meeting people's basic needs, asylum is the wrong tool to accomplish that broad humanitarian mission. Nor, contrary to the suggestion of Hathaway, Neve, and Schuck, should asylum be abandoned in favor of other refugee policy tools. Asylum responds to the distinctive situation of persecuted people, who have been expelled from their political communities, by expressing condemnation of persecutory regimes and by providing a remedy – surrogate membership abroad – that matches the special harm they have suffered. These unique characteristics of asylum explain why, despite its inefficiency as a form of humanitarian relief, it is nonetheless a valuable instrument in the refugee policy toolkit.

A political approach to asylum has deep historical roots. Chapter 1 explores asylum's origins in ancient Greece and early modern Europe, and concludes that asylum originally was a legal defense to extradition. By granting it, a state conferred immunity against another state's attempt to exercise jurisdiction. States justified their decision to grant asylum, rather than extradite, by highlighting the injustice that fugitives would face were they returned to their state of origin. Asylum, in other words, depended upon a judgment that another state targeted the asylum seeker for harm in a manner inconsistent with its rightful authority. The persecution requirement reflects the historic centrality of such a judgment to asylum.

Chapter 2 argues that we should continue to think about asylum's purpose in political, rather than humanitarian, terms. Asylum's expressive dimension differentiates it from other modes of refugee assistance, which are focused exclusively on meeting refugees' need for protection, and reflects the recognition that persecution is a distinctive kind of harm that calls for confrontation and condemnation. Chapter 2 outlines the advantages of treating asylum as expressive of political values. First, asylum can facilitate the further development and entrenchment of international norms against oppression and violations of human rights. These norms in turn can affect state behavior, either by leading states to conform their behavior to human rights norms in order to achieve domestic and international legitimacy, or by socializing political elites to internalize human rights values.

Second, asylum's expressive character allows it to play an important role in the enforcement of international norms against outlaw states. States that produce large numbers of asylum seekers could be placed on a kind of probation for failing to respect their citizens' basic human rights. Asylum thus serves as a low-level sanction against such states, cautioning them that if abuse continues, more powerful sanctions, such as sponsorship of opposition groups or even direct military intervention (for example, in the case of genocide), may be forthcoming. Such a role would make asylum an integral part of the emerging doctrine of "conditional sovereignty": states that are unwilling to protect their citizens from serious harm cannot rely on the doctrines of sovereignty and non-intervention to prevent interference by the international community. Third, an expressive asylum policy can provoke reflection and dialogue in receiving states about their own political values, and about whether their foreign policy corresponds to those political values.

Chapters 3 and 4 consider in greater detail what constitutes "persecution" and the consequences of a political approach to asylum for applicants like Angela, Alain, and Rodi. Chapter 3 focuses on harm carried out by governments. It contends that the label "persecution" describes conduct sufficiently odious that bystander states are justified in interfering in the internal affairs of the persecutory state. When such harm is inflicted on a substantial portion of a state's population, asylum by itself is an inadequate response. More damaging sanctions are appropriate, including (in extreme cases) military intervention. But when such harm is inflicted on only a few, system-wide sanctions may be disproportionate. Instead, bystander states should resort to more targeted sanctions, and asylum is one such sanction. It enables states to protect victims of extreme abuse while at the same time communicating condemnation for that abuse.

This interpretation of "persecution," linked to the minimum standards for international legitimacy, can help guide adjudicators when faced with a number of hard cases. For example, how should receiving states distinguish between legitimate criminal prosecution and persecution? Is the jailing of a coup plotter justified punishment or political persecution? How should one regard laws that require women to be veiled when in public? What about laws of general application that disproportionately affect certain groups, for example, military draft laws with no exception for conscientious objectors? Are Jehovah's Witnesses persecuted when they are punished under such laws? These questions, and others like them, are most sensibly analyzed by asking whether the state has acted consistent with minimum standards for international legitimacy.

Chapter 4 considers the circumstances in which victims of harm inflicted by private (non-government) parties – for example, victims of gang violence like Angela and battered women like Rodi – should be eligible for asylum. Courts have increasingly adopted what is called the "protection approach": serious harm inflicted by a private party can constitute persecution if the state is unwilling *or unable* to protect the victim. The disfavored alternative, called the "accountability approach," maintains that some degree of state culpability is a necessary element of persecution. It would thus limit asylum to cases where the state is *unwilling*, for illegitimate reasons, to protect victims from harm. I argue that the accountability approach better reflects asylum's expressive dimension.

The cases I draw upon come mainly – though not exclusively – from American law and American experience, since it is the system I know best. But the basic structure of American asylum law – such as the persecution requirement – shares much in common with the law of other Western states and the European Union. Where American law diverges significantly, for instance, in its treatment of persecution by non-government actors, I consider the law of other jurisdictions as well, including Canada, Britain, Australia, New Zealand, and to a lesser extent France and Germany. The argument I advance about the way asylum should be understood is by no means limited to the American context.

Chapter 5 addresses the question of what remedy asylum should provide to its recipients. Traditionally, recipients of asylum have received membership in the state of refuge, not merely temporary protection. In recent years, however, that practice has been under attack. I argue that the remedy of surrogate membership matches the distinctive harm that persecuted people have suffered. It also dramatizes the critical judgment that asylum expresses: that the persecutory regime has treated the refugee in such a reprehensible manner that the political relationship between that regime and the refugee has been sundered. In that respect, victims of persecution are differently situated than other, non-persecuted refugees, who retain political standing in their states of origin despite their displacement. While the former need surrogate membership, the latter can be adequately assisted through other refugee policy tools, such as temporary protection.

Finally, in Chapter 6, I argue that the greatest threat to refugee protection today stems from the variety of measures that states have undertaken to prevent asylum seekers from filing for asylum in the first place. These policies have been justified under the banner of preventing fraudulent or bad faith applications, but they have had the effect of excluding genuine refugees as well. These measures have found public support in part, I suggest, because the dominant humanitarian approach to asylum fails to recognize that persecuted people face a distinctive kind of harm and, therefore, have a special claim to the surrogate political membership that asylum has historically offered. The theory of asylum offered in the first five chapters offers a rationale for ensuring that asylum remains available to the persecuted, and, therefore, for rolling back some of the restrictive measures adopted over the last fifteen years.

Of course, states will inevitably face a tension between two goals: on the one hand, remaining open to persecuted people; and on the other hand, deterring bad faith applications by those who wish to circumvent ordinary immigration controls. But that balance should be struck, to the greatest extent possible, by adopting policies that remove the incentives for filing bad faith applications without imposing burdens on asylum applications by persecuted people. For example, rather than erecting barriers to entry or procedural rules that eliminate entire classes of applicants without regard to the strength of their claims, states should focus on speeding processing times to reduce the incentives for filing asylum claims in bad faith.

A brief note on terminology

The term "refugee" carries several meanings. Most narrowly, it refers to people who are outside their states of origin and are unwilling or unable to return home because of a well-founded fear of persecution for reasons of race, religion, nationality, social group membership, or political opinion. Such refugees are called "Convention refugees," referring to the UN Convention Relating to the Status of Refugees, which defines "refugee" in this way. More broadly, the term "refugee" can in common parlance refer to all people who are forced to leave their homes because of a threat to their well-being or freedom, whether due to persecution, famine, extreme poverty, generalized violence, or any other of a number of reasons. In subsequent chapters, when I use the term "refugee," I mean it in this ordinary sense. I will use the term "Convention refugee" to refer to refugee status within the meaning of the UN Convention. I also use the term "persecuted people" as shorthand to refer to Convention refugees.

The UN Convention does not place states under any international legal obligation to grant asylum to persecuted people, but it does impose a somewhat narrower duty known as "non-refoulement": states may not expel or return Convention refugees to territories where their lives or freedom would be threatened on account of race, religion, nationality, membership of a particular social group, or political opinion.[44]

An "asylum seeker" is someone who seeks admission to another state by claiming to be a Convention refugee, but whose status is not yet determined. Only a fraction of the world's Convention refugees are asylum seekers in the West. Most live in refugee camps along the borders of their country of origin, or have succeeded in proving their refugee status and have already received asylum. Likewise, only a fraction of the world's asylum seekers are Convention refugees; the majority do not qualify.

An asylum seeker who is recognized as a Convention refugee and who therefore receives asylum is called an "asylee." An applicant who fails to qualify for asylum, but who nonetheless makes a strong case that he should not be returned to his state of origin – a "non-Convention refugee" – is sometimes eligible for "temporary protection" or "humanitarian protection," a status that typically (though not in every country) offers fewer rights and benefits than asylum does, and presumptively offers no opportunity for permanent settlement.[45] There is no established international law obligation to shelter non-Convention refugees.

Notes

1. *A* v. *Secretary of State for the Home Department* [2003] EWCA Civ. 175 (CA). I have used the name Angela to refer to the asylum seeker in this case; she is called Miss A by the British court.

2. Alain Baptiste's name has been changed to protect his identity.

3. *In re R – A –*, 22 I. & N. Dec. 906, 908–9 (BIA 1999), vacated by order of the Attorney General, January 19, 2001.

4. See, for example, Joseph H. Carens, "Aliens and Citizens: The Case for Open Borders" in Ronald Beiner (ed.), *Theorizing Citizenship* (Albany, NY: SUNY Press, 1995), pp. 229–53; Bruce Ackerman, *Social Justice in the Liberal State* (New Haven, CT: Yale University Press, 1980), p. 95; Peter Singer and Renata Singer, "The Ethics of Refugee Policy" in Mark Gibney (ed.), *Open Borders? Closed Societies? The Ethical and Political Issues* (New York: Greenwood Press, 1988), pp. 111–30; and various articles collected in Brian Barry and Robert Goodin (eds.), *Free Movement* (University Park, PA: Pennsylvania State University Press, 1992).

5. See, for example, Michael Walzer, *Spheres of Justice* (New York: Basic Books, 1983), pp. 38–41; David Miller, *On Nationality* (New York: Oxford University Press, 1995); Yael Tamir, *Liberal Nationalism* (Princeton University Press, 1993); John Rawls, *Law of Peoples* (Cambridge, MA: Harvard University Press, 1999; and Michael Blake, "Immigration" in R. G. Frey and Christopher Health Wellman (eds.), *A Companion To Applied Ethics* (Malden, MA: Blackwell Publishing, 2003), pp. 224–37.

6. See, for example, Walzer, *Spheres of Justice*, p. 33, and Matthew J. Gibney, *The Ethics and Politics of Asylum* (Cambridge University Press, 2004), pp. 231–49.

7. UN Convention Relating to the Status of Refugees [UN Convention], July 28, 1951, 189 U.N.T.S. 137, art. 1(A)(2).
8. Aristide R. Zolberg, Astri Suhrke, and Sergio Aguayo, *Escape From Violence* (New York: Oxford University Press, 1989), pp. 269–70.
9. Zolberg *et al.* qualify this statement somewhat, maintaining that "victims of economic, that is, structural, violence must be helped first in their own country ..." Ibid., p. 271. I discuss this subject in Chapter 5.
10. In addition to Zolberg *et al.*, *Escape From Violence*, p. 269, see Joseph H. Carens, "Who Should Get In? The Ethics of Immigration Admissions," *Ethics and International Affairs*, 17 (2003), p. 101; Joseph H. Carens, "The Philosopher and the Policymaker: Two Perspectives on the Ethics of Immigration with Special Attention to the Problem of Restricting Asylum" in Kay Hailbronner *et al.* (eds.), *Immigration Admissions: The Search for Workable Policies in Germany and the United States* (Providence, RI: Berghahn Books, 1997), p. 18; Michael G. Heyman, "Redefining Refugee: A Proposal for Relief for the Victims of Civil Strife," *San Diego Law Review*, 24 (1987), p. 449; Adam Roberts, "More Refugees, less Asylum: A Regime in Transformation," *Journal of Refugee Studies*, 11 (1998), p. 381; Andrew Shacknove, "Who is a Refugee?," *Ethics*, 95 (1985), pp. 274–84; and Astri Suhrke, "Global Refugee Movements and Strategies of Response" in Mary M. Kritz (ed.), *U.S. Immigration and Refugee Policy: Global and Domestic Issues* (Lexington, MA: Lexington Books, 1983), pp. 159–60.
11. 1000 U.N.T.S. 46, at 47, reprinted in Guy Goodwin-Gill, *The Refugee in International Law*, 2nd edn. (New York: Oxford University Press, 1996), p. 430.
12. OAS.Ser.L/V/II.66, doc. 10, rev. 1, at 190–3, reprinted in Goodwin-Gill, *The Refugee in International Law*, p. 446.
13. UNHCR, "Note on International Protection," A/AC/96/830 (September 7, 1994).
14. UNHCR, *The State of the World's Refugees 1997–8: A Humanitarian Agenda* (New York: Oxford University Press, 1997), p. 24.
15. Jerzy Sztucki, "Who is a Refugee? The Convention Definition: Universal or Obsolete?" in Frances Nicholson and Patrick Twomey (eds.), *Refugee Rights and Realities* (Cambridge University Press, 1999), p. 67.
16. See, for example, *R. v. Immigration Appeal Tribunal and another, ex parte Shah* [1999] 2 A.C. 629 (UK, battered women); *Salibian* v. *Canada*, [1990] 3 F.C. 250 (Canada, ethnic conflict); *In re H –*, 21 I. & N. Dec. 337 (BIA 1996) (US, ethnic conflict).
17. James C. Hathaway, *Law of Refugee Status* (Toronto: Butterworths, 1991), pp. 104–5. See, for example, *Canada (Attorney General)* v. *Ward* [1993] S.C.R. 689; New Zealand Refugee Status Appeals

Authority, Refugee Appeal No. 71427/99, [2000] N.Z.A.R. 545; *Horvath* v. *Secretary of State for the Home Department* [2001] 1 A.C. 489 (UK); and *Minister for Immigration and Multicultural Affairs* v. *Khawar* [2002] H.C.A. 14 (Australia).

18. Immigration Rules, section 339C. This reflects an EU asylum directive that requires member states to offer what is called "subsidiary protection" on the bases quoted above (with the addition of "extralegal killing"). "EU Qualifications Directive," Council Directive 2004/83/EC of April 29, 2004 on minimum standards for the qualification and status of third country nationals or stateless persons as refugees or as persons who otherwise need international protection and the content of the protection granted, art. 15. However, the EU directive requires states to grant subsidiary protection to a qualified applicant only for a renewable one-year term. Ibid., art. 24.

19. Immigration and Refugee Protection Act (2001, c. 27), section 97(1).

20. Gil Loescher, *Beyond Charity* (New York: Oxford University Press, 1993), p. 21.

21. Declaration on Territorial Asylum, G. A. Res. 2312 (II), U.N. GAOR, 22nd Sess., Supp. No. 16, at 81, U.N. Doc. A/6716 (1967), reprinted in Goodwin-Gill, *Refugee in International Law*, p. 413.

22. The 1969 Organization of African Unity Convention concurred, "The grant of asylum to refugees is a peaceful and humanitarian act and shall not be regarded as an unfriendly act by a Member State." 1000 U.N.T.S. 46, art. II. The 1984 Cartagena Declaration on Refugees, a non-binding resolution endorsed by Latin American states, also called attention to the "peaceful non-political and exclusively humanitarian nature of grant of asylum or recognition of the status of refugees and … the importance of the internationally accepted principle that nothing in either shall be interpreted as an unfriendly act towards the country of origin of refugees." OAS/Ser.L/V/II.66, doc. 10, rev. 1, at 190–3, reprinted in Goodwin-Gill, *Refugee in International Law*, p. 446. And the Council of Europe has referred to asylum as an "humanitarian act." Council of Europe, Recommendation 1088 on the right to territorial asylum, October 7, 1988, para. 1.

23. For example, Atle Grahl-Madsen, *The Status of Refugees in International Law*, vol. 2 (Leiden: A. W. Sijthoff, 1972), p. 27, wrote that "a finding by the authorities of one State to the effect that persecution is taking place in the territory of another State, cannot be construed as a censure on the government of the latter State, and that such a finding does not constitute any interference or intervention in the domestic affairs of that State." See also Gilbert Jaeger, "A Comment on the Distortion of the Palliative Role of Refugee Protection," *Journal of Refugee Studies*, 8 (1995), p. 300;

Walter Kälin, "Non-State Agents of Persecution and the Inability of the State to Protect," *Georgetown Immigration Law Journal*, 15 (2001), p. 423; Ben Vermeulen *et al.*, "Persecution by Third Parties," unpublished paper commissioned by the Research and Documentation Centre of the Ministry of Justice of the Netherlands, May 1998, p. 17. Jaeger, "Comment," p. 301, emphasizes that asylum is properly called "territorial asylum" rather than "political asylum" in light of its humanitarian nature.

24. James C. Hathaway, "Reconceiving Refugee Law as Human Rights Protection," *Journal of Refugee Studies*, 4 (1991), p. 113.

25. UNHCR, "Asylum Levels and Trends in Industrialized Countries, 2006" (March 23, 2007), table 1 (for the year 2002); UNHCR, *UNHCR Statistical Yearbook 2001* (October 2002), table C.2 (for the years 1985 and 1997); and UNHCR, "Asylum Applications in Industrialized Countries: 1980–1999" (November 2001), tables V.1, VI.4, VI.5 (for the years 1970–82). This increase has been attributed variously to the paroxysm of ethnic violence that followed the crumbling of Cold War client states in Africa and Eastern Europe; globalization, which has made it easier and more attractive for migrants to move West to better their economic circumstances; and the elimination in Europe of guest-worker programs, leaving asylum as the only avenue for admittance other than family reunification. David Held *et al.*, *Global Transformations: Politics, Economics and Culture* (Stanford University Press, 1999), pp. 283–326; UNHCR, *The State of the World's Refugees 1997–8*, p. 27.

26. Illegal Immigration Reform and Immigrant Responsibility Act of 1996, Pub. L. No. 104–208. The Act imposed a one-year deadline for filing asylum applications, introduced expedited removal procedures, and expanded the national security grounds for excluding asylum seekers, among other things.

27. National Commission on Terrorist Attacks Upon the United States, *The 9/11 Commission Report* (July 2004), pp. 161, 177–8, www.9–11 commission.gov (last visited March 2, 2008); "Porous Borders: Terrorists May Be Among Refugees Heading to Europe," *Wall Street Journal*, July 5, 2002, p. A1.

28. The estimated size of the human smuggling and trafficking trade is $6 billion annually. Patrick Twomey, "Europe's Other Market: Trafficking in People," *European Journal of Migration and Law*, 2 (2000), p. 18; John Morrison and Beth Crosland, "The Trafficking and Smuggling of Refugees: the End Game in European Asylum Policy?" (UNCHR New Issues in Refugee Research Working Paper no. 39, 2001). The terrorist group Ansar al-Islam has been suspected of raising funds through immigrant smuggling in Europe. Glenn R. Simpson *et al.*, "Group in Europe is

Suspected of Forgery, Smuggling Immigrants," *Wall Street Journal*, April 14, 2004, p. A13.

29. UNHCR, "Asylum Levels and Trends in Industrialized Countries, 2006," table 1; UNHCR, *Statistical Yearbook 2001*, table C.1.

30. The peak in the early 1990s was caused by the break-up of Yugoslavia. The data come from UNHCR, "Asylum Levels and Trends in Industrialized Countries, 2006," table 1 (for the year 2006); UNHCR, *UNHCR Statistical Yearbook 2005* (April 2007), table C.1 (for the years 1996–2005); UNHCR, *UNHCR Statistical Yearbook 2001*, table C.1 (for the years 1982–95); and UNHCR, "Asylum Applications in Industrialized Countries: 1980–1999" (November 2001), tables V.1, VI.4, VI.5 (for the years 1970–82).

31. On the growth of temporary protection, see Daniele Joly, "A New Asylum Regime in Europe," in Nicholson and Twomey, *Refugee Rights*, p. 345; Matthew J. Gibney, "Between Control and Humanitarianism: Temporary Protection in Contemporary Europe," *Georgetown Immigration Law Journal*, 14 (2000), pp. 689–707; Joan Fitzpatrick, "Flight From Asylum: Trends Toward Temporary 'Refuge' and Local Responses to Forced Migrations," *Virginia Journal of International Law*, 35 (1994), pp. 13–70; Joan Fitzpatrick, "Temporary Protection of Refugees: Elements of a Formalized Regime," *American Journal of International Law*, 94 (2000), pp. 279–306.

32. Gibney, "Between Control," p. 690.

33. UN Convention, art. 33.

34. UNHCR, *Statistical Yearbook 2001*, table C.2; UNHCR, "Asylum Levels and Trends in Industrialized Countries, 2006," table 1. For a list of the steps taken by Britain in response to growing numbers, see Home Office, "Home Office Statistical Bulletin: Asylum Statistics: United Kingdom 2003" (August 24, 2004), p. 10, www.homeoffice.gov.uk/rds/pdfs04/hosb1104.pdf (last visited March 1, 2008). They include transit visa requirements; a "white list" of safe countries from which applications are presumed to be "clearly unfounded"; non-suspensive appeals for applicants from white list countries; restricted access to social support; and expedited processing of applications.

35. ICM/News of the World, February 16, 2004, and YouGov, August 14, 2003, both from *Polling the Nations*, www.poll.orspub.com.

36. The Refugee Council, "Attitudes Toward Refugees and Asylum Seekers: A Survey of Public Opinion" (May 2002), p. 4, www.refugeecouncil.org.uk/downloads/mori_report.pdf (last visited February 24, 2008).

37. Andrew Shacknove, "From Asylum to Containment," *International Journal of Refugee Law*, 5 (1993), p. 521. See also B. S. Chimni, "Globalization, Humanitarianism and the Erosion of Refugee

Protection," *Journal of Refugee Studies*, 13 (2000), pp. 243–63; Geoff Gilbert, "Rights, Legitimate Expectations, Needs and Responsibilities," *International Journal of Refugee Law*, 10 (1998), p. 351.

38. David A. Martin, "The Refugee Concept: On Definitions, Politics, and the Careful Use of a Scarce Resource," in Howard Adelman (ed.), *Refugee Policy: Canada and the United States* (Toronto: York Lanes Press, 1991), p. 35.

39. Gibney, "Between Control," p. 690.

40. See, for example, Arthur C. Helton, *The Price of Indifference* (New York: Oxford University Press, 2002), pp. 15, 299.

41. Alan Travis, "Asylum Service Criticised," *The Guardian* (UK), July 16, 2003.

42. UNHCR, "UNHCR Global Report 2003," pp. 30, 33, www.unhcr.org/publ/PUBL/40c6d74f0.pdf (last visited March 1, 2008).

43. James C. Hathaway and R. Alexander Neve, "Making International Refugee Law Relevant Again: A Proposal For Collectivized and Solution-Oriented Protection," *Harvard Human Rights Journal*, 10 (1997), p. 148; see also Peter H. Schuck, "Refugee Burden-Sharing: A Modest Proposal," in Peter H. Schuck (ed.), *Citizens, Strangers, and In-Betweens* (Boulder, CO: Westview Press, 1998), p. 297.

44. UN Convention, art. 33.

45. Temporary protection regimes include Temporary Protected Status (TPS) in the United States, exceptional leave to remain (until 2003) and humanitarian protection in the UK, tolerated status or *Duldung* in Germany, "B" status in Sweden, and Provisional Permission to Remain in the Netherlands. Since 1992, the number of asylum seekers in Europe who have been granted asylum has been smaller than the number refused asylum but granted one of these alternative forms of protection. See Joly, "A New Asylum Regime," p. 345.

1 | *Recovering Asylum's Political Roots*

Historiography plays an important role in debates over the proper conception of asylum. Critics of the persecution requirement have widely assumed it to be a Cold War artifact without any historical basis – a deviation from a humanitarian tradition that addressed the needs of the asylum seeker without making any judgment about the actions of the origin state. The persecution requirement, it is claimed, is a "product of recent Western history," framed to cast a spotlight on Soviet deficiencies with regard to political rights, while leaving in the shadows Western deficiencies regarding "socio-economic human rights."[1] On this view, the persecution requirement distorted asylum into a political instrument to be wielded against the Soviets at the cost of addressing the urgent needs of refugees.

Gervase Coles, for example, says that the persecution requirement was "specifically devised for a particular geographic problem at a particular time" – namely post-war Europe. It was, he writes, "adopted as being the essential characteristic of the new refugee in the belief that this would satisfactorily define European asylum seekers, the majority of whom were from Eastern Europe ... Both in its conception, and in practice, the *ad hoc* and partisan character of this approach was incontrovertible."[2] Jerzy Sztucki states that "the Convention with its definition is sometimes described as a Cold War product, 'Eurocentric' and, if only for these reasons, obsolete."[3] James Hathaway labels it "incomplete and politically partisan."[4] Historian Claudena Skran calls the persecution requirement a "deviation from the humanitarian principles of the early phase of refugee law."[5]

Before the late nineteenth century, historian Michael Marrus writes, "refugees seldom were a bone of contention among states and ... rarely preoccupied people in positions of authority. Until the second quarter of the nineteenth century there was no mention of refugees in international treaties, and states made no distinction between those fleeing criminal prosecution and those escaping political repression."[6] Ben Vermeulen *et al.* state that "asylum has always been seen as a matter to be viewed separately from criticism of the state of origin. The granting of asylum is not in itself an unfriendly act, and should not be construed as a censure of the government of the state of the asylum seeker."[7]

In a post-Cold War world, the critique continues, asylum can be returned to its historically humanitarian purpose. Astri Suhrke bluntly asks: "The [persecution requirement] is vulnerable to attack ... as a product of Western liberal thinking and Western political supremacy in the 1950s [and] reflects particularist notions of needs and rights. Can this be the basis for a definition that aspires to universality?"[8]

In fact, for most of its history, asylum has been viewed in political, rather than humanitarian, terms. The persecution requirement is deeply rooted in, not a departure from, asylum's long history. Asylum's origins lie in international criminal law: a recipient of asylum enjoyed immunity to extradition. Typically, such immunity was granted only when the requesting power was deemed to have abused its authority, for example, by seeking to punish the asylum seeker unjustly (i.e., persecute him). The extension of asylum to protect persecuted people generally, whether sought for extradition or not, occurred as states closed their borders to migrants. In a world of open borders, asylum was needed only by those facing extradition; other persecuted people were admitted as migrants. However, in a world of closed borders, the refusal to admit persecuted people could be functionally equivalent to extradition: it effected the return of those people to their states of origin, where they would be unjustly harmed. Asylum was thus transformed from an element of international criminal law (a defense to extradition) to a subset of immigration policy (a defense to deportation). But the class of intended beneficiaries – persecuted people – remained the same. These origins have largely gone unrecognized by contemporary commentators.

Because asylum historically depended upon a judgment about the rightfulness of another power's exercise of authority, and because granting asylum interfered with that exercise of authority, asylum was enmeshed in the high politics of international relations. Often, asylum produced international tension, which sometimes boiled over into open conflict. In order to dampen conflict, asylum was occasionally framed in humanitarian terms – for example, by those seeking asylum and by weak states granting asylum. But its political resonance was rarely far from the surface.

Thus, the political conception of asylum – as limited in focus to persecuted people, as expressing condemnation of the persecuting regime, and as linked to a broader strategy to reform that regime – is deeply rooted in asylum's history. The persecution requirement is not an aberrant product of the Cold War, but rather is inextricably connected with the way in which asylum has historically been understood and practiced.

Asylum and authority in ancient Greece

The word "asylum" is Latin, and comes from the Greek *asylia*, or "inviolability." In ancient Greece, inviolability was possessed by people whose work necessitated travel outside their own state – such as envoys, merchants, athletes, and others – and was recognized by all states as a matter of comity.[9] Inviolability was also a characteristic of certain places – namely, temples, altars, and other sanctuaries, called *asyla hiera*.[10] A person in need of protection from a pursuer could enter an *asylon hieron* and perform the rite of *hiketeia*, or supplication.[11] This rite is the ancient origin of what we today would call "seeking asylum."*

---

* In addition to its origins in ancient Greece, asylum also had origins in the Biblical cities of refuge. See Numbers 35:9–34; Deuteronomy 4:41–43, 19:1–13; and Joshua 20:1–9. Although the cities of refuge were not meant as havens for asylum seekers from abroad, nonetheless they share what we shall see are the main features of Greek asylums: claiming refuge involved a contest to the authority claimed by a pursuer, it initiated a legal proceeding, and a successful claim immunized the claimant against their pursuer.

The Bible sanctions the revenge killing of a murderer: it gives the "blood redeemer" the privilege to kill the murderer wherever he may find him. Numbers 35:19. But revenge killing was too serious a punishment for someone guilty of involuntary or accidental manslaughter, such as the man who "goes into the forest with his neighbor to cut wood, and his hand swings the axe to cut down a tree, and the head slips from the handle and strikes his neighbor so that he dies." Deuteronomy 19:5. Therefore, Numbers 35:9–15 commanded the Israelites to establish six cities of refuge scattered throughout the land of Canaan to which those guilty of involuntary manslaughter could flee, so that they would be protected from a blood redeemer.

The Talmud explains that after a killing, whether intentional or accidental, the killer would flee to a city of refuge. The court would send for the killer under guard, and he would be brought "before the assembly for judgment," Numbers 35:12, to "state his case," Deuteronomy 20:4, in order to determine the validity of his claim for protection from the blood redeemer. If the death was in fact unintentional, the killer would be brought back to the city of refuge under guard, in case the blood redeemer tried to kill him on the way. Makkot 9b. He would then enjoy immunity from vengeance so long as he stayed within the city of refuge. "But if the murderer will ever leave the border of the city of refuge to which he had fled, and the avenger of the blood shall find him outside ..., and the avenger of the blood will kill the murderer – he has no blood-guilt." Numbers 35:26.

Hiketeia was initiated when a person entered a temple, sat in an altar, or held on to an image of a god while grasping a broken twig or wool, the signs of a supplicant. By declaring oneself a supplicant, one could claim provisional immunity against one's pursuer. Such a declaration was a public act: "anonymous stay on sacred land was not tolerated."[12] Ulrich Sinn gives the example of the Amphiaraion at Oropos, at which anyone entering would have to post their name on a wooden tablet outside the entrance.[13]

Reaching sacred space alone, however, was not enough for supplicants to secure immunity. They also had to convince the god's priest that they deserved protection, and if they failed to do so, they could be turned away. Kent Rigsby explains, "The god was not obliged to accept and protect every supplicant, only those who had a just claim."[14] There are famous examples in Greek history of supplicants being rejected from asylum. The Athenian statesman Lycurgus approved of the execution of Callistratus, who sought refuge at the Altar of the Twelve Gods in Athens after returning from exile. He was executed, "Justly: for lawful treatment for wrongdoers is punishment, and the god rightly returned the guilty man to those wronged for punishment. It would be a terrible thing if the same signs were manifested to the pious and to evildoers."[15] Lycurgus also thought that Pausanias, a Spartan prince who was accused of Persian sympathies and of conspiring with Sparta's serfs, was rightly starved in Sparta's temple of Athena because "this proves that gods do not help traitors."[16]

As one might expect, over time the privilege of asylum came to be abused, encouraging lawlessness and undermining civil authority. Most supplicants were local criminals or slaves who hoped to be spared punishment. Tacitus reported that the number of temples offering asylum multiplied, and "were crowded by the most abandoned slaves; debtors screened themselves from their creditors, and criminals fled from justice. The magistrates were no longer able to control a seditious populace, who carried their crimes, under a mask of piety, to the altar of their gods."[17] When the Romans took over Greece, they curtailed the right of temples to grant asylum in the interest of order. Under the reign of Tiberius in 22 CE, the Roman Senate required temples to produce to the Senate legal proof of their right to grant asylum, which most temples were hard-pressed to do. The majority were stripped of their status as *asylia*.[18]

Hiketeia's international political importance, however, stemmed less from the refuge it afforded to local criminals, or to exiles who had been forced to leave their home states, than from the shelter it gave to fugitives who had fled abroad and were sought for extradition.[19] Just as a temple was considered to be inviolable space with respect to the *polis*, the concept of territorial sovereignty made one *polis'* territory inviolable with respect to others.[20] By granting asylum, a ruler was able to make inviolable a foreign supplicant who arrived within his territory (usually at a temple or altar, though not necessarily[21]) seeking protection from the supplicant's city of origin. Asylum acted as a defense to extradition, placing a fugitive beyond the requesting city's authoritative reach.[22]

Stories of such supplicants abound in ancient Greek drama. One of the most famous of these is the *Oresteia*, a trilogy written by Aeschylus. The second play in the trilogy, *The Libation Bearers*, ends with Orestes, who had just murdered his mother, Clytemnestra, fleeing to the temple at Delphi pursued by the terrifying Furies.[23] As the third play in the trilogy, the *Eumenides*, begins, Orestes is brought by Hermes from Delphi to the Parthenon, where he wraps himself around Athena's idol and begs to be protected from the Furies. The Furies have a claim of rightful authority on their side: their job is to avenge matricides, and here the facts are uncontested as by all accounts, Orestes did kill his mother.[24] Orestes, however, thinks the killing was justified, not a crime – it was in vengeance for Clytemnestra's slaughter of Agamemnon, Orestes' father.

Athena initially agrees to reach a verdict in the matter herself, but then decides to establish a human institution to do so – the Areopagus, the Athenian homicide court, presided over by "the finest men of Athens" who will "decide the issue fairly truly – / bound to our oaths, our spirits bent on justice." When the legal proceeding begins, the Furies argue for enforcing the letter of the law: matricide is matricide. Apollo, serving as Orestes' lawyer, argues that the killing was just vengeance commanded by Zeus. The judges are split evenly, but a tie vote yields an acquittal. The Furies are wildly angry, and lamenting their "power stripped, cast down," threaten to destroy the land. But Athena persuades them to put aside their anger and become guardians of Athens.[25]

The action of the *Oresteia* highlights three characteristics of *hiketeia*. First, when one claimed asylum through supplication, one *contested the rightfulness with which authority was exercised* in one's particular case. Thus, while Orestes has no objection to the Furies' mandate on the whole, he objects to its application in his case: his is not the normal case of matricide, he claims. A temple was a natural setting for contesting the rightfulness of authority, because, as Karl Schumacher points out, it is "an intermediary zone between the divine and the human world ...

suitable for communication between both worlds."[26] Grasping an idol dramatized the appeal made by a suppliant to a higher authority.

Second, *hiketeia* initiated a *legal proceeding* in which the suppliant was given the opportunity to make a plea on his own behalf, to put forward an argument as to why the punishment he faced was undeserved. Athena says to Orestes, "Tell us your land, your birth, your fortunes. / Then defend yourself against their charge, / if trust in your rights has brought you here to guard / my hearth and idol ..."[27]

Third, the result of *hiketeia*, if successful, was that the suppliant was given *immunity* from the authority of those who pursued him. The Furies are helpless to override the decision of the Areopagus and carry out their punishment against Orestes. Instead, they must redirect their complaints to the competing authority – Athens – that granted Orestes' claim.

These three elements of *hiketeia* are present in plays dealing with asylum from earthly authority as well. In Euripides' *The Heracleidae*, for example, Iolaus and the children of Heracles enter the temple of Zeus, seeking asylum in Athens from their Argive pursuers. An Argive messenger is caught by the Athenians trying to tear the children of Heracles out of the temple. He defends himself by appealing to the legitimacy of his claim to authority, saying: "I have / Authority for all I do or say; Since, as an Argive, I'm recovering / These Argive nationals who've run away, / Though legally condemned to death at home. / We have a perfect right to carry out / The laws we make for our sovereign land." The Athenians give Iolaus a chance to tell his side of the story, and he contests Argive authority, claiming that "we're expatriates. / What earthly right has he to drag us all / Back to the town that drove us out, as though / They still had claims on us. We're aliens now."[28] Demophon, the Athenian king, decides to side with Iolaus, effectively granting him and the children of Heracles immunity against the Argive claim to authority. The Argives are left with no choice but to redirect their grievance to the Athenian protectors, and they do so by unsuccessfully trying to invade Athens.

In Aeschylus' *The Suppliants*, the daughters of Danaos, fleeing forced marriage to the sons of Aigyptos, ask the Argive ruler Pelasgos to grant them asylum. Otherwise, they say, "The sons of Aigyptos will claim us. Don't hand us over!" Pelasgos is initially skeptical of the Danaids' claim for asylum (and no doubt intimidated by the prospect of a military confrontation with the sons of Aigyptos). Why, he asks, have they fled their native land? "Not to be slaves to the sons of Aigyptos." Pelasgos presses them: "Because you hate them? Or because it would be unlaw-ful?" In other words, Pelasgos requires that the Danaids frame their claim for asylum as a complaint about the legitimacy with which the Aigyptioi exercise authority over them. He says, "If the sons of Aigyptos claim to rule / you as next of kin, in accord with the law / of your land, how can I oppose them? / You must show that those same laws / give them no power over your lives."[29] Pelasgos eventually agrees to grant asylum to the Danaids (after they threaten to kill themselves upon the altar if he refuses), immunizing them against the authority claimed by the sons of Aigyptos.

When the Aigyptioi arrive to drag off the Danaids forcibly, Pelasgos prevents them from doing so. The Aigyptioi demand to know what could justify such inhospitable behavior. Their Herald asks, "Are my actions unjust? What gives offense? / ... I am just recovering lost property."[30] By framing the issue in this way, the Herald forces Pelasgos to stake a stand on whether the Aigyptioi's treatment of the women is consistent with the rightful exercise of authority. If the women are indeed "lost property," what right does Pelasgos have to stand in the way of those who come to collect them? As far as the Aigyptioi are concerned, the decision to grant asylum to the Danaids amounted to an unreasonable rejection of their claim of ownership and an unwarranted interference with their exercise of authority.

Because granting asylum to a supplicant involved interfering with the authoritative processes of the supplicant's city of origin, asylum had international political significance. When a fugitive on the lam from a foreign city asked for asylum, the leaders of the city of refuge often faced a troublesome dilemma. A decision to shelter a fugitive would be inter-preted as an affront to the foreign power and could sometimes precipi-tate war. However, a refusal to grant asylum was impious, and could be construed as a sign of political weakness.

In real life, leaders seeking to avoid confrontation more often declined to protect supplicants who might bring trouble. A famous example involved Pacytes, wanted by the Persian king Cyrus for having organized a failed revolt. When Pacytes fled to Cyme and sought asylum, the Cymeans were placed in a bind: they wanted neither to surrender the supplicant for fear of divine punishment nor to grant him protection for fear of war with the more powerful Persians. They decided to pass the buck by sending Pacytes to Mytilene, presumably expecting the Mytilenians to offer him protection. But Mytilene agreed to hand Pacytes over to Persia for a ransom. The Cymeans, feeling responsible for his safety, sent a ship to take him to Chios. The Chians then tore him away from the shrine of Athena and surrendered him to Persia in exchange for territory.[31]

Another method of avoidance, which at least paid lip service to the principle of asylum, was to seek advice from an oracle on whether to protect a supplicant. The oracle would then give an ambiguous answer that could be interpreted to the supplicant's disadvantage.[32] Another strategy was interdiction: Athens went so far as to place a police station near the Acropolis so as to intercept "undesirable suppliants" before they could reach the sanctuaries to initiate *hiketeia*.[33]

Sanctuary: Rome and the Middle Ages[34]

In Rome, asylum provided temporary immunity from prosecution until evidence could be gathered and a formal trial could be held.[35] Its major function was the protection of slaves. Roman law distinguished between two types of people: those who were *sui juris*, under their own jurisdiction; and those who were *alieni juris*, under the jurisdiction of others. Slaves fell into the latter category – they were in the *potestas*, or authority, of their master, which extended to the "power of life or death over" a slave.[36] As a general matter, harboring a runaway slave was considered theft; if one caught a runaway, one had to turn him over to magistrates, who would chain the slave pending his appearance before the city prefect or governor.[37]

A slave who fled from his master to a temple or to a statue of a caesar, however, was not considered a fugitive, because the intention was not to run away, but rather to seek asylum.[38] The prefect of the city was duty-bound to provide him a hearing in which the slave could protest the treatment given by his master.[39] The slave could contend, in other words, that the particular treatment inflicted upon him lay outside his master's authority over him, and seek immunity against it. Thus, Antoninus Pius (who ruled from 138–161 CE) decreed that "those who make just complaint be not denied relief against brutality or starvation or intolerable wrongdoing." He charged Aelius Marcianus, the procon-sul of Baetica, to:

judicially examine those who have fled the household of Julius Sabinus to take refuge at the statue and if you find it proven that they have been treated more harshly than is fair or have been subjected to infamous wrongdoing, then issue an order for their sale subject to the condition that they shall not come back under the power of their present master.[40]

If the master disobeyed the order to sell his slaves, Marcianus was to threaten the master with severe retribution.[41]

According to Tacitus, however, the privilege of asylum was abused. As mentioned above, Rome curtailed the Greek asylum privileges in 22 CE on the ground that they had become permanent sanctuaries for criminals; and in Rome itself, "[i]t had become a practice for the most abandoned characters to assume the privilege of slandering and maligning good men under the protection of Caesar's statute, to which they fled as a sanctuary ... Against this abuse it was argued by Caius Sestius a senator 'that princes were indeed as the gods; but by the gods just petitions only were heard ...' Others urged similar complaints."[42]

After Constantine's Edict of Toleration in 313 CE, Christian churches became places for asylum. In addition to slaves complaining of mistreatment, churches began to shelter debtors and accused criminals for whom bishops would use their influence to intercede and plead for leniency. "Sanctuary" – the name given to church-based asylum – is first mentioned in Roman law in 392 CE, when Theodosius stipulated that those who sought sanctuary in churches could not be removed by force.[43] Although church sanctuary was initially limited, especially in the East, churches in the West became increasingly powerful as the empire's authority crumbled.[44]

At stake in the struggle between the empire and the Church over control of sanctuaries was the meaning of asylum itself. For the empire, the purpose of asylum was to further earthly justice – it was tolerated within the empire, despite its abuse, because it was a useful avenue of appeal for those who ordinarily would not be able to contest the authority exercised over them. These included most obviously slaves, but also those who had been the victims of error or favoritism at trial. As in Greece, asylum was meant to protect the innocent, not the guilty. Implicit in granting asylum was a judgment that the recipient had been subjected to an abuse of authority and that the punishment he or she faced was unfair.

For the Church, the purpose of asylum was very different. Rather than being an instrument of justice, it was a vehicle for mercy. Clerics pleaded for leniency not only for the wrongly accused, but for anyone who had been sentenced by Roman courts.[45] Augustine even argued that the more detestable the crime committed by the accused, the more important sanctuary and intercession became.[46] A crime was viewed, first and foremost, as an offense against God, and thus could be repaired only through repentance, not through earthly punishment.

This Christian perspective governed the practice of asylum in medieval Europe. Nowhere is this more evident than in the medieval approach to murderers who sought sanctuary. Even though intentional murderers were explicitly excluded from the biblical cities of refuge as well as the sanctuaries of Rome, in 511 the Council of Orléans included "homicides, adulterers, and thieves" as potential recipients of sanctuary. In Germanic law as well, intentional murderers were frequently given immunity inside churches.[47]

At the same time as asylum was expanded to provide protection for people who had traditionally been excluded (like intentional murderers), the number of sites offering asylum proliferated. "The places of asylum were increasingly expanded to include convents, monasteries, cemeteries, places of bishops and Canons, hospitals, such establishments as those of the Knights of Saint-John of Jerusalem and of Templars, and even the crosses placed along the way."[48]

By the twelfth century, the Christian conception of asylum was under strain. An increase in crime – and in particular, in criminal acts committed by clerics, who were immune to secular authority – had led to the famous showdown over clerical immunity between Henry II and Thomas Becket in 1163. Clerics were tried in ecclesiastical courts before the bishop rather than in secular courts, and if found guilty, received more lenient punishments than they would otherwise have received. In particular, they were not punished by death or mutilation. The King demanded that Thomas, then Archbishop of Canterbury, assent to the Constitutions of Clarendon, which asserted the King's right to punish clerics. Thomas initially agreed but later revoked his agreement. Ultimately, the disagreement culminated in Thomas' murder in the cathedral at Canterbury.

Forty years later, Pope Innocent III, responding to inquiries from the Bishop of London about the extent of clerical immunity, declared that *"publicae utilitatis intersit, ne crimina remaneant impunita"* – in the interest of public utility, no crimes remain unpunished – for impunity encourages further wickedness. The pronouncement "became a standard catch-phrase" in the generation following, and issued a sea change in the role of the criminal law.[49] Hostiensis, among the most influential canonists in the thirteenth century, picked up on Innocent's statement, and reformulated it: "It is in everyone's interest that crimes should not remain unpunished." This reformulation had the effect of recognizing a general public interest in the punishment of crime.[50]

These developments had a devastating effect on the Church's sanctuary privileges. In response to a question posed by the King of Scotland as to what should be done with those who flee to churches to evade punishment, Innocent began by quoting the rule that no one should be dragged from a church, no matter how guilty he was. But then he stipulated a striking exception: "That is, unless the fugitive was a public thief or destroyer of fields by night, who often had insidiously and aggressively beset public highways ... [F]or wrongdoing of this magnitude (which both impedes public utility and noxiously molests everyone) the fugitive can be extracted, not succeeding in impunity."[51] This response would have been unintelligible to people just a few generations before, who saw earthly punishment as serving no useful purpose. By the middle of the fifteenth century, "public thieves, nocturnal marauders, sacrilegious persons, armed fugitives, those who commit crimes within churches, Jews, heretics, ravishers of maidens, traitors, blasphemers, murderers, exiles, those who kill clerics, prison escapees, assassins, highway robbers, and anyone convicted before a judge" were all excluded from sanctuary.[52] In England, the privilege of church asylum was finally removed by an Act of Parliament in 1625.[53]

On the Continent, Catholic kings tried to persuade the Court of Rome to limit the practice even further, and when Rome was unresponsive, they abolished it themselves. In France, Louis XII cut back on sanctuary in 1515, and in 1547, Henry II decreed that churches would provide no protection against the search and seizure of fugitives.[54] Elsewhere, kings began to consider the individual's reasons for requesting asylum rather than simply guaranteeing protection to anyone who had managed to enter a sanctuary.[55]

At the same time, religious wars broke out among Protestants and Catholics following the Reformation. They led to large-scale population transfers in Europe, as people fled religious persecution and sought refuge in a place where their religion was dominant. For example, following Sir Thomas Wyat's unsuccessful Protestant insurrection in 1554, Mary Tudor burned more than 300 Protestants at the stake; more than 30,000 fled to Holland during her reign.[56] Protestants also began to flee from France in 1585 when Henry III demanded that they convert to Catholicism or leave.[57] It was against this background of religious persecution, and the development of an inter-state system founded on territorial sovereignty, that the natural law jurists began to consider what place asylum ought to have in international law.

Grotius: asylum and international criminal law

In *De Jure Belli ac Pacis*, written in 1625, Hugo Grotius (1583–1645) sought to articulate rules to govern an international society of states – rules that dictated when states may and may not resort to force to pursue their ends – so as to reduce conflict.[58] He began his treatise by noting that his subject had yet to be addressed "in a comprehensive and systematic manner; yet the welfare of mankind demands that this task be accomplished."[59] Importantly, Grotius signaled asylum as one cause of war: "among the evils that arise from differences between states" is "the fact that 'It is possible for those who have done wrong to one state to flee for refuge to another.' "[60] This passage is significant because it suggests that the location of asylum had changed. Churches no longer offered the setting within which asylum was granted. Instead, a ruler granted asylum to fugitives fleeing another jurisdiction under the cover of his territorial sovereignty. And, as in ancient Greece, interfering with another polity's authoritative processes could create strife.

Grotius sought to minimize the possibility for conflict by arguing for a duty upon states to extradite or punish (*aut dedere aut punire*) fugitives who came within their borders. Failure to perform this duty made one an accessory to the crime and, therefore, liable to punitive war waged by the state seeking extradition.[61] The source of the duty to extradite or punish was found in the law of nature, which included the principle of commutative justice: "it is right for every one to suffer evil proportioned to that which he has done."[62] The justifications for that principle included the reform of offenders, the security given to those who are injured by wrongdoing, and "general utility," which is enhanced by the deterrent effects of punishment.[63] We hear echoes here of Innocent's proclamation several centuries earlier.

The duty to extradite, however, did not encompass *every* fugitive who fled abroad. It was limited by the "so much talked of rights of suppliants, and the inviolable nature of asylums ..." Grotius drew on a number of Greek sources to emphasize that asylum was deserved only by "those whose mind is innocent," not those "whose life is full of wicked acts."[64]

It was "for the benefit of those who suffer from undeserved enmity [*immerito odio laborant*], not those who have done something that is injurious to human society or to other men."[65] Only those offenders who fell into the former category were sheltered from the state's duty to "extradite or punish." In other words, asylum served as a defense against extradition, granted when the requesting state sought to inflict punishment unjustly.[66]

For Grotius, "unjust punishment" largely meant the punishment of people who had not actually committed the crime of which they had been accused. He provided two biblically-inspired examples of fugitives deserving of asylum: the accidental killer whose weapon slipped from his hand; and the slave who escaped from his master. Both were wrongfully accused: the accidental killer was sought for murder even though he did not intend to kill; and the slave had escaped subjugation to a master who could claim no rightful authority over him.

Those two cases, according to Grotius, were examples of the more general principle that asylum was to be available to all innocent people "who are beaten down by the hard and oppressive strokes of ill fortune."[67] As the two examples make clear, Grotius meant by this phrase a specific *kind* of "ill fortune" – namely, exposure to "undeserved enmity." Thus, Grotius gave the example of Nauplius, who received shelter from the Chalcidians once he had "adequately cleared himself from the charges brought by the Achaeans."[68]

Grotius' focus on supplicants who were innocent of the charges against them led him to state that "the case must be judged according to the ... law of [the supplicant's] own country."[69] According to that rule, states were to determine only whether a fugitive had in fact violated the criminal law of the requesting state. If so, then extradition was required, no matter how oppressive or noxious that criminal law was.

In other passages, however, Grotius recognized that asylum could be appropriate when a requesting state sought to punish conduct that, according to natural law, could not justly be made criminal. For example, Grotius recognized that "to obstruct the teachers of Christianity by pains and penalties is undoubtedly contrary to natural law and reason," and added that "[i]t seems unjust to persecute with punishments those who receive the law of Christ as true, but entertain doubts or errors on some external points."[70] Religious persecution would seem to fall within the description "undeserved enmity," warranting asylum. One might also expect asylum to be made available to those fleeing regimes that "provoke their peoples to despair and resistance by unheard of cruelties, having themselves abandoned all the law of nature."[71] Such people were innocent victims of tyrants who exercised political power in a manner inconsistent with the constraints imposed by natural law. In a footnote, Grotius cited the example of Frankish King Pepin, who "refused to surrender those who fled to him from Neustria to escape the tyranny."[72] Interestingly, Grotius even described himself in the Prologomena as "undeservedly forced out from my native land"; he had been sentenced for his involvement in a failed coup in the United Provinces, and sought asylum in France after escaping from prison in 1621 hidden in a trunk of books.[73]

The Grotian view of asylum was thus strikingly political. Determining whether a fugitive ought to be extradited or protected as a supplicant required the recipient state to make a potentially controversial normative judgment about the practices of the requesting state. Granting asylum expressed the view that the foreign state had exceeded the bounds of rightful authority, so that its claim to punish should not be honored.[74] Accordingly, asylum interfered with the internal affairs of another state. By granting asylum, a receiving state effectively acted as judge in a dispute between another state and one of its subjects. Having determined that the requesting state had no right to punish its subject, the receiving state provided him or her with immunity.

Asylum consequently bore a family resemblance to more forceful sanctions that could be employed against governments that treated their citizens cruelly. Grotius noted the "rule established by the law of nature and of social order, and ... confirmed by all the records of history, that every sovereign is supreme judge in his own kingdom and over his own subjects, in whose disputes no foreign power can justly interfere." Nonetheless, he argued, regimes can be so barbaric that "they lose the rights of independent sovereigns, and can no longer claim the privilege of the law of nations."[75] When regimes violated the natural law, Grotius sanctioned the waging of punitive wars against them.[76] He reasoned that, although citizens of a repressive government were bound by a pledge of loyalty to the sovereign and, therefore, could not revolt themselves, foreign governments were not bound by any such pledge and thus could intervene to aid the oppressed. Grotius provided the example of Constantine, who "took up arms against Maxentius and Licinius, and other Roman emperors [who] either took, or threatened to take them up against the Persians, if they did not desist from persecuting the Christians."[77]

On the Grotian view, asylum and punitive wars followed similar sorts of judgments – that authority was being exercised wrongfully. They differed in the degree of the sanction they imposed. Punitive war, the more severe sanction, should be waged only in cases where another regime's wrongdoing was so excessive that the regime as a whole had lost its authority to govern. Asylum was an appropriate response to particular instances in which authority was wrongfully exercised. Grotian asylum policy was thus enmeshed with high international politics.

Wrestling with Grotius: Pufendorf, Wolff, Vattel

Later international jurists, such as Samuel von Pufendorf (1632–94),[78] Christian Wolff (1679–1754),[79] and Emerich de Vattel (1714–67),[80] rejected Grotius' idea that states had the power to enforce the natural law against violators. Pufendorf instead theorized that the power to punish stemmed from sovereignty.[81] Because the international system had no sovereign, states were not fit to punish one another for violations of the natural law committed against third parties. A state was only justified in fighting a war when it had been harmed itself; and even then the state's motive could not be to punish, but rather to seek reparations for the harm done to it.[82] Nor were states under any duty to extradite or punish fugitives from another state; punishment was a matter between the criminal and his own sovereign.[83] Pufendorf argued that his view would promote a more peaceful international system. "For a person to thrust himself forward as a kind of arbitrator of human affairs," as Grotius' theory required, "is opposed even to the equality granted by nature, not to mention the fact that such a thing could easily lead to great abuse, since there is scarcely a man living against whom this could not serve as an excuse for war."[84]

Pufendorf: underprotecting refugees

Pufendorf's comparatively pacific view of the international system had important consequences for his treatment of asylum. On Grotius' account, states were under an obligation to extradite or punish criminals who fled from other states. Asylum was an exception to this obligation, warranted only when the requesting state sought to inflict an undeserved injury. Grotian asylum policy was thus premised on states "thrusting themselves forward as arbitrators of human affairs." Pufendorf rejected the proposition that states should make judgments of this kind. But how then should one understand asylum?

Pufendorf's approach was to collapse asylum into the general duty to "admit ... strangers, as well as ... kindly provid[e] travelers with shelter and hospitality."[85] He reached this conclusion by citing several authorities that appeared to equate supplicants and strangers.[86] Grotius had also argued for a duty of hospitality to strangers, saying that "individual subjects, who wish to remove from the dominions of one power to those of another" should be free to do so. Indeed, Grotius regarded the possibility of such migration as a "principle of natural liberty."[87] But for Grotius, asylum was a different matter than hospitality. Supplicants were wanted for extradition by their states of origin; they were not simply sojourners seeking a new home. The relevant duty regarding supplicants was to extradite or punish – unless, of course, the punishment faced by the supplicant was undeserved. Because Pufendorf did not accept the duty to extradite or punish, he saw no need to differentiate between supplicants and other strangers seeking a new home. All should be received with hospitality.

Pufendorf's duty of hospitality, however, could give way to interests of state. "If the duty of hospitality is to be an obligation of natural law," Pufendorf wrote, "it is required that the stranger shall have an honourable or necessary reason for being away from his home. Furthermore, he should be an upright man, and one from whom no danger or disgrace will come to our house."[88] Thus, he concluded, states merely needed to admit "a few strangers, who have not been driven from their homes for some crime," and they remained at liberty to restrict entry except to those who were "industrious or wealthy, and will disturb neither our religious faith nor our institutions."[89]

For Pufendorf, then, whether supplicants would be admitted turned not on justice or desert, as it had for Grotius; instead, admittance turned on the contribution supplicants could make to the receiving state. Will they be productive members of the local economy? Will they help the country grow more powerful? Are they religiously compatible? If the answer was no, admission could be refused – and supplicants would be returned to face unjust punishment. Pufendorf concluded:

Every state may reach a decision, according to its own usage, on the admission of foreigners who come to it for ... reasons [other than temporary passage, a brief visit, or trade] that are necessary and deserving of sympathy ... [W]hen these people are worthy of our sympathy, and no reasons of state stand in the way, it would certainly be an act of humanity on our part to confer a kindness on them, that will not be too onerous on us, or the cause of later regret. If they are not, our pity should be so restrained that we may not later become an object of pity to others.[90]

Asylum was thus decoupled from the controversial judgments about other states' authority that had been, for Grotius, at asylum's core. From Grotius' standpoint, Pufendorf's approach thus risked the under-protection of supplicants: in pursuit of self-interest, states were free to turn away people deserving of protection.

Wolff: overprotecting refugees

Like Pufendorf, Christian Wolff rejected Grotius' ideas that states could enforce the natural law against one another and that they had a duty to extradite or punish fugitives. "[A] wrongful act committed in one state," Wolff wrote, "does not affect another state ..."[91] Wolff also followed Pufendorf in viewing asylum as linked to the duty of hospitality. But he went to greater lengths than Pufendorf in urging states to take this duty seriously.

Admonishing his readers to "be compassionate toward exiles,"[92] he wrote that:

exiles do not cease to be men, because they are driven into exile, consequently compelled to depart from the place where they have domicile ... [S]ince by nature all things are common ... the right of living anywhere in the world cannot be absolutely taken away from one, by nature the right belongs to an exile to live anywhere in the world.[93]

In a reprise of medieval Christian attitudes toward punishment, Wolff even endorsed giving refuge to ordinary criminals as an act of love that recognized the possibility of redemption: "Since the act cannot be undone by us or by them, it is rather incumbent on us that we bring them back to a better moral life, and that, if they should desire to reform of their own accord, we should not stand in the way to prevent it."[94] From the Grotian standpoint, Wolff thus urged the overprotection of supplicants: asylum was to be granted even to criminals who deserved to be punished.

While Wolff urged states to be open to foreigners, he stopped short of requiring them to be. Permanent residence, Wolff wrote, could not be "denied to exiles by a nation, unless special reasons stand in the way";[95] but the list of "special reasons" was long – in effect, states had discretion to deny admittance for any reason related to the public welfare – and in the end, exiles had no recourse but to accept a state's decision. "[A]n exile is allowed to ask admittance," Wolff wrote, "but he cannot assuredly according to his liking determine domicile for himself, wherever he shall please, and if admittance is refused, that must be endured."[96]

Vattel: a middle path

Vattel presented his *Le Droit des Gens* as an explication, expansion, and correction of Wolff's work. But his view of asylum was much more subtle than Wolff's. On the one hand, he agreed with Wolff that states should err on the side of overprotecting fugitives. "[N]o Nation," he wrote, "may, without good reason, refuse even a perpetual residence to a man who has been driven from his country,"[97] even one who was escaping punishment. Although there was a long list of "good reasons" that could justify exclusion – as there was for Wolff and Pufendorf – at the same time states should not lightly invoke them. The right to asylum, Vattel wrote, was:

in the abstract ... a necessary and perfect one, [but] it must be observed that it is only an imperfect one relative to each individual country; ... By reason of its natural liberty it is for each Nation to decide whether it is or is not in a position to receive an alien. Hence an exile has no absolute right to choose a country at will and settle himself there as he pleases; he must ask permission of the sovereign of the country, and if it be refused, he is bound to submit.[98]

However, "[p]rudence should not take the form of suspicion nor be pushed to the point of refusing an asylum to the outcast on slight grounds and from unreasonable or foolish fears. It should be regulated by never losing sight of the charity and sympathy which are due to the unfortunate."[99]

Moreover, Vattel emphasized, when asylum seekers could not find a refuge anywhere else, a state was required to take them in without regard to its national interests:

The Nation to which they present themselves should grant them lands in which to dwell, at least for a time, unless it has very serious reasons for refusing ... But, after all, these fugitives must find an asylum somewhere, and if every Nation refuses to grant it to them, they may justly settle in the first country where they find sufficient land without having to deprive the inhabitants.[100]

Vattel thus argued for an even more robust right of asylum than Wolff. It was animated not only by a sense of compassion – which could always be overridden by national interest – but also by a duty of justice, to which national interest sometimes needed to give way. In that sense, Vattel took overprotection one step further than Wolff: not only were states entitled to grant asylum to criminals (who, Grotius argued, should be extradited, not sheltered), they could be *required* to do so.

Certain criminals, however, were so dangerous that no state could reasonably be expected to absorb them. The principle of asylum had its practical limits. Criminals "who by the character and frequency of their crimes are a menace to public security everywhere," Vattel concluded, ought to be extradited and punished, not sheltered. Such criminals included "poisoners, assassins, [and] incendiaries ...; for they direct their disastrous attacks against all Nations, by destroying the foundations of their common safety." Pirates also fell into this category, as did robbers. The state of refuge, said Vattel, ought to "deliver [such criminals] up to the injured State, so that it may inflict due punishment upon [them]"[101] – indeed, they ought to do so even when such criminals were one's own citizens. We hear strains of Grotius – but only for the worst of criminals. No state should be required to accept criminals who "violate the laws and menace the safety of all Nations alike."[102]

Confining the duty to "extradite or punish" to crimes that fell within the *delicta majora* – like murder, piracy, and arson[103] – was quite clever. Asylum could be extended to the vast majority of fugitives, as Wolff had advocated; but at the same time, public safety could be preserved by requiring that the most dangerous of criminals be extradited. And, because everyone agreed on the narrow set of crimes that constituted the *delicta majora*, the decision whether to grant asylum to a criminal or to extradite him would not involve the state of refuge in any controversial judgments about another state's authority to punish. Extradition could reasonably be demanded only when a supplicant was wanted for a crime that everyone could agree should be punished. In all other cases, asylum was the appropriate response.

In fact, however, Vattel's approach could not entirely avoid controversial judgments about other states. Although states were likely to agree in the abstract about which crimes fell into the *delicta majora*, they might disagree for several reasons about whether a particular asylum seeker was extraditable. First, oppressive countries could have criminal procedures regarded by free states as insufficiently protective of liberty. They might admit secret evidence, presume guilt rather than innocence, or violate due process in some other way. Even someone accused of piracy still had certain due process rights that provided limits on a state's rightful authority. If an oppressive state routinely exceeded those limits, a free state that took due process seriously might wish to grant asylum even to an accused pirate. The extradition of those who "menace the safety of all" thus depended upon a tacit judgment that the requesting state's criminal procedure would accord due process to the accused.

Second, even if due process were guaranteed, a foreign state's punishments might be too harsh to be acceptable. This difficulty could arise even with respect to an extradition treaty between two free states. Thomas Jefferson, for example, objected to a treaty with Britain that would extradite thieves, because "In England, and probably in Canada, to steal a hare is death, the first offence; to steal above the value of 12*d*, death the second offence. All excess of punishment is a *crime*; to remit a fugitive to excessive punishment is to be *accessary* to the crime."[104] Today we see this problem arise in the unwillingness of European states to extradite to the United States a fugitive who will potentially be subject to the death penalty if found guilty. The extradition of serious criminals thus also depended upon a judgment that the punishment faced by a fugitive, if found guilty, would be reasonable.

Finally, states could disagree about what counted as a crime for the purposes of extradition. For example, Britain was reluctant to return to the United States for punishment fugitive slaves who had killed their masters. In 1841, it refused to extradite about 100 slaves who had anchored the American ship *Creole* in the Bahamas after having staged a mutiny. Britain viewed these slaves as having engaged in justified rebellion. The United States, needless to say, disagreed, and viewed the slaves as murderers and mutineers. A decision to extradite, therefore, depended upon a judgment that the requesting government was correct in classifying an act as a crime rather than as an act of justified rebellion.

Vattel's approach – granting asylum to all except those who had committed serious crimes abroad – was thus premised upon a series of potentially controversial judgments about other states' authoritative processes: Would the serious criminal be tried fairly? Would he be punished fairly? And did his act really constitute a serious crime? If not, then asylum was warranted and extradition should be refused.

Vattel seemed to have acknowledged at least the first problem. When a regime made a practice of disregarding the due process rights of fugitives who were extradited to it, Vattel regarded further extraditions to that regime as inappropriate: "[I]f he should find from constant experience that his subjects are being persecuted by the magistrates of the neighboring States when appearing before them, he would doubtless be justified ... in refusing requisitions until satisfaction had been made for the injustice done and its recurrence provided against."[105] And if a state refused to extradite a criminal when extradition was expected, Vattel maintained that the refusing state needed clearly to express its qualms by "set[ting] forth [its] reasons for taking such action and mak[ing] them perfectly plain."[106] In other words, if asylum was granted to someone wanted for a serious crime, the state of refuge was required to justify its actions through criticism of the requesting state.

The English tradition

Concerns about the criminal procedure of other states animated the English policy between the seventeenth and nineteenth centuries of granting asylum to virtually every refugee who arrived on its shores, without regard to his reason for flight, and no matter how odious his crime. Even by 1870, Britain had signed only a handful of extradition treaties.[107]

Beginning in 1174, England had entered into numerous treaties with Scotland, Ireland, and France providing for the mutual rendition of fugitives who had fled across the border.[108] Writing in the early seventeenth century, Sir Edward Coke (1552–1634) objected strongly to this practice, especially insofar as it involved handing over English subjects to a foreign government for punishment. He wanted to protect England's comparatively demanding requirements of due process against circumvention, and extradition made it possible for English subjects to be tried and convicted for crimes under procedures that would be unacceptable in England. Thus, Coke argued in his comments on the Magna Carta that English subjects could not be forcibly sent abroad except by Act of Parliament.[109]

Coke's objections were not limited to the extradition of English subjects, however. He also favored a rule granting asylum to foreigners who sought refuge in England. "Divided kingdomes under severall kings in league with another," he wrote, "are sanctuaries for servants or subjects flying to safety from one kingdome to another, and upon demand made by them, are not by the laws and liberties of kingdomes to be delivered: and this (some hold) is grounded upon the law in Deuteronomy. *Non trades fervum domino fuo, qui ad te confugerit* [Thou shalt not deliver unto his master the servant which is escaped from his master unto thee]."[110]

Coke's position was reflected in the Habeas Corpus Act of 1679, which stipulated that an "inhabitant" or "resident" of England could not legally be sent prisoner abroad.[111] Although this language perhaps left ambiguous the applicability of the Act to foreigners taking refuge in England, it nonetheless prepared the way for an English reluctance to enter into extradition treaties. By 1791, Thomas Jefferson could report to George Washington that "England has no such convention with any nation, and their laws have given no power to their executive to surrender fugitives of any description."[112]

Britain at last agreed to extradite murderers and forgers to the United States in 1794 and to France, the Netherlands, and Spain in 1802. Extradition treaties covering a few additional offenses – assault with intent to commit murder, piracy, arson, and robbery – were signed with the United States and France in 1843.[113] But in practice these treaties were ineffectual, since the British were often unwilling to accept warrants issued by French or American magistrates as sufficient for extradition. Contrary to British law, French warrants could be issued based on an accusation without proof; consequently, no criminal was extradited from Britain to France between 1843 and 1863. And it was feared that the Americans would accuse escaped slaves of fictitious crimes to bring about their recapture.[114]

England's willingness to become, as Jefferson put it, "the asylum of the Paolis, the La Mottes, the Calonnes, in short, of the most atrocious offenders as well as the most innocent victims, who have been able to get there,"[115] thus stemmed from its respect for criminal procedure as a basic ingredient of liberty. It had made a categorical judgment that the criminal procedure of other states offered the accused inadequate protection and permitted the criminal law to be used as an instrument of political repression. Asylum served as a prophylactic measure against the possibility that a fugitive would be treated unjustly if extradited. Other governments – with the limited exceptions of the United States, France, and later Denmark – could not be trusted to observe the procedural protections to which the English thought all accused criminals were entitled, and which ensured that political dissidents would be fairly treated.

The young United States adopted the English approach toward extradition. Thomas Jefferson wrote in 1792 that an extradition treaty between a free government and a despotic government was unworkable:

Two neighboring and free governments, with law equally mild and just, would find no difficulty in forming a convention for the interchange of fugitive criminals. Nor would two neighboring despotic governments, with laws of equal severity. The latter wish that no door should be opened to their subjects flying from the oppression of their laws. The fact is, that most of the governments on the continent of Europe have such conventions; but England, the only free one till lately, has never yet consented either to enter into a convention for this purpose, or to give up a fugitive. The difficulty between a free government and a despotic one is indeed great.[116]

So long as a gap existed between free countries and despotic regimes in terms of the crimes for which one could be punished, the due process required to convict, and the kind of punishment exacted, Jefferson thought it was better to provide asylum for fugitives and wrongdoers than to return them for prosecution. "The laws of this country," he explained to Minister Genet of France in 1793:

take no notice of crimes committed out of their jurisdiction; The most atrocious offender, coming within their pale, is received by them as an innocent man, and they have authorized no one to seize or deliver him. The evil of protecting malefactors of every dye is sensibly felt here, as in other countries; but until a reformation of the criminal codes of most nations, to deliver fugitives from them, would be to become their accomplices: the former therefore is viewed as the lesser evil.[117]

Aside from the Jay Treaty of 1794 entered into with Britain, which was allowed to lapse, the United States did not conclude another extradition treaty until 1842 (with Britain) and 1843 (with France).

The Anglo-American approach to asylum shared much with that of Grotius. While Britain and the United States readily extended asylum without regard to the innocence or guilt of the asylum seeker (unlike Grotius), they did so for a reason that Grotius would have appreciated: a categorical judgment that other states' authoritative processes could not be relied upon to limit punishment to those who deserved it. Jefferson acknowledged that asylum was a second-best solution; that sheltering criminals was an evil; and that in principle extradition ought to be carried out. But, he argued, that principle could not be justly implemented in a world full of despotic governments. Protecting individuals from unjust prosecution was too important a task to entrust to the kangaroo courts of despotic regimes.

Cesare Beccaria, the eighteenth-century Italian penal reformer (1738–94), shared this view. As a general matter, he opposed the existence of sanctuaries within countries, since "[i]mpunity and asylum differ only in degree ... [A]sylums encourage crimes more than punishments deter them."[118] But he was reluctant to endorse an end to asylum, despite its corrosive effect on law and order. Asylum was an unfortunate but necessary policy in a world full of oppressive regimes:

But, whether international agreements for the reciprocal exchange of criminals be useful, I would not dare to decide until laws more in conformity with the needs of humanity, until milder punishments and an end to dependence on arbitrary power and opinion, have provided security for oppressed innocence and hated virtue – until universal reason, which ever tends the more to unite the interests of throne and subjects, has confined tyranny altogether to the vast plains of Asia, though, undoubtedly, the persuasion that there is not a foot of soil upon which real crimes are pardoned would be a most efficacious means of preventing them.[119]

In other words, if governments could be trusted to exercise their authority rightfully, asylum would be a malicious interference with justice. But in a world where many regimes exercise power arbitrarily, asylum was necessary to effectuate justice.

Protecting revolutionaries: the political offense exception

While Britain had a long tradition of hostility toward extradition, the Continent had adopted a different approach. Rulers regularly extradited criminals – including political offenders, who were least likely to receive a fair trial – to their allies. Indeed, the return of fugitives accused of *lèse-majesté* was the main purpose of extradition. Crimes affecting the "public weal," as Grotius put it, were considered to be more serious than "private" crimes.[120]

The French Revolution brought about major changes in the way Europeans, both on the Continent and in Britain, approached extradition and asylum. While for Grotius and Coke asylum was aimed largely at protecting innocent people from unfair criminal procedures, by the early nineteenth century the focus of asylum had changed from criminal justice to political morality. On the Continent, and soon afterwards in England and the United States, states began to grant asylum in order to protect those who were wanted abroad for political offenses. At around the same time in England and the United States, extradition courts, wary of creating diplomatic difficulties for the executive, began to embrace the "rule of non-inquiry," according to which courts refused to inquire into the adequacy of the requesting state's criminal procedures.[121]

The first state to proclaim the principle of asylum for political offenders was revolutionary France, and it had unabashedly political aims in doing so. The French Constitution of 1793 guaranteed asylum to any foreigner forced to flee his land for advancing the cause of liberty.[122] This principle was often honored in the breach, however, as France continued to extradite political offenders until the 1830s. Treaties with Switzerland in 1798, 1803, and 1828 all called for the extradition of fugitives whose crimes undermined state security.[123]

In 1833, Belgium became the first state to pass a law barring the extradition of a foreigner wanted for "any political crime antecedent to the extradition, or for any act connected with such a crime."[124] By the mid-nineteenth century, the Belgian text had been adopted by most European states. Even autocracies adopted a political offense exception; without it, the liberal states were unwilling to extradite ordinary criminals to them.[125]

The idea that political offenders should be sheltered from extradition resonated in England as well. In 1815, the government was roundly criticized following the Governor of Gibraltar's surrender of political fugitives to Spain. Sir James Mackintosh appealed on the floor of Parliament to the "venerable principle" of the non-extradition of political offenders.[126] By the late nineteenth century, political morality had become the main focus of asylum in England as well. Opponents of extradition treaties expressed concern that illiberal states would use the criminal law as a pretext for persecuting political dissidents. In 1847, the Home Office opposed a proposed extradition treaty with Naples primarily on that ground:

> With France & America we have made Treaties of Extradition for many good reasons; having Confidence in the Governments of those Countries, that they would not use the provisions of the Treaty covertly for *political* purposes … But could we have the same Confidence in the *Neapolitan* Government? … Besides, a convention of the kind proposed with the Neapolt Govt c^d scarcely ever be carried into effect, on account of the irregularities or looseness w^h w^d probably be found to exist in their Criminal Proceedings. – **But the principle Objection is the danger that such a Convention will be perverted to** *political* **purposes.**[127]

John Stuart Mill and his Liberal Party, offering a similar argument, were able to block a proposed extradition treaty in 1852 between England and France that would have returned to France anyone who had fled a conviction or an arrest warrant. Mill warned that the French criminal law was too susceptible to political manipulation, so that political dissidents might be punished under the pretense of prosecution for an ordinary crime. "The depositions which are taken preparatory to a criminal trial in France by the *juge d'instruction* are taken in secret," he argued. "It is … the easiest thing in the world to get up a false charge against a person, if … there is the slightest disposition to do so."[128]

On its face, the political offense exception appeared impartial: it gave asylum to any political offender, regardless of the offender's ideological goals. The political offender exception was, in its phrasing, indifferent between despotism and democracy, autocracy and liberalism. On at least one account, this seeming neutrality was the major advantage of the political offense exception: it allowed countries to avoid having to determine whether the offender's crimes had been legitimate resistance to tyranny. Heinrich Lammasch, the last Prime Minister of Imperial Austria, wrote in the mid-1880s that a blanket exception for political offenders was a corollary of the principle of non-intervention, avoiding the need for foreign states to pick sides in the internal disputes of other states.[129]

Despite the appearance of neutrality, the political offense exception was in fact premised upon a categorical judgment about the legitimacy of foreign governments. The political offense exception was first enacted in revolutionary France to support and shelter radical democrats oppressed by neighboring autocracies. It furthered a particular political aim and was grounded in a particular view about legitimate authority. States sought to protect political offenders whose goals were sympathetic, and deny protection to those whose goals they opposed, by manipulating the definition of "political offense" to encompass only "legitimate" resistance.

One way to define "political offense" was to focus on the elements of the offense itself. Thus, acts such as treason or sedition – which were aimed at the government – were political, while common law offenses – like murder or robbery – were not. But that answer seemed to be unduly narrow, since common law offenses could be politically motivated and connected to an uprising or rebellion. For example, one could murder a political official or rob to obtain funds for a political group.

On the other hand, if an offense could be regarded as "political" due solely to its motivation or objective, the category of "political offenses" would be disturbingly broad: terrorists who indiscriminately harmed innocents in pursuit of a political objective would enjoy protection from extradition. As Sir James Fitzjames Stephen put it in his treatise on English criminal law, such an approach "would have protected the wretch Fieschi, whose offence consisted in shooting down many persons in the streets of Paris in an attempt to murder Louis-Philippe."[130]

Stephen and John Stuart Mill both preferred a definition centered on the context in which an act was committed. The phrase "political offense," argued Stephen, "ought to be interpreted" to pertain to crimes that "were incidental to and formed a part of political disturbances."[131] But that definition was also unsatisfying. It was underinclusive, since it would omit a "legitimate" act, performed with a political purpose, committed prior to the beginning of a political disturbance. It also risked overinclusion because it labeled "political" any criminal act committed in the course of an insurrection. Thus, it too might protect offenders like "the wretch Fieschi," who showed little regard for innocent human life.

In the end, whether an act of resistance was regarded as a "political offense" depended implicitly on a judgment about whether certain *tactics* could be legitimately employed in carrying out political resistance.[132] Thus, Mill contended that "in rebellion, as in war, ... a distinction should be made between fair weapons or modes of warfare and foul ones."[133] He therefore argued in favor of extraditing from France two suspects in the 1867 Clerkenwell Prison bombing, which was carried out to facilitate the escape of two Irish Fenians, but killed fourteen others.[134]

Of course, whether one regarded resistance tactics as "legitimate" often depended in part on one's view of the regime against which resistance was directed. An act might be regarded as a legitimate tactic of rebellion when carried out by a democratic revolutionary against an autocracy, but not when carried out by a socialist or anarchist against a liberal democracy. Thomas Jefferson drew upon that distinction in explaining his reluctance to extradite Spanish fugitives wanted for treason:

Treason ... when, real, merits the highest punishment. But most codes extend their definitions of treason to acts not really against one's country. They do not distinguish between acts against the *Government* and acts against the *oppressions of the Government.* The latter are virtues, yet have furnished more victims to the executioner than the former: because real treasons are rare, oppressions frequent. The unsuccessful strugglers against tyranny have been the chief martyrs of treason laws in all countries. Reformation of government with *our* neighbors is as much wanting now, as reformation of religion is or ever was any where. We should not wish, then, to give up to the executioner the patriot who fails and flees to us.[135]

Jefferson's argument, of course, turned on implicit substantive criteria that allowed him to distinguish between "real treasons" against legitimate governments, on the one hand, and justified resistance against oppressive governments, on the other hand.

Along similar lines, a British court ruled that Theodule Meunier, an anarchist wanted by France for the 1892 bombings of a barracks and of the Café Véry in Paris, was extraditable. His acts of resistance could not be regarded as "political offenses," the court held, because anarchism was not a political movement. To be political, the court said, an offense must at least aim at replacing one kind of government with another; but anarchists rejected all governments.[136]

In sum, the definition of "political offense" did not simply fall from the sky. It was rooted in value judgments about what counted as legitimate resistance to government and legitimate punishment by government, and was designed to "get it right," morally speaking, as often as possible. And the policy of sheltering political offenders not only followed from, and expressed, such value judgments, but also advanced the cause of liberty by sheltering its partisans from punishment.

From extradition to deportation: reconceiving asylum as immigration policy

The historical account offered in the preceding pages recovers asylum's political roots. Asylum's historical function was to immunize fugitives against unjust punishment. It therefore depended upon a potentially controversial judgment about the manner in which another regime exercised its authority. The persecution requirement follows naturally from that historical function. To "persecute" means to "pursue with harassing or oppressive treatment," precisely the kind of treatment that historically gave rise to a valid claim for asylum against extradition. Today, of course, extradition and asylum are separate areas of law, and asylum is usually viewed as a subset of immigration policy rather than international criminal law. But the purpose of asylum – to shelter those exposed to persecution – remains the same.

The recasting of asylum – from a defense against extradition to a defense against deportation – occurred as states began to close their borders. In a world of open borders, asylum was needed only as a defense to extradition; persecuted people who were not sought for extradition could easily find a home elsewhere. But in a world of closed borders, refusing admittance was functionally equivalent to extradition: in either case, the foreigner was returned to his state of origin.[137] It followed that, if asylum's historical purpose was to be served in a world of closed borders, asylum needed to be made available to all those who were persecuted and who would otherwise be excluded or deported, and not merely those who were actually sought for extradition. The persecution requirement served to distinguish between refugees deserving of asylum on the one hand, and ordinary migrants excluded by the new immigration restrictions on the other hand.

In Britain, for example, immigration controls were first put into place in 1793, partly in response to fears that French spies had infiltrated the country and were organizing a revolt. Britain went to war with France a few weeks later. The 1793 Act excluded "undesirable aliens," required foreigners to arrive at particular ports of entry, and limited their freedom of movement once they were within the country.[138] But the bill's sponsor, Lord Grenville, stressed that it was not intended to exclude refugees fleeing the Terror; it was aimed only at those "who would pull down church and state, religion and God, morals and happiness."[139] Notwithstanding the Act, Britain received a large number of refugees over the next decade – though exact figures are unavailable – and spent in excess of £2.9 million on their support.[140]

Nonetheless, as the Napoleonic Wars came to an end, the 1793 Aliens Act came under increasing criticism from those who felt it was insufficiently protective of democrats fleeing Continental autocracies. Asylum seekers were seen as heroic freedom fighters, whose only crime, as John Cam Hobhouse put it on the floor of Parliament in 1822, was "the longing of expatriated friends of liberty to overthrow tyrants at home."[141] England's policy of sheltering political offenders from extradition enjoyed broad public support; many felt that revolutionary activity was a legitimate response to the pervasive autocracy on the Continent. By 1826, the Act had been repealed and replaced with a less restrictive alien registration provision. Britain's borders remained effectively open for the next eighty years, and aliens resident there could not be deported.[142]

The 1905 Aliens Act, Britain's next attempt at regulating immigration, was directed at reducing the large number of Eastern European Jews who had begun to enter Britain in the 1880s. Opponents of the legislation argued that it represented a perversion of Britain's national traditions. One Liberal MP appealed:

[t]o all who are anxious to preserve the right of asylum, and all who are devoted to that traditional great policy of this country, to vote against a measure which renders it possible that mere officialdom shall be able to exclude the political refugee from this country ... I have inherited traditions which compel me to vote against a measure which I think would tend to impair the world-wide and historical reputation which this country has enjoyed for centuries as being a sanctuary for the politically distressed.[143]

In the end, the 1905 Act barred criminals and those likely to become public charges. But it exempted:

an immigrant who proves that he is seeking admission ... solely to avoid prosecution or punishment on religious or political grounds, or for an offence of a political character or persecution involving danger of imprisonment or danger to life or limb on account of religious belief.[144]

Asylum, which historically had sheltered fugitives wanted for extradition, had been reconceived as a defense to exclusion or deportation. Immigration restrictions had the same practical effect as extradition: the return of foreigners to their home state. The traditional rationale for asylum – to protect foreigners from unjust punishment – therefore applied equally to foreign victims of persecution who were not fugitives, but who merely sought refuge abroad. The persecution requirement served to distinguish among refugees who were deserving of an exemption from the Act's requirements and ordinary immigrants who were not.

A similar pattern unfolded in the United States. Beginning in the late nineteenth century, faced with increasing numbers of immigrants, particularly from Central and Eastern Europe, the United States began for the first time to restrict immigration from Europe. In 1891, Congress passed a measure excluding paupers and other persons likely to become a public charge.[145] This was followed by a nearly twenty-year campaign to enact a statute requiring new immigrants to pass a literacy test. Progressives supported the literacy test on economic grounds, nativists on racialist grounds. Congress first passed a literacy bill in 1895, but it was vetoed by President McKinley; unsuccessful attempts followed in 1906 and 1912 (the latter due to a veto by President Taft).

In 1915, a literacy test was passed yet again, and this time was vetoed by President Wilson on the ground that it "seeks to all but close entirely the gates of asylum which have always been open to those who could find nowhere else the right and opportunity of constitutional agitation for what they conceived to be the natural and inalienable rights of man."[146] Wilson also objected that the literacy requirement excluded people who had been denied the opportunity to become educated, without regard to their natural capacities.

Finally, in 1917, Congress passed a revised version of the bill that exempted from the literacy test victims of religious persecution, "whether such persecution be evidenced by overt acts or by laws or governmental regulations that discriminate against the alien or the race to which he belongs because of his faith."[147] Victims of political persecution, however, received no such exemption; lawmakers feared that the beneficiaries of such an exemption would be radicals whom the United States sought to exclude. And, as pointed out by Jewish groups who supported the exemption for victims of religious persecution, political dissidents were in any event not likely to be illiterate.[148] Interestingly, President Wilson again vetoed the Bill; this time, he *objected* to the exemption for victims of religious persecution on the ground that it forced American officials to perform the "invidious function" of judging other states, thereby risking diplomatic embarrassment or dispute.[149]

By the early 1920s, restrictionist sentiments overcame respect for the principle of asylum. Bills enacted in 1921 and 1924 imposed immigration quotas based on national origin; no exception to the quota caps was made for victims of persecution. That policy, together with (until 1935) a strict interpretation of the rule excluding those likely to become public charges, which also had no exception for victims of persecution, tragically limited the number of German Jews accepted by the United States in the years leading up to the Second World War.[150]

On the Continent, the story was more complex but the upshot similar: as immigration controls were tightened over the course of the nineteenth century, asylum was reconceived as an exception to those restrictions and was made available to those who would be persecuted were they returned to their countries of origin.

Unlike Britain, countries on the Continent had long policed foreigners within their borders with an eye toward expelling undesirable aliens, such as political dissidents, deserters, peddlers, vagabonds, and beggars. In Austria, a special police division was established in 1794 to register foreigners, and undesirables were expelled if found traveling within the country.[151] Similarly, in the German states passport legislation was introduced at the beginning of the nineteenth century and the authorities kept careful track of foreigners' movements in the interior. Travelers staying over night were required to register at the local police station, and police visas were required for onward travel. Deviation from the approved route risked arrest. In larger Prussian cities, any travelers staying longer than a few hours needed to purchase a residence permit to be carried with them at all times.[152] Foreigners could be deported not only for crimes, but also for such offenses as "competing with citizens in overcrowded labour markets, or for becoming a burden on public funds."[153] Foreign vagrants deported from Bavaria alone between 1836 and 1850 numbered between 5,700 and 12,700 per year.[154]

In France, royal decrees dating from the fifteenth century required innkeepers to report the identities of their guests to the authorities, and passports were required of travelers entering and leaving cities.[155] In the 1790s, regulations were strengthened: property owners were required to report the names of foreigners residing or staying in their property; foreigners needed to declare their presence or face expulsion; and passport controls were tightened.[156]

However, throughout much of the nineteenth century, the liberal European states – namely, France, the Netherlands, and after 1830,

Belgium – offered aliens subject to expulsion a choice of a border from which to be expelled. As Frank Caestecker has explained, this "provision was the result of a liberal ideology which acknowledged the very different regimes in Europe and the resulting different conceptions of what a crime was."[157] Because aliens could choose the border from which they would be expelled, the expulsions were not seen as a threat to the principle of asylum: deportees could choose to be expelled to a third country if they would face persecution at home.

In 1849, Prussia began to request that the liberal states expel to it only those foreigners who were either of German origin or who had to pass through the German states to return to their countries of origin and who possessed money for the transit fare. This plea was ignored, and in 1884, the German Reich decided to begin returning all others to the border from which they had entered. This unilateral move forced the liberal states to revise their expulsion policies, since it was no longer possible to offer all expellees the border of their choice. Over the next twenty years, France, Belgium, and the Netherlands entered into bilateral treaties with Germany and with each other providing that third-country nationals could not be expelled into neighboring states without the consent of those states. At the same time, the treaties obligated states to accept their own nationals and to give free passage to others who needed to pass through to reach their countries of origin.[158] Foreigners facing expulsion were now returned to their states of origin.

As Caestecker explains, this change in expulsion policy forced states to reconceive of asylum as a subset of immigration policy. When refugees facing expulsion could choose their border, expulsion did not necessarily expose them to persecution. But "from the 1880s onwards, when unwanted aliens were deported to their country of origin which was for most refugees their country of persecution, this possibility was excluded."[159] Asylum became the mechanism by which an alien could claim a reprieve from expulsion to his state of origin, and to qualify, he needed to demonstrate a fear of persecution. The liberal regimes, Caestecker reports:

immediately and explicitly forbade the expulsion of refugees ... Special facilities were provided for the (politically) persecuted. All aliens who were to be expelled had to be questioned about whether they were pursued for political reasons. If so, the central authorities had to be informed about those who claimed to be refugees. Their allegations had to be verified and genuine refugees were not to be deported.[160]

In one sense, this new arrangement left refugees better off: whereas before they faced expulsion, albeit to a country other than their country of origin, now they could avoid deportation altogether through asylum.[161]

Conclusion

The historical account put forward in this chapter offers a needed response to those who criticize the persecution requirement as a Cold War creation, designed to advance the ideological interests of the West by directing attention to Soviet deficiencies. While the West undoubtedly viewed the 1951 UN Convention's persecution requirement as to its political advantage, it is mistaken to think that the standard was an ad hoc invention crafted from whole cloth for partisan purposes. The Convention, which was born on the ashes of the Holocaust, did not define into existence a "new" refugee. To the contrary, historically, asylum and persecution were inextricably connected: asylum's function was to protect unfortunates from specifically political harms; granting asylum reflected the judgment that the state of origin had abused its authority; and asylum was connected to other tactics for reforming or challenging abusive regimes (e.g., military intervention for Grotius, support for liberal revolutionaries by the European liberal states in the nineteenth century).

Originally, asylum served this function as a defense to extradition and was focused largely on protecting innocent fugitives from unfair criminal procedures. But beginning in the late eighteenth and early nineteenth centuries, asylum's focus shifted from procedural criminal justice to the promotion of substantive political morality: asylum benefited "political offenders" who had justifiably rebelled against autocratic rule and were sought for extradition; and it no longer benefited ordinary criminals who might be subjected to unfair criminal procedures, because the "rule of non-inquiry" forbade courts from inquiring into the criminal procedure of other states. Asylum's focus on political morality was not altogether novel. It was in harmony with the ancient Greek practice and the theory espoused by Grotius, and it was also consistent with the general historical function of asylum to immunize people who faced unjust punishment. But, nonetheless, it did mark a shift in emphasis: asylum now protected *refugees*, not fugitives.

That trend was reinforced as states began to close their borders over the course of the nineteenth century. As states began to return unwanted foreigners to their countries of origin, asylum was reconceived as a defense to deportation. But its function remained the same: a reprieve for those who would face unjustified punishment if returned to their respective states of origin. The eventual identification of "persecution" as the essential criterion for refugee status in the Convention thus followed naturally from asylum's historical purpose (a tradition that was tragically displaced by xenophobia and isolationism during the years leading up to the Second World War). In short, the political conception of asylum has deep historical roots.

Of course, that does not alone provide an argument for retaining a political view of asylum today, as against a humanitarian alternative. But it does invite us to take seriously the question of whether there might be sound moral and practical reasons to do so.

Notes

1. James C. Hathaway, *Law of Refugee Status* (Toronto: Butterworths, 1991), pp. 1, 8.
2. Gervase Coles, "Approaching the Refugee Problem Today" in Gil Loescher and Laila Monahan (eds.), *Refugees and International Relations* (New York: Oxford University Press, 1989), pp. 374–5. See also: Gil Loescher, *Beyond Charity* (New York: Oxford University Press, 1993), p. 57, who claims that the persecution requirement was designed to fit a Western notion of the refugee.
3. Jerzy Sztucki, "Who is a Refugee? The Convention Definition: Universal or Obsolete?" in Frances Nicholson and Patrick Twomey (eds.), *Refugee Rights and Realities: Evolving International Concepts and Regimes* (Cambridge University Press, 1999), p. 55.
4. Hathaway, *Law of Refugee Status*, p. 8.
5. Claudena M. Skran, *Refugees in Inter-War Europe: The Emergence of a Regime* (New York: Oxford University Press, 1995), p. 112 n. 33.
6. Michael Marrus, *The Unwanted* (New York: Oxford University Press, 2002), pp. 7, 9. See also: Loescher, *Beyond Charity*, p. 33, who claims that refugees are a "distinctly modern problem" and that before the twentieth century, "asylum was a gift of the crown, the church, and municipalities; and fugitive individuals and groups could expect no response to claims of asylum or protection premised on human or political right."
7. Ben Vermeulen *et al.*, "Persecution by Third Parties," unpublished paper commissioned by the Research and Documentation Centre of the Ministry of Justice of the Netherlands, May 1998, p. 17. See also: Gilbert Jaeger, "A Comment on the Distortion of the Palliative Role of Refugee Protection," *Journal of Refugee Studies*, 8 (1995), p. 300, and Walter Kälin, "Non-State

Agents of Persecution and the Inability of the State to Protect," *Georgetown Immigration Law Journal*, 15 (2001), p. 423.

8. Astri Suhrke, "Global Refugee Movements and Strategies of Response" in Mary M. Kritz (ed.), *U.S. Immigration and Refugee Policy: Global and Domestic Issues* (Lexington, MA: Lexington Books, 1983), p. 159.

9. Ulrich Sinn, "Greek Sanctuaries as Places of Refuge" in Nanno Marinatos and Robin Hägg (eds.), *Greek Sanctuaries: New Approaches* (London: Routledge, 1993), p. 90.

10. After 300 BC, cities also began to declare themselves "inviolable," although there is considerable scholarly debate over exactly what purpose this served. Some have argued that claims of inviolability resulted from mutual defense agreements between states or non-belligerency agreements between coastal cities and pirates. See Rob W. M. Schumacher, "Three Related Sanctuaries of Poseidon" in Marinatos and Hägg, *Greek Sanctuaries*, p. 69. More recently, Rigsby has called this conventional wisdom into question, arguing that cities declared themselves inviolable for honorific or expressive purposes, in the same way that an American city might declare itself a nuclear free zone. Kent J. Rigsby, *Asylia: Territorial Inviolability in the Hellenistic World* (Berkeley, CA: University of California Press, 1996), p. 24. In any event, unlike the inviolability of sanctuaries, the inviolability of cities did not correspond to a practice of supplication.

11. Schumacher, "Three Related Sanctuaries," pp. 68 et seq.

12. Sinn, "Greek Sanctuaries," p. 91.

13. Ibid.

14. Rigsby, *Asylia*, p. 10.

15. Quoted in Rigsby, *Asylia*, p. 10 n. 33.

16. Quoted in Rigsby, *Asylia*. For a full account of the story of Pausanias, see Thucydides, *History of the Peloponnesian War*, trans. Rex Warner (New York: Penguin, 1972), Book 1, paragraphs 128–35.

17. Tacitus, *Historical Works, Vol. 1: The Annals*, trans. Arthur Murphy (London: J. M. Dent, 1908), p. 168.

18. S. Prakash Sinha, *Asylum and International Law* (The Hague: Martinus Nijhoff, 1971), p. 9.

19. Although there was no duty of extradition in ancient Greece, it nonetheless often took place by the consent of both states, particularly in the case of offenses of a public character. See Coleman Phillipson, *International Law and Custom of Ancient Greece and Rome*, vol. 1, 1911 (reprinted Buffalo, NY: William S. Hein, 2001), p. 361; Rigsby, *Asylia*, p. 11; and Christopher L. Blakesley, "The Practice of Extradition from Antiquity to Modern France and the United States: A Brief History," *Boston College International and Comparative Law Review*, 4 (1981), pp. 41 et seq.

20. Rigsby explains, "The legal immunity of a Greek temple is a negative fact, the absence of secular jurisdiction; so too the legal immunity of a city with respect to other sovereign states, which had no say about what went on within its boundaries ... In cases of supplication doubtless Zeus Xenios was watching, and the decision was not idle. But no foreign government had a say in the matter." Rigsby, *Asylia*, pp. 9–10.

    A number of ancient Greek plays reflect that principle. In Sophocles' *Oedipus at Colonus*, for example, the Athenian ruler, Theseus, tells Creon, who has attempted to tear Oedipus away from the altar, "[Y]ou're plundering me, plundering our gods, / dragging away their helpless suppliants by force. / Never, I tell you, if I'd set foot on your soil, / even if I'd the most just claims on earth – / never without the sanction of your king, / ... I'd never drag and plunder. / I would know how a stranger should conduct himself / in the midst of citizens." Sophocles, *Oedipus at Colonus*, trans. Robert Fagles as *Three Theban Plays* (New York: Penguin, 1982), lines 1049–56. Similarly, in Euripides' *Heracleidae*, the supplicant Iolaus tells his foreign pursuer, Copreus, that "I'm well protected by / God's temple and this free and sovereign state," and the Chorus rebukes Copreus for trying to rip Iolaus from the altar. "Instead of kidnapping these refugees / So brazenly," it scolds, "you should have seen the king / And shown respect for Athens' sovereign rights." Euripides, *The Heracleidae*, trans. David Grene and Richard Lattimore as *Four Tragedies* (University of Chicago Press, 1955), lines 61–2, 111–13.

21. Rigsby explains that "this act was portable and not restricted to sacred space." *Asylia*, p. 10.

22. I am indebted to Matthew Stephenson for helpful discussions on this point.

23. Aeschylus, "Libation Bearers," in *The Oresteia*, trans. Robert Fagles (New York: Penguin Books, 1984), lines 1032–60.

24. Aeschylus, "Eumenides," in ibid., lines 234, 206–7.

25. Ibid., lines 503–5, 613–14, 620 et seq., 767, 805, 898–900.

26. Schumacher, "Three Related Sanctuaries," p. 74.

27. Aeschylus, "Eumenides," lines 451–4.

28. Euripides, *The Heracleidae*, lines 137–43, 186–9.

29. Aeschylus, *The Suppliants*, trans. Peter Burian (Princeton University Press, 1991), lines 326, 320–3, 374–8.

30. Ibid., lines 940–2.

31. Herodotus, *The History*, trans. David Grene (University of Chicago Press, 1987), at I.157–61. For another historical example of such a dilemma, see Thucydides' account of the flight of Themistocles. Thucydides, *History*, paragraphs 135–8.

32. Sinn, "Greek Sanctuaries," p. 92.
33. Ibid.
34. This section is deeply indebted to Karl Blaine Shoemaker, "Sanctuary Law: Changing Conceptions of Wrongdoing and Punishment in Medieval European Law," unpublished Ph.D. thesis, University of California-Berkeley (2001).
35. The practice of asylum, of course, is part of Rome's founding myth: Romulus supposedly built the population of his city by turning Palatine Hill into an asylum for fugitives.
36. Justinian, *Digest*, trans. Alan Watson as *Digest of Justinian*, vol. 1 (Philadelphia, PA: University of Pennsylvania Press, 1998), at 1.1.6.1.
37. Ibid. at 1.11.4.1.3–8.
38. Ibid. at 1.21.1.17.12.
39. Ibid. at 1.1.12.1.1.
40. Ibid. at 1.1.6.2; see also Gaius, *The Institutes of Gaius*, trans. Francis de Zulueta (Oxford: Clarendon Press, 1946), at 1.53.
41. Justinian, *Code of Justinian*, trans. S. P. Scott as *The Civil Law* (Cincinnati, OH: Central Trust Co., 1932), at 1.6.2.
42. Tacitus, *The Annals*, trans. Henry G. Bohn as *The Works of Tacitus: The Annals*, vol. 1 (Oxford, 1854), at III.36.
43. Ibid. at 1.12.2; see also *Theodosian Code*, 9:45.
44. See Sinha, *Asylum*, pp. 11 et seq., for a discussion of the growth of church sanctuary in the late Roman Empire.
45. Shoemaker, "Sanctuary Law," p. 46.
46. Augustine, "Letter 153," in *Patrologia Latina* 33:653, quoted in Shoemaker, "Sanctuary Law," pp. 48–50.
47. Shoemaker, "Sanctuary Law," p. 116.
48. Sinha, *Asylum*, p. 11.
49. Richard M. Fraher, "Theoretical Justification for the New Criminal Law of the High Middle Ages," *University of Illinois Law Review*, 1984 (1984), p. 580.
50. Ibid.
51. Quoted in Shoemaker, "Sanctuary Law," p. 251.
52. Shoemaker, "Sanctuary Law," p. 253.
53. Sinha, *Asylum*, p. 12.
54. Ibid.
55. M. Cherif Bassiouni, *International Extradition: United States Law and Practice*, 3rd edn. (Dobbs Ferry, NY: Oceana Publications, 1996), p. 139.
56. Sinha, *Asylum*, p. 18.
57. Henry IV issued the Edict of Nantes in 1598, which allowed the Protestants and Catholics to both practice their religions freely. The Edict was revoked by Louis XIV in 1685, giving rise to the first

group to be called "refugees," Huguenots fleeing renewed Catholic persecution.

58. Hugo Grotius, *De Jure Belli ac Pacis Libri Tres* (1625), trans. Francis W. Kelsey (Oxford: Clarendon Press, 1925). On the significance of Grotius, see Hedley Bull, "The Importance of Grotius in the Study of International Relations" in Bull *et al.* (eds.), *Hugo Grotius and International Relations* (New York: Oxford University Press, 1990), pp. 71 et seq. Richard Tuck, *Rights of War and Peace* (New York: Oxford University Press, 1999), was an invaluable reference for this section.

59. Grotius, *De Jure Belli ac Pacis*, at Prolegomena, paragraph 1.

60. Ibid., II.21.4.6.

61. Ibid., II.21.1–4.

62. Hugo Grotius, *Rights of War and Peace*, trans. A.C. Campbell (Westport, CT: Hyperion Press, 1979), II.20.1.

63. Ibid., II.20.9.

64. Grotius, *De Jure Belli ac Pacis*, II.21.5.1.

65. Grotius, *De Jure Belli ac Pacis*, II.21.5. The Campbell translation, see Grotius, *Rights of War and Peace*, II.21.5, renders "*immerito odio laborant*" as "unmerited persecution," a translation considerably more favorable from the point of view of my argument. But I have chosen nonetheless to stick to the more literal "undeserved enmity."

66. Thanks to Matthew Stephenson for an invaluable and inspirational discussion on this point.

67. Grotius, *De Jure Belli ac Pacis*, II.21.5.

68. Ibid.

69. Grotius, *Rights of War and Peace*, II.21.6.2, citing Aeschylus, *The Suppliants*, for support.

70. Ibid., II.20.49–50.

71. Ibid., II.25.8.

72. Grotius, *De Jure Belli ac Pacis*, II.21.5.1.

73. Grotius, *Rights of War and Peace*, Prologomena, paragraph 30 ("*Nunc quod mihi indigne e patria ... ejecto ...*"). For details of Grotius' flight to France, see W.S.M. Knight, *The Life and Works of Hugo Grotius* (London: Sweet and Maxwell, 1925), pp. 161–3.

74. Two passages could be viewed as inconsistent with the interpretation of Grotius that I have offered. First, Grotius stated, "Nor is it contrary to the relations of amity to receive individual subjects, who wish to remove from the dominions of one power to those of another. For that is not only a principle of natural liberty, but favourable to the general intercourse of mankind. On the same grounds a refuge given to exiles may be justified." Grotius, *Rights of War and Peace*, III.20.41. Elsewhere, Grotius argued, "To those who pass through a country, by water or by land, it ought to be

permissible to sojourn for a time, for the sake of health, or for any other good reason ... Furthermore a permanent residence ought not to be denied to foreigners who, expelled from their homes, are seeking a refuge, provided that they submit themselves to the established government ..." Grotius, *De Jure Belli ac Pacis*, II.2.15–16.

These passages have been interpreted as endorsing a politically neutral conception of asylum, born of compassion for exiles. Atle Grahl-Madsen, *The Status of Refugees in International Law*, vol. 2 (Leiden: A. W. Sijthoff, 1972), p. 26. But that reading confuses hospitality with asylum. Receiving sojourners and exiles according to a principle of hospitality is not the same as receiving supplicants for asylum. Exiles had been expelled and were no longer counted as members of their states, often for having committed a crime. They needed to find somewhere else to live. But they did not necessarily flee from "unmerited persecution," since banishment was sometimes viewed as a justified punishment, and they were not wanted for extradition, as refugees or supplicants were. Thus, it was not "contrary to the relations of amity" between states to receive exiles who had been justly banished for crimes they committed, because such exiles were no longer wanted by their state of origin. They had been rightfully excommunicated, as it were. By contrast, receiving *supplicants* wanted for extradition was justified only if the punishment were "unmerited" – a determination that rested upon a controversial judgment about the requesting state's exercise of authority and implied condemnation of that state.

75. Grotius, *Rights of War and Peace*, II.25.8.

76. This is because in a state of nature, states act as the executors of the natural law: "[K]ings and those who are possessed of sovereign power have a right to exact punishment not only for injuries affecting immediately themselves or their own subjects, but for gross violations of the law of nature and of nations, done to other states and subjects." Grotius, *De Jure Belli ac Pacis*, II.20.40.

77. Grotius, *Rights of War and Peace*, II.25.8.

78. Samuel Pufendorf, *De Jure Naturae et Gentium Libri Octo* (1672), trans. C. H. Oldfather and W. A. Oldfather (Oxford: Clarendon Press, 1934).

79. Christian Wolff, *Jus Gentium Methodo Scientifica Pertractatum* (1764 edn.), trans. Joseph H. Drake (Oxford: Clarendon Press, 1934).

80. Emer de Vattel, *The Law of Nations or the Principles of Natural Law* (1758), trans. Charles G. Fenwick (Geneva: Slatkine Reprints – Henry Dunant Institute, 1983).

81. Pufendorf, *De Jure Naturae*, VIII.3.7.

82. Pufendorf argued that a state is only justified in going to war when it *itself* has been harmed. See Pufendorf, *De Jure Naturae*, VIII.3.7, VIII.6.5, and

VIII.6.14. Wolff agreed, as did Vattel. See Wolff, *Jus Gentium*, at sections 169, 256–8, and 636; and Vattel, *Law of Nations*, II.1.7 and II.4.54–5.

83. See Pufendorf, *De Jure Naturae*, VIII.6.14.

84. Ibid.

85. Ibid., III.3.9.

86. These sources include the *Odyssey*, from which Pufendorf draws the quotation, "In a brother's place stands the stranger and the suppliant"; and Lucian's *De Dea Syria*, which, Pufendorf says, lists "among the sins for which mankind was destroyed in Deucalion's flood ... 'They did wicked deeds, for they kept not their oaths, nor harboured strangers, nor received fugitives.' " Finally, Pufendorf cites Philo Judaeus, *On the Life of Moses*, who, Pufendorf says, "remarks that 'strangers, in my opinion, should be looked upon as refugees.' " Pufendorf, *De Jure Naturae*, III.3.9.

87. Grotius, *Rights of War and Peace*, III.20.41.

88. Pufendorf, *De Jure Naturae*, III.3.9.

89. Ibid., III.3.10.

90. Ibid.

91. Wolff, *Jus Gentium*, section 151.

92. Ibid., section 150. Above I criticized Grahl-Madsen for conflating Grotius' distinction between supplicants (who flee to escape punishment) and exiles (who are banished). See note 74, above. Wolff, unlike Grotius, used the term "exile" to refer both to a "voluntary" exile, who "for the purpose of escaping a penalty or disaster departs of his own accord from the place where he has domicile," and to an "involuntary" exile, who is "compelled to depart by the decree of a judge or order of a ruler." Wolff, *Jus Gentium*, section 145.

93. Wolff, *Jus Gentium*, section 147.

94. Ibid., section 150.

95. Ibid., section 149.

96. Ibid., section 148.

97. Vattel, *Law of Nations*, I.19.230.

98. Ibid., I.19.230; see also ibid., I.19.228, 232.

99. Ibid., I.19.231.

100. Ibid., II.9.125.

101. Ibid., I.19.232-233 and II.6.76. Vattel added, however, that "states which are on more intimate terms of friendship and comity" extradite even those wanted for misdemeanors or civil prosecution. He thought that this "practice is an excellent one, for it enables neighboring States to live together in peace, so that they seem to form but one Republic." Ibid., II.6.76.

102. Ibid., II.6.76.

103. The *delicta majora* approach to extradition was not merely theoretical: many treaties were designed along these lines. For example, the Webster-Ashburton Treaty between the United States and Britain, enacted in 1842, identified seven offenses which were extraditable: murder; assault; forgery; counterfeiting; piracy; robbery; and arson. These seven were chosen because they were thought to form a *delicta majora*. See Clive Parry (ed.), *British Digest of International Law*, Part VI (London: Stevens and Sons, 1965), pp. 653–4.

104. *American State Papers, Documents, Legislative and Executive, of the Congress of the United States*, vol. 1, 1789–1815 (Washington, DC: Gales and Seaton, 1832), p. 258 (emphasis in original).

105. Vattel, *Law of Nations*, II.6.76. This quote refers to the case where one extradites one's *own* citizens to a foreign state for punishment. But the same argument might be thought to apply to the case where a foreign citizen is returned to his own state for punishment, since Vattel thought that "it is proper that the guilty should be convicted after a trial conducted with due process of law." Ibid., I.19.233.

106. Ibid., II.6.76.

107. Christopher H. Pyle, *Extradition, Politics, and Human Rights* (Philadelphia, PA: Temple University Press, 2001), pp. 85–6.

108. See Paul O'Higgins, "History of Extradition in British Practice, 1174–1794," *Indian Yearbook of International Affairs*, Part II (1964), pp. 78–115; Parry, *British Digest*, pp. 444–5; and Blakesley, "Practice of Extradition."

109. Coke thought that the extradition of English subjects contravened Chapter 29 of the Magna Carta, which guaranteed that "no freeman shall be taken imprisoned or disseised of his freehold … but by lawful judgment of peers or the law of the land." Commenting on that clause, Coke wrote, "By the Law of the Land no man can be exiled, or banished out of his native Countrey, but either by authority, or in the case of abjuration for felony by the Common Law …" Sir Edward Coke, *The Second Part of the Institutes of the Laws of England*, 5th edn. (London: Streater *et al.*, 1671), p. 47. Abjuration was a practice that allowed accused felons who had taken sanctuary in a church to receive safe passage abroad, and immunity from future requests for extradition, by leaving England from the nearest port. For a discussion of these points, see Pyle, *Extradition*, pp. 10 and following.

110. Sir Edward Coke, *The Third Part of the Institutes of the Laws of England* (London: Flesher, 1644), p. 180 (citing Deuteronomy 23:15).

111. Habeas Corpus Act of 1679, 31 Ch. 2 c. 2, section XII.

112. Thomas Jefferson, "Letter to Washington, Nov. 7, 1791," in Thomas Jefferson Randolph (ed.), *Memoir, Correspondence, and Miscellanies*

from the Papers of Thomas Jefferson, vol. 3, 2nd edn. (Boston, MA: Gray and Bowen, 1830), p. 131.

113. Andreas Fahrmeir, *Citizens and Aliens: Foreigners and the Law in Britain and the German States 1789–1870* (New York: Berghahn Books, 2000), p. 185.

114. Ibid., p. 186.

115. Jefferson, "Letter to Washington," p. 131.

116. Thomas Jefferson, "Letter to Governor Pinckney, April 1, 1792" in Randolph, (ed.), *Memoir*, vol. 3, p. 160 (emphasis added).

117. *State Papers and Publick Documents of the United States: 1789–96*, vol. 1 (Boston, MA: T.B. Wait and Sons, 1815), p. 146 (emphasis added).

118. Cesare Beccaria, *On Crimes and Punishments* (1764), trans. Henry Paolucci (Indianapolis, IN: Bobbs-Merrill, 1963), p. 60.

119. Ibid., p. 61.

120. Grotius, *De Jure Belli ac Pacis*, II.21.5. The same point was made by Thomas Hobbes, *Leviathan* (New York: Penguin, 1977), pp. 347, 350–1. For a brief discussion of this issue relating to asylum, see Sinha, *Asylum*, pp. 170–1.

121. For a discussion of the emergence of the rule of non-inquiry, see Pyle, *Extradition*, pp. 118–29.

122. "Il donne asile aux étrangers bannis de leur patrie pour la cause de la liberté." Constitution de l'An I, art. 120 (1793).

123. Sinha, *Asylum*, pp. 171–2.

124. Ibid., p. 172.

125. Pyle, *Extradition*, p. 83.

126. Ibid., p. 80.

127. Quoted in Fahrmeir, *Citizens and Aliens*, pp. 185–6 (bold emphasis added).

128. Pyle, *Extradition*, p. 85

129. Otto Kirchheimer, *Political Justice: The Use of Legal Procedure for Political Ends* (Princeton University Press, 1961), p. 383; see also: Christine Van den Wijngaert, *The Political Offence Exception to Extradition* (Boston, MA: Kluwer-Deventer, 1980), p. 3.

130. Sir James Fitzjames Stephens, *History of the Criminal Law of England*, vol. 2 (London: Macmillan, 1883), p. 70.

131. Ibid., p. 71.

132. See generally Van den Wijngaert, *The Political Offence Exception*.

133. Quoted in Pyle, *Extradition*, p. 88.

134. Ibid.

135. *American State Papers*, vol. 1, p. 258.

136. *In re Meunier* [1894] 2 Q.B. 415.

137. *Matter of Doherty*, 599 F. Supp. 270 (S.D.N.Y. 1984), offers a modern example of the interrelationship between extradition and asylum. Doherty, an IRA terrorist wanted by Britain for the murder of a British officer during an ambush, was determined by a US court to be non-extraditable; the murder he had committed was regarded as a "political offense" because it was committed amidst a political uprising. But because he had entered the United States illegally, and because he was ineligible for asylum on account of his terrorist activities, he was deported to Ireland, which then extradited him to Britain. See also *INS v. Doherty*, 502 U.S. 314 (1992).

138. Margrit Schulte Beerbühl, "British Nationality Policy During the Napoleonic Wars" in Andreas Fahrmeir *et al.* (eds.), *Migration Control in the North Atlantic World* (New York: Berghahn Books, 2003), p. 57.

139. Ibid., quoting *The Parliamentary History of England, from the Earliest Period to the Year 1803*, vol. 30, p. 188.

140. Ibid., p. 58.

141. *Parliamentary Debates* (2nd series), vol. 7 (1822), p. 1442, quoted in Bernard Porter, *The Refugee Question in Mid-Victorian Politics* (Cambridge University Press, 1979), p. 68.

142. Fahrmeir, *Citizens and Aliens*, p. 194.

143. *Parliamentary Debates* (4th series), vol. 145, p. 793, quoted in David Feldman, "Changes in Nineteenth-Century Immigration Controls" in Fahrmeir *et al.* (eds.), *Migration Control*, at p. 168.

144. 5 Edw. VII c. 13; N. W. Sibley and Alfred Elias, *The Aliens Act and the Right of Asylum* (London: W. Clowes and Son, 1906), p. 85.

145. 26 Stat. 1084.

146. "Veto Message, January 28, 1915," *Compilation of the Messages and Papers of the Presidents*, vol. 18 (New York: Bureau of National Literature, 1917), p. 8043.

147. 39 Stat. 874.

148. Aristide R. Zolberg, *A Nation By Design: Immigration Policy in the Fashioning of America* (Cambridge, MA: Harvard University Press, 2006), p. 240.

149. Quoted in Zolberg, *A Nation by Design*, p. 240.

150. Ibid., pp. 273, 277.

151. Birgitta Bader-Zaar, "Foreigners and the Law in Austria" in Fahrmeir *et al.* (eds.), *Migration Control*, p. 143.

152. Fahrmeir, *Citizens and Aliens*, pp. 107–8.

153. Ibid., p. 187.

154. Ibid., p. 191.

155. Olivier Faron and Cyril Grange, "Foreigners in Late Eighteenth-Century Paris" in Fahrmeir *et al.* (eds.), *Migration Control*, p. 40.

156. Ibid., p. 41.
157. Frank Caestecker, "The Transformation of Nineteenth-Century West European Expulsion Policy, 1880–1914" in Fahrmeir *et al.* (eds.), *Migration Control*, p. 123.
158. Ibid., pp. 126–7.
159. Ibid., p. 128.
160. Ibid., pp. 128–9.
161. Ibid., p. 127.

2 | *Promoting Political Values through Asylum*

A sylum's political roots highlight its expressive character: asylum is intertwined with the evaluation and condemnation of other states' internal practices. That expressive dimension sets asylum apart from other policy tools that policymakers in the West can use to aid refugees, which are "palliative," that is, focused solely on addressing refugees' urgent needs.[1] Other refugee policy tools include relief aid provided directly to refugees or through intermediaries such as the state of origin, intergovernmental organizations like the United Nations High Commissioner for Refugees (UNHCR), or nongovernmental organizations; and development aid of various kinds designed to ameliorate the root causes of refugee flows.

States also offer various forms of protection abroad other than asylum. Some states have overseas refugee resettlement programs, under which a limited number of refugees are selected abroad, often by the UNHCR, and resettled in host states. Many states also offer protection – usually on a temporary basis – to certain non-persecuted refugees who do not qualify for asylum. In the United States, for example, the Attorney General is authorized to grant temporary protected status (TPS) to aliens from a country or region experiencing "ongoing armed conflict" when "requiring the return of aliens" to that area "would pose a serious threat to their personal safety"; to aliens for whom an "earthquake, flood, drought, epidemic, or other environmental disaster" has resulted in a "substantial, but temporary, disruption of living conditions"; and to aliens who are unable to "return[ ] to [their] state in safety" due to other "extraordinary and temporary conditions."[2] European Union guidelines require member states to offer "subsidiary protection" to asylum seekers who face a "real risk" of torture, inhuman or degrading punishment, the death penalty, or a "serious and individual threat to a civilian's life or person by reason of indiscriminate violence in situations of international or internal armed conflict."[3] The United Kingdom has implemented these guidelines by making available what it calls "humanitarian protection" to qualifying refugees, who include not only those identified by the EU guidelines, but also people who face a "real risk" of "unlawful killing."[4] Canada also offers refuge to non-persecuted refugees who are nonetheless "persons in need of protection," including those who face a substantial risk of torture or an individualized risk to their lives against which the origin state is unable or unwilling to protect – unless that risk is caused by the inability of the origin state to provide adequate medical care.[5]

The insight that asylum is just one of several tools in the refugee policy toolkit is crucial. Limiting asylum to persecuted people does not mean leaving behind other refugees. Other refugee policy tools can be used to address their needs. The question, then, is what asylum contributes to the refugee policy toolkit. What sets it apart from other refugee policy tools, and what do its unique characteristics tell us about its scope?

Asylum not only provides refugees with protection, but also has an expressive dimension:[6] it directs condemnation toward other states for having egregiously mistreated the refugees it protects. The persecution requirement is intertwined with asylum's expressive character. The term "persecution" describes not only a refugee's vulnerability to harm; it also describes a particular *kind* of harm – one inflicted maliciously and unjustifiably, usually by the state or with official sanction. Further, the term "persecution" captures the opprobrium that should attach to such mistreatment.

In expressing condemnation, asylum also advances an instrumental goal, namely, the reform of persecutory regimes. Asylum is thus part and parcel of a broad political program aimed at solving the root causes of refugee flows by promoting the rule of law and human rights. In this sense, asylum bears a family relationship to another refugee policy tool (one to be used only in dire circumstances, such as genocide): military intervention. As Doris Meissner, the former Commissioner of the US Immigration and Naturalization Service, has put it: "Toward antagonist nations, political asylum and refugee decisions represent one of many methods for registering disapproval of a nation's leadership or political system."[7]

Recognizing asylum's expressive, political character is controversial. Scholars and international bodies have repeatedly sounded the refrain that asylum is palliative, not political. For example, in 1967, the United Nations General Assembly passed a resolution declaring that "[t]he grant of asylum by a State is a peaceful and humanitarian act and ... as such, it cannot be regarded as unfriendly by any state."[8] Atle Grahl-Madsen, an authoritative commentator on refugee law, concurred that "a finding by the authorities of one State to the effect that persecution is taking place in the territory of another State, cannot be construed as a censure on the government of the latter State, and ... such a finding does not constitute any interference or intervention in the domestic affairs of that State."[9] And Deborah Anker, a prominent lawyer, activist, and scholar, has stated that refugee law "does not attempt to set a corrective agenda, tell another country how to act, or propose plans for eradicating particular practices."[10]

Many have argued that the 1980 Refugee Act, which revamped American refugee and asylum policy, was intended to separate asylum from politics and place it on a purely humanitarian footing.[11] Along these lines, the US Board of Immigration Appeals has written:

It is also important to remember that a grant of political asylum is a benefit to an individual under asylum law, not a judgment against the country in question ... A decision to grant asylum is not an unfriendly act precisely because it is not a judgment about the country involved, but a judgment about the reasonableness of the applicant's belief that persecution was based on a protected ground. This distinction between the goals of refugee law (which protects individuals) and politics (which manages the relations between political bodies) should not be confused ...[12]

It is true that when an adjudicator determines whether an applicant is eligible for asylum, she should be focused on whether the applicant himself has a well-founded fear of persecution. The asylum adjudication process is not an appropriate forum for issuing broad-gauged criticism of other states disconnected from the particular case at hand. Nor are asylum adjudicators or judges the appropriate actors to issue such general pronouncements. At the same time, however, in considering the claim of a particular applicant, the adjudicator inescapably must assess the legitimacy of another state's actions. A decision to grant asylum rests on a judgment that another state has persecuted; such a judgment is by definition critical; granting asylum, therefore, entails the expression of condemnation; and that condemnation aims at reforming the abusive state. To deny that is either to engage in double-talk or implicitly to deny that asylum should be limited to persecuted people. A humanitarian conception of asylum – according to which eligibility would turn on exposure to harm generally, rather than to persecution in particular – would eliminate from asylum any expressive valence. Refugees may face many types of harm that are nobody's fault.

Asylum's expressive character has advantages, but also dangers. Frequently, commentators emphasize the dangers: that states will be unwilling to grant asylum to people persecuted by friendly countries for fear of damaging good relations; that they will be all too willing to grant asylum to people – whether persecuted or not – from hostile countries in order to express condemnation of an enemy regime; and that weak states may be reluctant to grant asylum to refugees from strong states. In all these scenarios, asylum becomes disconnected from the genuine normative judgments that ought to underlie it, and the interests of refugees are subordinated to the interests of state.

These dangers are as old as asylum itself. In Euripides' *Heracleidae*, for example, the children of Heracles – fleeing Argos – reach Athens only after being turned away from the rest of the Greek city-states, who fear antagonizing the powerful Argives. Iolaus, the guardian of the children of Heracles, laments: "Anywhere / We go, when [the Argive king] finds out, he sends someone / To bully them into expelling us, / And claims his town's too strong and he's too rich / To risk offending. When our hosts recall / That these are orphans, that I've no support, / They cringe and end up sending us away."[13]

But there are advantages as well as dangers to an expressive asylum policy, and these advantages are rarely appreciated. And the dangers, though real, can be minimized through institutional design that insulates asylum adjudicators from political interference, so that asylum decisions reflect genuine normative judgments about the nature of the harm faced by applicants.

The distinctive harm of persecution

To further motivate the distinction between persecution and other sorts of harms, and to explain why asylum policy should distinguish between them, consider John Rawls' typology of "burdened societies" and "outlaw states." Burdened societies aspire to meet their citizens' basic needs, but their "historical, social, and economic circumstances make their achieving [such a regime] difficult if not impossible."[14] Their leaders are motivated by a desire to secure decent treatment for their citizens and by a "common good" idea of justice – that is, when formulating policy, they "take[ ] into account … the fundamental interests of everyone in society."[15] But they may be too weak to possess a monopoly on violence and consequently be wracked by civil conflict, or they may lack the infrastructure to offset food shortages or lack the resources to redress severe poverty. Burdened societies recognize that their citizens are entitled to protection from harm, but due to exigencies beyond their control, are unable to provide it. Citizens of burdened societies lack protection of their basic rights, but they retain standing as members. The appropriate stance of outsiders to burdened societies is to lend assistance, not to condemn their failures. Asylum is an inappropriate tool for addressing the needs of those fleeing burdened societies. The label "persecution" is inapposite to describe their situation; and to grant asylum would be to issue a condemnation where none is warranted.

By contrast, consider what Rawls calls an "outlaw state." This type of regime flouts the requirements for international legitimacy by violating basic human rights – such as the peremptory human rights norms recognized by customary international law, including the prohibitions on slavery, torture, genocide, prolonged arbitrary detention, and the murder or disappearance of persons – or by harming citizens for illegitimate reasons.[16] Toward such states, a confrontational strategy is appropriate. Outsiders "may pressure outlaw regimes to change their ways" by "firm[ly denying] economic and other assistance" or by refusing to "admit [them to] mutually beneficial cooperative practices." If an outlaw state fails to respond to these measures, and "the offenses against human rights are egregious," forceful "intervention in the defense of human rights would be acceptable and would be called for."[17] Asylum responds to the harms perpetrated by outlaw states by providing shelter to their victims in a manner that also expresses the condemnation that is deserved.

Of course, not every citizen of an outlaw state is exposed to the kind of treatment that makes the state an outlaw. Often outlaw states reserve such treatment for those who challenge their authority by expressing contrary political opinions, or for those who, by virtue of their different race, religion, or nationality, are made into scapegoats or marginalized in order to generate solidarity among others. Nor, in the real world, is the distinction between burdened societies and outlaw states always clear. Outlaw elements may exist within burdened societies. Indeed, one way for a society to be burdened is that, despite its best efforts, it is unable entirely to control these outlaw elements. For example, a British court found that the government of Slovakia – despite reasonable diligence – was unable to reduce a Roma's exposure to skinhead attack beneath the level of well-founded fear.[18]

A state may also be both burdened and outlaw: it may be unable to protect some citizens despite its best efforts, and be unwilling to protect others whom it is capable of protecting. Nigeria serves as an example. On the one hand, "[t]he weakness of the Nigerian police force, its apparent inability to maintain law and order, and the lack of public confidence in its effectiveness ... have given many armed groups the freedom to operate according to their own rules, and to carry out serious human rights abuses with impunity."[19] But at the same time, the Nigerian government has carried out politically motivated arbitrary arrests, detentions, and torture.[20] A country might also be unable to protect some rights (for example, rights to economic subsistence) and be unwilling to protect other rights (for example, rights to physical security).

Arendt's concept of the "right to have rights,"[21] which Seyla Benhabib glosses as a right to membership,[22] helps further to distinguish between persecution and other harms. Arendt wrote:

> No matter how they have once been defined (life, liberty, and the pursuit of happiness, according to the American formula, or as equality before the law, liberty, protection of property, and national sovereignty, according to the French); no matter how one may attempt to improve on an ambiguous formulation like the pursuit of happiness, or an antiquated one like unqualified right to property; the real situation of those whom the twentieth century has driven outside the pale of the law [i.e. refugees] shows that these are rights of citizens whose loss does not entail absolute rightlessness. The soldier during war is deprived of his right to life, the criminal of his right to freedom, all citizens during an emergency of their right to the pursuit of happiness, but nobody would ever claim that in any of these instances a loss of human rights has taken place ... The calamity of the rightless is not that they are deprived of life, liberty, and the pursuit of happiness, or of equality before the law and freedom of opinion ... but that they no longer belong to any community whatsoever.[23]

Arendt's distinction between a deprivation of rights and "the calamity of the rightless" tracks Rawls' distinction between burdened societies and outlaw states. A state may be unable to secure its citizens' rights for any number of legitimate reasons, including national emergencies that require citizens to sacrifice some of their rights, natural disasters like earthquakes or droughts that destroy their livelihood, and civil wars that engulf their neighborhoods. Such citizens nonetheless retain their membership in what Rawls calls a "people" and what Arendt calls a "community":[24] their burdened society recognizes their entitlement to rights, but is unable to deliver what it acknowledges is owed. By contrast, to be persecuted is to have one's rights go unprotected *because* they are unrecognized. Asylum recognizes the distinctive nature of the harm suffered by persecuted people. It not only grants them protection from the insecurity they face, but also points an accusing finger at the persecutory state that is responsible.

Asylum and foreign policy

To view asylum as palliative – as limited to addressing the urgent needs of the asylum seeker – is thus to draw its function too narrowly. Historically, after all, asylum not only immunized the supplicant against the illegitimate exercise of authority; it was also an element of a broader political program designed to reform the abusive state. For Grotius, the circumstances that justified asylum in an individual case also justified, in the aggregate, military action undertaken to punish the abusive regime. For the English, the blanket asylum policy stemmed from their unwillingness to be a partner in the operation of tyrannical systems of law. And the political offense exception was intended to provide shelter for liberal revolutionaries who were wanted by autocratic regimes, with the goal of undermining those regimes. According to the political approach, asylum not only shelters the persecuted from illegitimate harm, but is also one element of a strategy to reform the abusive practices of the state of origin.

International relations scholars have identified three main mechanisms for changing the behavior of other states: coercion, persuasion, and what Ryan Goodman and Derek Jinks have called acculturation. Coercion influences state conduct by changing the cost–benefit calculation associated with certain actions "through material rewards and punishments."[25] Persuasion affects state conduct by leading states, through argument and deliberation, to "internalize new norms and rules of appropriate behavior and redefine their interests and identities accordingly ... [A]ctors are consciously convinced of the truth, validity, or appropriateness of a norm, belief, or practice."[26] Finally, acculturation leads states to conform to the norms adopted by a reference social group with which they identify through "peer pressure"; conformity is induced by the "generalized pursuit of social legitimacy."[27] Asylum has a role to play in facilitating all three mechanisms for influencing state behavior.

Coercion

The most obvious way to alter the behavior of other states is to force change through the levers of military and economic power. Asylum resides on a continuum with other means of sanctioning foreign governments, such as diplomatic letters of protest, the recalling of ambassadors, economic embargo, sponsorship of opposition groups, and direct military intervention. It differs from these other forms of sanction in that it is individuated. While these other forms of sanction follow from a *system-wide* judgment about the legitimacy of a regime, a grant of asylum follows from a judgment about the legitimacy of a state's exercise of coercive power *in a particular case*. The availability of such a sanction is useful, particularly in a world increasingly wary of economic sanctions and military intervention, and in search of alternative ways to sanction foreign governments for mistreating their citizens.

Asylum acts as a warning that if abusive practices continue, more powerful sanctions may be forthcoming. As Mark Gibney explains, granting asylum may be "merely a precipitating event that prompts a wide array of responses by the receiving country."[28] Judgments in particular cases are connected to system-wide judgments insofar as they provide the data points upon which a system-wide judgment of illegitimacy can be made. It is through many individual acts of persecution that a state becomes an outlaw state.

States which produce large numbers of asylum seekers are, therefore, placed on a kind of probation. If they continue to mistreat their citizens, they become liable to other forms of sanction, such as "diplomatic initiatives, economic and trade sanctions, ... complaints lodged in regional and international fora,"[29] possible criminal prosecution in an international criminal tribunal, and, in extreme cases, the sponsorship of opposition groups or even direct military intervention.

The political approach thus views asylum as linked to a particular view of sovereignty's place in the international system: sovereignty cannot serve as a shield of immunity behind which unjustified harm can be inflicted with impunity. As Richard Haass, the former director of Policy Planning at the US State Department and now president of the Council on Foreign Relations, has remarked, "Sovereignty is not absolute. It is conditional. When states violate minimum standards by committing, permitting, or threatening intolerable acts against their own people or other nations, then some of the privileges of sovereignty are forfeited."[30]

Usually, the number of people persecuted by any given government is sufficiently small that they can be absorbed abroad without much difficulty, and more coercive interference would be grossly disproportionate to the harms that would be prevented. In the majority of cases, asylum is an appropriate method of doing something to protect victims of persecution while registering disapproval and issuing a warning to the persecutory regime. However, if persecution is widespread and cruel enough – as in cases of ethnic cleansing or genocide – then the proportionality calculations must be revised. Coercive interference in the form of military intervention may indeed satisfy the proportionality principle, despite the harm to innocents that would result. In such cases, military intervention becomes a viable substitute for asylum.[31]

The 1994 UN Security Council Resolution authorizing military force against Haiti offers a prototype for how military intervention can act as a more potent substitute for asylum. The resolution, which expressly listed "violations of civil liberties" and "the desperate plight of Haitian refugees" as justifications for authorizing the use of all necessary means to overthrow the Haitian regime, was significant as the first UN Security Council Resolution to mandate regime change of a UN member state.[32] The creation of a Kurdish safe zone in northern Iraq offers another excellent example of a case in which military intervention substituted for asylum. In that case, the UN Security Council Resolution cited the "repression of the Iraqi civilian population in many parts of Iraq, including most recently in the Kurdish populated areas which led to a massive flow of refugees towards and across international frontiers" as a threat to international peace justifying military action to create a safe haven.[33] In cases of ethnic cleansing, the justification for substituting military intervention for asylum is even stronger, since, as the Bosnian war taught, granting asylum can inadvertently facilitate ethnic cleansing.[34]

In sum, when numbers are small, states should help the persecuted on a retail basis, one-by-one, through asylum. But when numbers increase, so that it is possible to infer not just that the state of origin has abused its citizens in particular cases, but rather that such abuse is its systematic policy, then, if the abuse is sufficiently severe and widespread, receiving states may be justified in assisting the persecuted wholesale by toppling the persecutory regime or by establishing a safe zone in which the persecuted can rebuild their political community.[35]

In another respect as well, asylum has a role to play in coercively enforcing the minimum conditions for legitimate government: it can serve not only as a warning that more invasive and damaging sanctions may be forthcoming, but can also be directly linked to those sanctions. Already, states tie material rewards to conformity with human rights standards by imposing conditions for military and economic assistance. For example, the United States bars security assistance to states that "engage[ ] in a consistent pattern of gross violations of internationally recognized human rights."[36] Another statute requires that the United States use its influence over multilateral development banks to "advance the cause of human rights, including by seeking to channel assistance toward countries other than those whose governments engage in a pattern of gross violations of internationally recognized human rights."[37] The World Bank, for its part, loans money only to countries that meet requisite standards of good governance. There is evidence suggesting that these policies can provoke recalcitrant states to improve their human rights practices.[38]

Asylum can be linked to conditional aid policies in several respects. Asylum decisions can be used as a source of information for government officials in determining whether the human rights prerequisites for aid have been met. Asylum law can also be a source for generating more precise, concrete standards of conduct against which other states' human rights performance can be measured. Asylum offers a unique resource in that respect: in deciding particular cases, asylum adjudicators are forced to move beyond slogans – like those in the international human rights covenants – and define the scope of a general standard as applied in concrete factual scenarios.

Asylum policy can also coerce a change in behavior by states eager to generate a reputation for rule of law and good governance, for example, those that seek membership in exclusive international organizations. For example, it is plausible to believe that states seeking accession to the EU or NATO would be extremely sensitive to asylum grants given to their citizens, and would revise their domestic policies to avoid that possibility. Hungary, for instance, was deeply distressed by the French decision to grant asylum to Roma from the town of Zamoly in 2000. A government spokesman condemned the decision as "unfounded, unfair, and unjust,"[39] and there was concern in Hungary that it would "threaten[ ] Hungary's reputation abroad" and delay Hungary's accession to the EU.[40] One would expect that Turkey likewise would be sensitive to asylum grants given to its citizens, and that the prospect of being labeled a persecutory state would provide it with an additional incentive to adopt policies conforming to those of the EU. One can imagine similarly conditioning membership in other international organizations – for instance, trade organizations – on human rights practices, and relying in part on asylum grants as an indicator of a state's compliance.

More generally, asylum policy contributes to international perceptions about whether a state is trustworthy or a rogue state. Being labeled a rogue state is costly: it "entails loss of reputation, trust, and credibility,"[41] making other states less willing to engage in economic and security cooperation. At the domestic level too, such a reputation undermines citizens' perceptions of their government's legitimacy, making it harder for leaders to assert their authority. Martha Finnemore and Kathryn Sikkink explain, "Increasingly, citizens make judgments about whether their government is better than alternatives ... by seeing what other people and countries say about their country." International condemnation is thus "important insofar as it reflects back on a government's domestic basis of legitimation and consent and thus ultimately on its ability to stay in power. This dynamic was part of the explanation for regime transitions in South Africa, Latin America, and southern Europe."[42]

Finally, even when more forceful sanctions are inappropriate or impracticable, asylum provides a means beyond mere words of condemnation for receiving countries to alter the relative costs and benefits of persecutory policies. For example, granting asylum to political activists gives them a safe haven from which they can organize and fundraise free from the threat of torture or disappearance. Dissident exile communities can be a powerful political force in their countries of origin, and granting asylum to those targeted for genocide frustrates the genocidal regime's goal of extermination.

One could also imagine states enabling recipients of asylum to file suits against their states of origin and its officials seeking civil damages for persecution. One precedent in the United States is the Torture Victim Protection Act of 1991, which creates civil liability for individuals who, acting in an official capacity for a foreign nation, subjected another to torture or extrajudicial killing.[43]

Another precedent is litigation in the United States under the Alien Tort Claims Act of 1789 (ATCA), prior to the US Supreme Court ruling cutting back the scope of that statute in the 2004 case *Sosa* v. *Alvarez-Machain*.[44] The ATCA gives US courts jurisdiction over civil suits "by an alien for a tort only, committed in violation of the law of nations or a treaty of the United States."[45] In a seminal case, *Filartiga* v. *Pena-Irala*,[46] the Second Circuit Court of Appeals permitted an ATCA suit by relatives of a Paraguayan, who had been kidnapped and tortured to death, against the responsible official, who also happened to be in the United States and thus was subject to the personal jurisdiction of US courts.

The Supreme Court has subsequently read the ATCA to remedy only "violations of ... international law norm[s] with [the] definite content and acceptance among civilized nations" comparable to "the historical paradigms familiar when [the ATCA] was enacted" – for example, the norm against piracy. Torture might still satisfy this standard, but arbitrary detention – the tort alleged in *Sosa* – does not.[47] One could, however, imagine Congress amending the statute to make clear its applicability to torture as well as to extend it to the violation of other peremptory international human rights norms.

Opening the courts to such civil suits would also be consistent with the spirit of universal criminal jurisdiction for crimes against humanity and genocide, as practiced by Belgium between 1993 and 2003. Universal jurisdiction permits courts to exercise authority over cases that otherwise have no connection to the forum state – for example, the prosecution of Rwandans by Belgium for their role in the Rwandan genocide – on the ground that certain acts are universally regarded as criminal and so fairly can be punished by any authority.[48] However, universal criminal jurisdiction is a highly controversial concept, and universal civil jurisdiction takes matters one step further by placing the decision to sue in the hands of private parties rather than state prosecutors.

Finally, one could imagine expanding the exceptions to foreign sovereign immunity, permitting victims of persecution to sue their former state directly. Currently, in the United States, the Foreign Sovereign Immunities Act of 1976 (FSIA) permits suit by US nationals against foreign governments for (among other things) "torture" and "extrajudicial killing," if the foreign state is designated as a state sponsor of terrorism at the time the act is committed.[49] To enable suits by victims of persecution, this exception to the FSIA would need to be expanded in three ways: first, to permit suits by non-US nationals who have received asylum in the US; second, to permit suits for other persecutory acts in addition to "torture" and "extrajudicial killing"; and third, to remove the "state sponsor of terrorism" limitation.

Persuasion

So far I have considered various ways in which asylum can be used by a receiving state as one component of a broader strategy to coerce reform of abusive practices. That possibility, however, assumes that international norms proscribing a certain practice already exist and that the receiving state has internalized norms enough to act on them.

When those conditions are lacking, asylum can help to foster the emergence, recognition, and internalization of new international human rights norms in both the state of refuge and the state of origin. It does so by "fostering structural opportunities for transnational networks to engage governments"[50] to persuade them of the existence and the importance of new norms. Once persuaded, states adopt policies reflecting these norms – both in their domestic law and in their foreign policies.

Finnemore and Sikkink emphasize that persuasion requires "[t]he construction of cognitive frames ... [that] resonate with broader public understandings and are adopted as new ways of talking about and understanding issues."[51] Asylum offers a ready-built cognitive frame for norm entrepreneurs, who "call attention to issues or even 'create' issues by using language that names, interprets, and dramatizes them."[52] It is an especially effective framing device for several reasons. First, asylum seekers are individuals, not abstractions: they have faces and stories that norm entrepreneurs can use to generate public interest in abusive practices abroad. Second, asylum has a bracing immediacy: because asylum seekers have asked for help from the receiving state, that state is now implicated in their fate. It is now an agent, not a bystander. A norm entrepreneur can use this complicity to connect a new human rights issue with already internalized norms. Third, because asylum involves a legal proceeding, it enables the immediate institutionalization of a new norm into law.

The issue of female genital mutilation (FGM) provides one good example of how asylum policy can be employed by norm entrepreneurs. Although advocates had been pressing US policymakers to take action against FGM for many years, legislation was finally passed in 1996 – contemporaneous with the asylum case of Fauziya Kasinga, who became a kind of poster child for the brutality of FGM.[53] Her story, which was widely reported in newspapers, made the issue concrete for the American public; and her asylum application forced the country to take a stand on the issue of FGM.

Senator Harry Reid, who was the driving force behind the FGM legislation, expressly used Kasinga's asylum application to dramatize the importance of the issue, and proposed taking action that would not only recognize her claim but also make FGM illegal in the United States and condition US foreign assistance on efforts to eradicate it abroad. In his view, Kasinga's application for asylum represented an opportunity for the United States to "take a stand and speak out against this horrid practice." In his remarks on the Senate floor, Reid deftly weaved together America's complicity in Kasinga's fate with its moral responsibility to take more wide-ranging action against FGM:

A young woman from Togo was recently called to our attention because this woman, a 20-year-old woman, was going to have this procedure. Fauziya Kasinga fled Togo and came to America in order to escape the torture of female genital mutilation. She is now seeking asylum based on the threat of this procedure being performed on her and she deserves it. She fled Togo, left behind people, and her family. She has been in the United States prisons for 2 years in order to escape this procedure. Women and children should not be forced to face this pain, potential death, and emotional scarring.

An amendment will be offered today to the pending immigration bill that would allow female genital mutilation to be the basis of asylum in this country, as well as to criminalize the act in the United States. We must join other countries in legally banning female genital mutilation. As immigrants from Africa and the Middle East travel to other nations, this practice travels with them. The United Kingdom, Sweden, and Switzerland have passed laws prohibiting this practice. France and Canada maintain that their laws will prevent this from happening. The United States is faced with the responsibility, I believe, of abolishing this specific practice within its borders as well as providing safe refuge for those in fear of having this torture inflicted upon them.

Mr. President, I think we should be very clear and precise in what we allow for asylum. I think we have been too lax in asylum cases. I do not think we have had the personnel to adequately handle these cases. People come and claim political asylum, and are lost in the vast bowels of this country.

Having said that, though, I believe there is no case clearer for demanding asylum than a woman or a girl saying I am here because if I stay in my country, they are going to rip out my genitalia. This practice is brutal, systematic, and it is a cultural practice. It has been endured by millions of young girls and women and its prevalence is just now being revealed to the world.[54]

In the end, Congress passed statutes criminalizing FGM in the United States and conditioning international lending on anti-FGM education.[55] Although Congress voted down Reid's proposal to add a presumption to the asylum statute that victims of FGM are persecuted on account of political opinion, the Board of Immigration Appeals took roughly that position in granting Kasinga asylum.

The American recognition and institutionalization of a norm against FGM likely was influential in changing the policies of African countries toward the practice. As Elizabeth Heger Boyle and Sharon Preves have pointed out: "Although a number of African countries had adopted policies or passed legislation prior to the U.S. legislation" – largely in response to pressure from European governments – "complete uniformity in national policies" (except for Sierra Leone and Somalia) "was achieved after the U.S. legislation was enacted."[56]

The sanctuary movement in the early to mid-1980s offers another example of the way asylum can be used by activists to promote a foreign policy oriented toward human rights. The movement, which began in a small Arizona church in 1981 and grew to include over 330 churches and synagogues across the country, created a kind of "underground railroad" to smuggle Salvadoran refugees across the Mexican border and illegally shelter them in the United States. The movement challenged as illegal – and inconsistent with America's rhetorical commitment to asylum – the government's practice of labeling virtually all Salvadorans fleeing civil war as "economic refugees." But the sanctuary movement was not only focused on sheltering those who sought refuge; it also used the refugees' plight to dramatize and bring to public attention the United States' role in fomenting strife through its support for the Salvadoran government.[57]

The movement was remarkably successful: it not only helped many hundreds of refugees, but also enlisted over 40,000 Americans in sheltering refugees or raising funds to help refugees in detention make bail. Member churches eventually sued the government for discriminating against Salvadoran and Guatemalan refugees in asylum hearings. As part of the legal settlement, reached in December 1990, the government agreed immediately to stop deporting Salvadorans and Guatemalans and to reconsider asylum denials made to those two groups since 1980. Altogether, the government agreed to rehear over 150,000 asylum cases.[58] The movement also raised public awareness of the atrocities carried out in the course of the civil war in El Salvador and of America's complicity through its support for the Salvadoran government.

Asylum can also provide a critical perspective on a receiving state's domestic practices. Take as an example recent debates over the eligibility of battered women for asylum. The possibility that such women will be deemed "persecuted" and receive asylum presents an opportunity for women's advocates to call attention to the pervasiveness of violence against women in Western society and the inadequacy of social resources devoted to their protection. That possibility should also lead one to reflect critically on the US Supreme Court's 1989 holding that "nothing in the language of the Due Process Clause itself requires the State to protect the life, liberty, and property of its citizens against invasion by private actors,"[59] and the implications of this holding for battered women who find the police unwilling to enforce restraining orders against their abusers.[60] If the United States is ready to apply the label "persecution" to such misconduct when it occurs in other countries (as it may soon be), perhaps American women should have standing in court to sue when it happens at home.

Acculturation

Acculturation is the final mechanism by which asylum can induce changes in state behavior. Some international relations scholars have argued that state behavior can be explained by reference to a state's identity within an institutional cultural context.[61] State leaders are engaged in "evaluative relationships" with the leaders of their state "peers."[62] States conform to norms because state leaders wish "to demonstrate that they have adapted to the social environment – that they 'belong.' ... In this sense, states [or, more accurately, state leaders] care about following norms associated with liberalism because being 'liberal states' is part of their identity in the sense of something they take pride in or from which they gain self-esteem."[63]

Identity-based socialization will be most likely to affect state behavior when the status of the state in question is tenuous. In such cases, states of origin may be especially sensitive to grants of asylum to their citizens. The official Israeli response to the first grant of asylum to an Israeli citizen by the United States is especially interesting in this regard.[64] The

Israeli Foreign Ministry spokesman called the decision "a troubling precedent ... It's not something that would harm relations between the countries, but in principle, there may be damage to Israel's image. It places Israel in the same category as countries whose citizens are persecuted and need shelter from the state – which, of course, is not the situation in Israel."[65] Were asylum granted to Israeli citizens with increasing frequency, Israel might be led to alter its domestic policies, lest its identity with the liberal states of the West become unsustainable.

***

In sum, by expressing condemnation of persecutory states, asylum advances a political agenda to end those practices. Asylum can play several roles in this program. First, asylum's expressive sanction can be connected to efforts at coercing other states to conform to established international norms against abusive state conduct. Second, when an international norm has not yet been established or internalized, asylum can be used by norm entrepreneurs to persuade policymakers to recognize that norm and revise domestic and foreign policies accordingly. Finally, asylum's expressive sanction can lead certain states of origin – those especially sensitive to their standing among other states they regard as peers – to reform their internal practices to conform to widely accepted norms.

Despite asylum's role in a foreign policy aimed at promoting human rights and rule of law abroad, human rights advocates have generally rejected asylum's expressive dimension. Deborah Anker, for example, writes that "refugee law is not aimed at holding states responsible; its function is remedial."[66] James Hathaway contends that, although asylum should provide protection to victims of human rights abuse, it should "retain a distinctly palliative orientation."[67] But granting asylum to victims of human rights abuses is hardly politically neutral. A state that has violated the human rights of its citizens has violated internationally recognized limits on legitimate state action. Such violation warrants criticism, condemnation, and corrective action, and asylum is the refugee policy vehicle for that response.

The dangers of a political approach

The primary objection to investing asylum with political significance is that it will be misused to serve foreign policy interests to the detriment of refugees: a state's interest in expressing (or not expressing) condemnation will come to determine the outcome of asylum proceedings. Asylum policy would thereby become detached from the substantive judgments concerning legitimacy that ought to underlie it. It is likely that this concern motivates refugee advocates to describe asylum as "remedial" or "palliative," and thus as disconnected from politics.

Such a concern is born out of experience. During the Cold War, for instance, American policymakers explicitly used asylum as a tool to accomplish ideological goals, granting asylum to those fleeing Communist states without regard to whether they had actually suffered persecution, and denying asylum to those fleeing persecution committed by US client states. Each Communist refugee was seen as a "ballot for freedom" whose defection served to demoralize those who were left behind.[68] A National Security Council document from 1953 made this strategy explicit, noting that the "escape of people from countries in the Soviet orbit inflicts a psychological blow on communism."[69]

Until 1965, refugees from Communist countries were selected overseas and admitted through parole, which allowed the Attorney General in his discretion to admit aliens temporarily "for emergent reasons or for reasons deemed strictly in the public interest."[70] The use of this discretionary provision was highly ideological: of the 232,711 persons who were paroled into the United States between 1952 and 1968, only 925 were from non-Communist countries.[71] The 1965 Amendments to the Immigration and Nationality Act created a statutory basis for refugee admissions for the first time. Up to 6 percent of the visas made available to immigrants from the eastern hemisphere – totaling 10,200 – were reserved for people who, "because of persecution ... on account of race, religion, or political opinion," had "fled ... from any Communist or Communist-dominated country or area, or ... from any country within the general area of the Middle East."[72] Those who qualified immediately received legal permanent residence.[73]

The Refugee Act of 1980 was meant to remedy the ideological and geographical biases that had infected earlier US refugee policy. It discarded the 1965 statute's geographic limitations on refugee eligibility, and adopted in its place a definition that closely tracked the UN Convention definition of the refugee.[74] The 1980 Act also for the first time created an explicit statutory basis for asylum. While asylum remained a discretionary grant, the Act specified that anyone who had a "well-founded fear of persecution on account of race, religion, nationality, membership in a particular social group, or political opinion" would be eligible for a favorable exercise of discretion. In Arthur Helton's words, the Act was meant to "establish[ ] a standard for uniform and nonideological refugee eligibility."[75]

Despite this goal, asylum continued to be harnessed to foreign policy throughout the 1980s, due to ideologically influenced interpretations of the persecution requirement. Mark Gibney and Michael Stohl compared 1985 asylum approval rates to the human rights performance of asylum seekers' countries of origin. They discovered a success rate of only 8 percent for applicants from countries where "murders, disappearances, and torture are a common part of life, [and] terror affects those who interest themselves in politics or ideas." By contrast, applicants from countries where "there is a limited amount of imprisonment for nonviolent political activity [but] few persons are affected, torture and beating are exceptional ... [and p]olitical murder is rare" enjoyed a 39 percent success rate. With respect to the overseas refugees program, Gibney and Stohl discovered a shocking *negative* correlation between refugee admissions from a country and the severity of human rights abuses committed in that country. They attributed this discrepancy to a bias in favor of applicants from Communist countries like Hungary, Poland, and Romania, and against applicants from ravaged Central American countries like El Salvador and Nicaragua.[76]

The end of the Cold War presented an opportunity for finally liberating asylum from an ideological bias. Given that opportunity, a humanitarian critic may argue that a political and expressive approach to asylum represents a step backwards. The Cold War experience suggests that it may be naive to expect asylum to remain attached to genuine normative judgments about the legitimacy of other states' conduct. If asylum has political significance, the humanitarian argument continues, inevitably the protection of the persecuted will take a backseat to realpolitik interests.

Asylum can become detached from the sort of judgment that ought to underlie it in two ways. First, receiving states might "overprotect" citizens from enemy states, without regard to whether they are really persecuted, in order to condemn those states. Second, states might "underprotect" refugees from friendly states that they wish not to criticize. The Cold War experience furnishes an example of each phenomenon, and each presents a different kind of problem.

Overprotection: applicants from Communist countries

Eastern bloc asylum seekers in the 1980s were systematically overprotected by the United States in order to achieve ideological goals. If grant rates were too low, the United States feared that an insufficiently condemnatory message would be sent to Communist governments. According to a 1982 Immigration and Naturalization Service (INS) study, asylum seekers from Communist countries were held to a less demanding burden of proof than other asylum seekers in order to boost their grant rates. Furthermore, in at least some instances, applicants were given asylum for ideological reasons regardless of the objective strength or weakness of their applications. The report noted:

In some cases, different levels of proof are required of different asylum applicants. In other words, certain nationalities appear to benefit from presumptive status, while others do not. For example, for an El Salvadoran national to receive a favorable advisory opinion, he or she must have a "classic textbook case." On the other hand [the State Department] sometimes recommends favorable action where the applicant cannot meet the individual well-founded fear of persecution test. This happened in December 1981 a week after martial law was declared in Poland. Seven Polish crewmen jumped ship and applied for asylum in Alaska. Even before seeing the asylum applications, a State Department official said "We're going to approve them." All the applications, in the view of INS senior officials, were extremely weak. In one instance, the crewman said the reason he feared returning to Poland was that he had once attended a Solidarity rally (he was one of the more than 100,000 participants at the rally). The crewman had never been a member of Solidarity, never participated in any political activity, etc. His claim was approved within 48 hours.[77]

Asylum regulations considered in 1986 would have formalized asylum's ideological role. Worried that the 38 percent approval rate for Polish applicants was too low given the Reagan Administration's intense opposition to Communism, the Justice Department proposed a legal presumption that all applicants from "totalitarian" governments were persecuted and thus eligible for asylum. An aide to Attorney General Meese explained the need for such a regulation, saying, "Our asylum policy is inconsistent with our foreign policy."[78]

The United States continues to employ a presumption of this sort for Cubans: the Cuban Adjustment Act of 1996 authorized the Attorney General to grant legal permanent residence to Cuban nationals who have been present in the United States for at least one year after admission or parole and are otherwise admissible, regardless of whether they can demonstrate a well-founded fear of persecution.[79]

How should one regard presumptions such as these? Critics of such presumptions often imply that they are unfair by contrasting the favorable treatment given to applicants fleeing Communist states with the unfavorable treatment given to Salvadorans or Haitians.[80] But one must be careful not to muddle the issue. Suppose (counterfactually) that Salvadoran and Haitian asylum cases were judged fairly on their individual merits. Would there then be anything unfair about the presumptions in favor of applicants from places like Communist Poland or Cuba?

One possibility is that such presumptions reflect genuine system-wide judgments about the legitimacy of other regimes – akin to England's blanket non-extradition rule – in place of the individualized judgments that ordinarily characterize asylum adjudication. Whether such a system-wide judgment is appropriate may depend on three questions. The first is one of probabilities. Is persecution so widespread in the state of origin that a presumption of persecution is sensible? Have the mine run of asylum applicants from that country experienced persecution? If so, then administrative convenience favors a presumption.* The second question involves a normative judgment, reflecting the fact that asylum involves an expression of condemnation. Is a system-wide sanction fitting? Is persecution really so pervasive that other sorts of system-wide sanctions would also be appropriate (even if imprudent for other reasons), such as trade sanctions, diplomatic protests, or (at the extreme) military intervention? The third question is a practical one. Is the political program with which asylum is connected – one aimed at transforming persecutory regimes – best served by a presumption implying system-wide condemnation? Or is it better served by tying condemnation to individual cases of malfeasance?

---

* Temporary protected status (TPS) in the United States effectively implements a presumption for administrative reasons. TPS provides protection to all aliens from a designated state or sub-national region who are present in the United States prior to a cut-off date. The rationale is that large-scale disturbances, like civil war or natural disaster, will produce large refugee flows; even though some migrants from a designated country or region may be able to return safely, the overwhelming majority will not. Administrative convenience favors a blanket rule granting protection in place of individualized determinations.

The desirability of any such presumption is offset by one important consideration: such a presumption will necessarily lead to overprotection, that is, granting asylum to some people who would not be eligible were their cases decided on their individual merits; and, when political or financial resources for helping refugees are scarce, overprotection can impose unacceptable costs on refugees from other countries. It is wrong to prefer a non-persecuted Cuban over a persecuted Salvadoran. System-wide presumptions should not come at the cost of leaving other refugee populations unassisted.

Reasonable people can disagree about whether, in light of these criteria, the presumption in favor of applicants from Eastern bloc states was justified. On the one hand, the INS report quoted above suggests that the mine run of applicants from those countries did *not* suffer persecution; indeed, the Reagan Administration proposed a presumption for exactly that reason! Moreover, their absorption may well have come at the expense of qualified Salvadorans and Haitians. On the other hand, one could reasonably conclude that persecuted Salvadorans and Haitians were denied asylum unjustifiably, but for unrelated reasons, so that non-persecuted Poles and Cubans were not really taking away scarce slots from them; that the persecution that did occur in Communist countries was sufficiently pervasive and severe to warrant system-wide sanctions; and that an asylum policy built around system-wide sanctions against Communist governments advanced the goal of regime change.

Underprotection: the case of the Salvadorans

Between 1980 and 1985, the United States granted asylum to only 561 out of 20,699 Salvadoran asylum applicants, despite the State Department's assessment that, during that period, political killings claimed several hundred lives per month.[81] Even Salvadoran torture victims were accepted for asylum at lower rates than were torture victims from ideologically hostile countries.[82] Arthur Helton attributed this discrepancy to the United States having "identified significant foreign policy interests with the government of El Salvador. As a matter of foreign policy, therefore, our Executive branch (which includes the State Department and the INS) has every incentive to characterize the situation in El Salvador as an improving one – an image that would be jeopardized by granting asylum to Salvadorans."[83] This ideological explanation for low grant rates was corroborated by Doris Meissner, the Executive Associate Commissioner of the INS during the Reagan Administration. She acknowledged the explicit political calculus that affected Salvadoran asylum decisions:

Because the United States was supporting the government of El Salvador, a low percentage of asylum grants served U.S. foreign policy objectives. A high percentage would have conveyed some disapproval behind the vote of confidence being given to its struggle for democracy. So the INS's emphasis on rapid case processing and illegal migration, combined with a lack of incentive for the State Department to dig into the difficult but critical issues of economic versus political flight, resulted in extremely low approval rates – about two percent – at the very time when public awareness of and revulsion over the death squad activity in El Salvador reached a peak.[84]

The underprotection of persecuted asylum applicants is clearly troubling. The exclusion of Salvadorans amounted to a moral disaster: people who should have received asylum were denied it and were sent back to be killed.

Humanitarians respond to the Salvadorans' plight by arguing for the separation of asylum from politics. But the problem with asylum policy toward Salvadorans was that it had become detached from its moral underpinnings, not that it involved the condemnation of other states. Doris Meissner put this point well:

Implementation of the [1980 Refugee] Act in a manner that meets the purpose and vision it evoked requires that refugee and asylum objectives be pursued *along with* foreign policy goals instead of chronically subordinate to them. The two can never be fully divorced nor should they be. Still, we must come to the point where, as a nation, we can say to an El Salvador: We support and will vigorously assist you in your efforts to bring democracy to your country. At the same time, we will give haven to those in your country who are persecuted and we implore you to make every effort to end the abuses that make this necessary. Or we can say to a Poland: We decry totalitarian systems and believe democratic institutions are the will of people worldwide. But we recognize that millions live under repressive regimes, and while they do not enjoy the liberty that is their due, they are also not all victims of persecution as described in international law.[85]

To solve the problem of underprotection, one must design a system of asylum adjudication that can be insulated from the sort of ideological hijacking that Meissner rightly criticizes. Already, the United States has taken significant steps in that direction. Prior to 1990, after a brief interview, INS examiners would send an applicant's file to the State

Department for an advisory opinion on whether asylum should be granted. The opinions were crafted by the State Department Bureau of Human Rights and Humanitarian Affairs after consultation with country desk officers. The desk officers, whose job is to maintain relations with their designated countries, were biased toward denying asylum to applicants from friendly countries and granting asylum to applicants from hostile countries. Richard Preston quotes one as saying about a denial of an asylum application, "We didn't grant him asylum because the United States government doesn't want to pass judgment on the internal conditions of allied countries. That would cause resentment on their part and hurt the bilateral relationship."[86] The INS tended to treat State Department recommendations with great deference – they were followed 95 percent of the time[87] – on the assumption that the State Department possessed greater knowledge than immigration judges about country conditions. The result was an asylum policy bent to accommodate foreign policy interests.

Reforms in 1990 ended the State Department's advisory role,[88] created a professional corps of asylum adjudicators trained in international human rights and refugee law, and established a documentation center for the collection of information on human rights practices in various states, including NGO reports in addition to State Department Human Rights Reports.[89] These institutional changes represented a profound step in the right direction: independent adjudicators do not answer directly to those in charge of foreign policy or immigration enforcement and are encouraged to develop a bureaucratic culture focused on assisting victims of persecution.

One might ask why, if asylum is invested with political significance, a state would ever turn adjudication over to an asylum corps insulated from the control of foreign ministry officials. There are several answers. First, in general, asylum is a more effective vehicle for condemnation if it appears to be impartially administered. Although asylum decisions will occasionally be in tension with a receiving state's foreign policy, that may be a cost worth paying. Second, there can be diplomatic advantages to an independent asylum corps whose decisions cannot be controlled by foreign ministry officials: policymakers can distance themselves from asylum decisions in order to carry out a policy of engagement toward a persecuting country, while still preserving a mode in which that country's abuses can be condemned. Finally, states may value the long-standing tradition of granting asylum to persecuted people, and may genuinely wish to maintain that tradition.

One might also question whether investing asylum with political significance would affect the way adjudicators decide cases. Perhaps they would be more reluctant to grant asylum when more than just the refugee's protection is at stake. But that concern can be met by proper training and the development of a bureaucratic culture focused on assisting persecuted people. Adjudicators can be taught to focus on the merits of the case in front of them.

There is the separate question of whether (in the United States) the federal judiciary would be willing to review asylum determinations made by the immigration agency's adjudicators if asylum's expressive dimension were made explicit. Federal judges may fear that such review would enmesh them in debates about foreign policy and force them to "make immigration decisions based on [their] own implicit approval or disapproval of U.S. foreign policy and the acts of other nations."[90] Indeed, some courts have deferred to agency determinations to avoid entangling themselves in "political questions."[91]

That concern is overstated. The purpose of judicial review is simply to ensure the legality of agency action. Federal courts are not supposed to make asylum policy, but instead are supposed to review policy decisions to ensure that they are not arbitrary or capricious and are grounded in a plausible interpretation of the governing statute, and to review adjudications to ensure that they are supported by substantial evidence in the record and comport with agency rules and precedent. That task requires courts to determine only whether the agency acted reasonably in finding that the applicant was or was not persecuted. It does not require them to make foreign policy.

Conclusion

Recognizing asylum's expressive dimension reinvests asylum policy with political significance at a time when it is increasingly under attack. The last fifteen years have seen an explosion in restrictive policies directed toward asylum seekers. These policies, which I shall consider in greater detail in Chapter 6, include visa requirements, carrier sanctions, and interdiction programs that make it harder for asylum seekers to reach territory from which they can file an asylum application; procedural rules such as filing deadlines and "safe third country" policies that make it harder for asylum seekers to have their case heard on its merits; and other policies, such as detention, intended to discourage claims. It is not surprising that support for these measures increased as the Cold War ended, and as asylum no longer had obvious ideological significance.

The humanitarian approach to asylum has encouraged the perception that asylum policy offers nothing to receiving states other than moral self-satisfaction. This, I have suggested, is a mistake. Properly understood, asylum continues to have political significance. By itself, asylum is a mild form of sanction for abuses committed by governments against their citizens. In some situations, for example, when directed at states especially sensitive to their international standing, the expressive sanction of asylum by itself might induce reform to end abusive practices. Asylum can also be used by activists to facilitate the emergence of new human rights norms and the institutionalization of those norms into policy. In other situations, asylum can be connected with more muscular sanctions, such as conditional aid and military intervention.

In sum, asylum should be viewed not only as a means of protecting refugees, but also as another arrow in the quiver of a human rights-oriented foreign policy, tied to the view that sovereignty is conditional on a state satisfying minimum conditions of international legitimacy. Sovereignty cannot serve as a shield of immunity behind which states can engage in persecution with impunity.

Notes

1. The idea of a "refugee policy toolbox" is borrowed from Arthur C. Helton, *The Price of Indifference* (New York: Oxford University Press, 2002), p. 154. The term "palliative" is borrowed from James C. Hathaway, "Reconceiving Refugee Law as Human Rights Protection," *Journal of Refugee Studies*, 4 (1991), p. 113.
2. 8 U.S.C. section 1254a(b).
3. "EU Qualifications Directive," Council Directive 2004/83/EC of April 29, 2004 on minimum standards for the qualification and status of third country nationals or stateless persons as refugees or as persons who otherwise need international protection and the content of the protection granted, art. 15.
4. Immigration Rules, section 339C.
5. Immigration and Refugee Protection Act (2001 ch. 27), section 97(1).
6. Legal scholars have increasingly called attention to the importance of judging the impact of law not only in light of its visible consequences,

but also in light of its expressive meaning. The seminal account of expressivism in the context of punishment is offered by Joel Feinberg, "The Expressive Function of Punishment" in Feinberg (ed.), *Doing and Deserving: Essays in the Theory of Responsibility* (Princeton University Press, 1970), pp. 95–118. For more recent analyses of expressive theory generally, see Elizabeth S. Anderson, *Value in Ethics and Economics* (Cambridge, MA: Harvard University Press, 1993), pp. 17–43; Elizabeth S. Anderson and Richard H. Pildes, "Expressive Theories of Law: A General Restatement," *University of Pennsylvania Law Review*, 148 (2000), p. 1504; and Cass R. Sunstein, "On the Expressive Function of Law," *University of Pennsylvania Law Review*, 144 (1996), p. 2021. For a critique of expressive theory, see Matthew D. Adler, "Expressive Theories of Law: A Skeptical Overview," *University of Pennsylvania Law Review*, 148 (2000), p. 1363.

7. Doris Meissner, "Reflections on the U.S. Refugee Act of 1980" in David A. Martin (ed.), *The New Asylum Seekers: Refugee Law in the 1980s* (Norwell, MA: Kluwer Academic, 1988), p. 63.

8. Declaration on Territorial Asylum, G. A. Res. 2312 (II), U.N. GAOR, 22nd Sess., Supp. No. 16, at 81, U.N. Doc. A/6716 (1967). See also the sources cited in note 23 to the Introduction.

9. Atle Grahl-Madsen, *The Status of Refugees in International Law*, vol. 2 (Leiden: A. W. Sijthoff, 1972), p. 27.

10. Deborah Anker, "Refugee Law, Gender, and the Human Rights Paradigm," *Harvard Human Rights Journal*, 15 (2002), p. 146.

11. See note 75 below.

12. *In re S – P –*, 21 I. & N. Dec. 486, 492–3 (BIA 1996).

13. Euripides, *The Heracleidae*, trans. David Grene and Richard Lattimore as *Four Tragedies* (Chicago, IL: University of Chicago Press, 1955), lines 15–25.

14. John Rawls, *Law of Peoples* (Cambridge, MA: Harvard University Press, 1999), p. 5.

15. Ibid., pp. 66–7.

16. Ibid., p. 109. Rawls himself offers two versions of the distinction between burdened societies and outlaw states. The first looks to the external conduct of a state toward other states: unlike outlaw states, burdened societies are "not expansive or aggressive." Ibid., p. 106. The second focuses on a state's internal conduct toward its citizens: thus, a state can qualify as an outlaw, even if it is "not dangerous and aggressive toward other states," if it engages in conduct that violates the human rights of its citizens. Ibid., pp. 93–4 n. 6. For purposes of this discussion, I emphasize the latter ground of distinction.

17. Ibid., pp. 93–4 and n. 6.

18. *Horvath* v. *Secretary of State for the Home Department* [2001] 1 A.C. 489.

19. Human Rights Watch, "The O'odua People's Congress: Fighting Violence with Violence" (2003), pp. 1–2, www.hrw.org/reports/2003/nigeria0203/nigeria0203.pdf (last visited April 2, 2008).

20. US Department of State, "Nigeria – 2004 Country Reports on Human Rights Practices" (2005), www.state.gov/g/drl/rls/hrrpt/2004/41620.htm (last visited April 2, 2008).

21. Hannah Arendt, *Origins of Totalitarianism* (San Diego, CA: Harcourt Brace, 1973), p. 297.

22. Seyla Benhabib explains that this phrase "invoke[s] ... a *moral claim to membership and a certain form of treatment compatible with the claim to membership.*" Seyla Benhabib, *Transformations of Citizenship* (Amsterdam: Koninklijke Van Gorcum, 2001), p. 16 (emphasis in original). See also Frank I. Michelman, "Parsing 'A Right to Have Rights,'" *Constellations*, 3 (1996), p. 200.

23. Arendt, *Origins*, p. 295.

24. Ibid.

25. Ryan Goodman and Derek Jinks, "How to Influence States: Socialization and International Human Rights Law," *Duke Law Journal*, 54 (2004), p. 633.

26. Ibid., p. 635.

27. Ibid., p. 645.

28. Mark Gibney, "The Divorce Between Refugee Determinations and Pursuit of Human Rights Objectives Through U.S. Foreign Policy: The Case of Female Genital Mutilation" in Lydio F. Tomasi (ed.), *In Defense of the Alien*, vol. XVIII (New York: Center for Migration Studies, 1996), p. 182.

29. Ibid.

30. Ambassador Richard N. Haass, "Sovereignty: Existing Rights, Evolving Responsibilities" (Remarks to the School of Foreign Service and the Mortara Center for International Studies, Georgetown University, Washington, DC, January 14, 2003), www.state.gov/s/p/rem/2003/16648.htm (last visited April 8, 2008); see also International Commission on Intervention and State Sovereignty, *Responsibility to Protect* (Ottawa: International Development Research Centre, 2001), www.iciss.ca/pdf/Commission-Report.pdf (last visited April 8, 2008).

31. For a cautionary note on the use of military power to establish a safe area, see T. Alexander Aleinikoff, "Safe Haven: Pragmatics and Prospects," *Virginia Journal of International Law*, 35 (1994), p. 71.

32. The preamble stated, "*Gravely concerned* by the significant further deterioration of the humanitarian situation in Haiti, in particular the

continuing escalation by the illegal *de facto* regime of systematic violations of civil liberties, the desperate plight of Haitian refugees and the recent expulsion of the staff of the International Civil Mission ..." S.C. Res. 940, U.N. SCOR, 49th Sess., 3413th mtg., U.N. Doc. S/RES/940 (1994) (original emphasis). See also Adam Roberts, "More Refugees, Less Asylum," *Journal of Refugee Studies*, 11 (1998), p. 387.

33. S.C. Res. 688, U.N. SCOR, 46th Sess., 2982d mtg., U.N. Doc. S/RES/688 (1991).

34. See International Federation of Red Cross and Red Crescent Societies, *World Disasters Report 1996*, p. 15, noting that in Bosnia, "moving people made the humanitarian programme an instrument of ethnic cleansing."

35. Thanks to Arthur Applbaum for a discussion on this point.

36. 22 U.S.C. section 2304(a)(2).

37. 22 U.S.C. section 262(a)(1).

38. Sarah H. Cleveland, "Norm Internalization and U.S. Economic Sanctions," *Yale Journal of International Law*, 26 (2001), p. 5. Cleveland cites a study by Gary Hufbauer and Jeffrey Schott, which demonstrated that US sanctions successfully influenced human rights practices in Brazil between 1977 and 1984, in Uganda under Idi Amin, and in Nicaragua under Somoza. See Gary Clyde Hufbauer *et al.*, *Economic Sanctions Reconsidered: Supplemental Case Histories*, 2nd edn, vol. 2 (Washington, DC: Institute for International Economics, 1990), pp. 463–6.

39. "Constitutional Watch: A Country-by-Country Update on Constitutional Politics in Eastern Europe and the ex-USSR – Hungary," *East European Constitutional Review*, 10 (Spring/Summer 2001), www. law.nyu.edu/eecr/vol10num2_3/constitutionwatch/hungary.html (last visited April 8, 2008).

40. US Committee for Refugees, "Country Reports: Hungary," *World Refugee Survey 2001* (Washington, DC: US Committee for Refugees, 2001).

41. Martha Finnemore and Kathryn Sikkink, "International Norm Dynamics and Political Change," *International Organization*, 52 (1998), p. 903.

42. Ibid.

43. Pub. L. 102-256 (March 12, 1992), 106 Stat. 73, codified at 28 U.S.C. section 1350 note.

44. *Sosa v. Alvarez-Machain*, 542 U.S. 692 (2004).

45. 28 U.S.C. section 1350.

46. *Filartiga v. Pena-Irala*, 630 F.2d 876 (2d Cir. 1980). See also *Kadic v. Karadzic*, 70 F.3d 232 (2d Cir. 1995); *In re Estate of Marcos Human*

Rights Litig., 978 F.2d 493 (9th Cir. 1992); *Tachiona v. Mugabe*, 234 F. Supp. 2d 401 (S.D.N.Y. 2002); and *Xuncax v. Gramajo*, 886 F. Supp. 162 (D. Mass. 1995).

47. *Sosa*, 542 U.S. at 732, 737.

48. See A. Hays Butler, "The Growing Support for Universal Jurisdiction" in Stephen Macedo (ed.), *Universal Jurisdiction: National Courts and the Prosecution of Serious Crimes Under International Law* (Philadelphia, PA: University of Pennsylvania Press, 2004), pp. 69–70. For a discussion of some of the difficult issues raised by universal jurisdiction, see Anne-Marie Slaughter, "Defining the Limits: Universal Jurisdiction and National Courts" in Macedo (ed.), *Universal Jurisdiction*, pp. 168–90.

49. 28 U.S.C. section 1605(7).

50. Goodman and Jinks, "How to Influence States," p. 693.

51. Finnemore and Sikkink, "International Norm Dynamics," p. 897.

52. Ibid.

53. *Matter of Kasinga*, 21 I. & N. Dec. 357 (BIA 1996).

54. Congressional Record 142 (104th Cong. 2d Sess., April 29, 1996), p. S4287.

55. 18 U.S.C. section 116 (criminal prohibition); 22 U.S.C. section 262k-2 (international lending).

56. Elizabeth Heger Boyle and Sharon E. Preves, "National Politics as International Process: The Case of Anti-Female-Genital-Cutting Laws," *Law and Society Review*, 34 (2000), p. 725.

57. On the sanctuary movement, see generally Ignatius Bau, *This Ground is Holy: Church Sanctuary and Central American Refugees* (New York: Paulist Press, 1985); Susan Bibler Coutin, *The Culture of Protest: Religious Activism and the U.S. Sanctuary Movement* (Boulder, CO: Westview Press, 1993); Ann Crittenden, *Sanctuary: A Story of American Conscience and the Law in Collision* (New York: Weidenfeld & Nicolson, 1988); Miriam Davidson, *Convictions of the Heart: Jim Corbett and the Sanctuary Movement* (Tucson, AZ: University of Arizona Press, 1988); Robert Tomsho, *The American Sanctuary Movement* (Austin, TX: Texas Monthly Press, 1987).

58. *American Baptist Churches v. Thornburgh*, 760 F.Supp. 796 (N.D. Cal. 1991).

59. *DeShaney v. Winnebago County Department of Social Services*, 489 U.S. 189, 195 (1989).

60. *Town of Castle Rock, Colo. v. Gonzales*, 545 U.S. 748 (2005).

61. This approach is known as "constructivism." See, for example, Peter J. Katzenstein, "Introduction: Alternative Perspectives on National Security" in Katzenstein (ed.), *The Culture of National Security: Norms and Identity in World Politics* (New York: Columbia University Press,

1996), pp. 1–32; Alexander Wendt, "Collective Identity Formation and the International State," *American Political Science Review*, 88 (1994), pp. 384–96; Alexander Wendt, "Constructing International Politics," *International Security*, 20 (1995), pp. 71–81. See also: Thomas P. Risse, Steven C. Ropp, and Kathryn Sikkink (eds.), *The Power of Human Rights: International Norms and Domestic Change* (Cambridge University Press, 1999); Alexander Wendt, *Social Theory of International Politics* (Cambridge University Press, 1999).

62. Finnemore and Sikkink, "International Norm Dynamics," p. 903.

63. Ibid., pp. 903–4.

64. *Baballah* v. *Ashcroft*, 335 F.3d 981 (9th Cir. 2003), amended by *Baballah* v. *Ashcroft*, 367 F.3d 1067 (9th Cir. 2004).

65. Vered Levy-Barzilai and Max Levitte, "Gimme Shelter," *Ha'aretz*, July 25, 2003, www.haaretz.com/hasen/pages/ShArt.jhtml?itemNo=322027 (last visited April 8, 2008).

66. Anker, "Refugee Law," p. 135.

67. James C. Hathaway, "Reconceiving Refugee Law as Human Rights Protection," *Journal of Refugee Studies*, 4 (1991), p. 121. See also James C. Hathaway, "New Directions to Avoid Hard Problems: The Distortion of the Palliative Role of Refugee Protection," *Journal of Refugee Studies*, 8 (1995), p. 293, stating, "We must not be shy to validate the palliative, the protective, the stop-gap role of refugee law. There is nothing shameful about addressing the human consequences of harm"; and Gilbert Jaeger, "A Comment on the Distortion of the Palliative Role of Refugee Protection," *Journal of Refugee Studies*, 8 (1995), p. 301, attributing Hathaway's position to "his adherence to the humanitarian nature of asylum."

68. Gil Loescher, *Beyond Charity* (New York: Oxford University Press, 1993), p. 21.

69. Quoted in Aristide R. Zolberg, Astri Suhrke, and Sergio Aguayo, *Escape From Violence* (New York: Oxford University Press, 1989), p. 273.

70. Immigration and Nationality Act of 1952 (June 27, 1952, ch. 477, 66 Stat. 163), section 212(d)(5). Section 243(h) of the 1952 Act also authorized the Attorney General to withhold the deportation of an alien "to any country in which in his opinion the alien would be subject to physical persecution." However, as interpreted by the Board of Immigration Appeals, an alien was eligible for withholding of deportation only if he could establish a "clear probability" of persecution, a demanding standard that was, in Arthur Helton's words, "stringently applied." Arthur C. Helton, "Political Asylum Under the 1980 Refugee Act: An Unfulfilled Promise," *University of Michigan Journal of Law Reform*, 17 (1984), p. 244.

71. Helton, "Political Asylum," p. 246. See also: Gil Loescher and John A. Scanlan, *Calculated Kindness* (New York: Free Press, 1986), p. 70 and Kevin R. Johnson, "A 'Hard Look' at the Executive Branch's Asylum Decisions," *Utah Law Review* (1991), p. 289.

72. Immigration and Nationality Act, section 203(a)(7) (as amended in 1965 by Pub. L. 89-236 section 3, 79 Stat. 911, 913) (repealed at 94 Stat. 102, 107 (1980)). Subsequent amendments permitted a portion of these refugee visas to be used by people who met the above definition, but had already been present in the United States for at least two years. 8 C.F.R. section 245.4 (1971).

73. David A. Martin, "Reforming Asylum Adjudication: On Navigating the Coast of Bohemia," *University of Pennsylvania Law Review*, 138 (1990), p. 1261 n. 37.

74. Refugee Act 1980, Pub. L. 96-212 section 1, 94 Stat. 102 (1980), codified at 8 U.S.C. section 1101(a)(42).

75. Helton, "Political Asylum," p. 250. See also Deborah E. Anker and Michael H. Posner, "The Forty Year Crisis: A Legislative History of the Refugee Act of 1980," *San Diego Law Review*, 19 (1981), pp. 9–89; Carolyn Patty Blum, "Political Assumptions in Asylum Decision-Making: The Example of Refugees from Armed Conflict" in Howard Adelman (ed.), *Refugee Policy: Canada and the United States* (Toronto: York Lanes Press, 1991), pp. 282–91; and Martin, "Navigating the Coast," p. 1262 n. 39.

76. Mark Gibney and Michael Stohl, "Human Rights and U.S. Refugee Policy" in Mark Gibney (ed.), *Open Borders? Closed Societies? The Ethical and Political Issues* (New York: Greenwood Press, 1988), pp. 163–70.

77. Immigration and Naturalization Service, "Asylum Adjudications: An Evolving Concept and Responsibility for the Immigration and Naturalization Service" (June and December 1982), p. 59 n.*, quoted in Helton, "Political Asylum," p. 254.

78. Doris Meissner, "Reflections on the U.S. Refugee Act of 1980" in David A. Martin (ed.), *The New Asylum Seekers: Refugee Law in the 1980s* (Norwell, MA: Kluwer Academic, 1988), p. 64.

79. Pub. L. 104-208, Div. C, Title VI, section 606 (September 30, 1996), 110 Stat. 3009-695; Pub. L. 89-732 (November 2, 1966), 80 Stat. 1161, codified at 8 U.S.C. section 1255 note.

80. See, for example, Norman Zucker and Naomi Zucker, *Desperate Crossings: Seeking Refuge in America* (Armonk, NY: M. E. Sharpe, 1996); T. Alexander Aleinikoff, David A. Martin, and Hiroshi Motomura, *Immigration: Process and Policy*, 4th edn. (St. Paul, MN: West Group, 1998), pp. 1162–7; and Charles J. Ogletree, Jr., "America's Schizophrenic Immigration Policy: Race, Class, and Reason," *Boston College Law Review*, 41 (2000), p. 761.

81. Gibney and Stohl, "Human Rights," pp. 153, 161.
82. "Torture victims from El Salvador had an approval rate of 4 percent, from Nicaragua 15 percent, from Iran 64 percent, and from Poland 80 percent." Zucker and Zucker, *Desperate Crossings*, p. 88. Another example of underprotection was the American reluctance to grant asylum to supporters of Allende following Pinochet's coup in Chile. Loescher, *Beyond Charity*, p. 100.
83. Helton, "Political Asylum," p. 254.
84. Doris Meissner, "Reflections," p. 63. The US Government later essentially admitted that Salvadoran and Guatemalan applicants had been forced to overcome an unfairly strong negative presumption in the settlement to a class action suit filed against the INS by eighty churches and refugee groups. See *American Baptist Churches* v. *Thornburgh*, 760 F. Supp. 796 (N.D. Cal. 1991). As part of the settlement, the Justice Department agreed to adjudicate *de novo* all Salvadoran and Guatemalan asylum claims filed between 1980 and 1991 under new regulations designed to limit the influence of foreign policy considerations on the asylum process. In part to address the large backlog of cases created by the ABC settlement, Congress subsequently passed the Nicaraguan Adjustment and Central American Relief Act (NACARA) in 1997, which permitted class members, as well as others, to adjust their status to legal permanent residence without having to undergo a new hearing. Pub. L. 105-100, Title II, 111 Stat. 2193 (1997). After receiving pressure from immigrant advocacy groups to offer a similar amnesty for Haitians, in 1998 Congress passed the Haitian Refugee Immigration Fairness Act (HRIFA), which allowed Haitians who were in the United States on December 31, 1995, and who met other requirements, to adjust their status to legal permanent residence. Pub. L. 105-277, Div. A, section 101(h) [Title IX], 112 Stat. 2681-538 (1998).
85. Meissner, "Reflections," pp. 64–5 (original emphasis).
86. Quoted in: Richard K. Preston, "Asylum Adjudications: Do State Department Advisory Opinions Violate Refugees' Rights and U.S. International Obligations?" *Maryland Law Review*, 45 (1986), p. 117.
87. Barbara M. Yarnold, *Refugees Without Refuge: Formation and Failed Implementation of U.S. Political Asylum Policy in the 1980s* (Lanham, MD: University Press of America, 1990), p. 87.
88. The immigration service must still forward applications to the State Department, which has the option of providing comment; see 8 C.F.R. section 208.11(b). However, a State Department opinion is no longer a necessary part of the adjudication process.
89. 8 C.F.R. section 208.1(b). See also 8 C.F.R. section 208.12(a), which expressly authorizes asylum officers to consider "material provided

by ... international organizations, private voluntary agencies, news organizations, or academic institutions," as well as the State Department, in
reaching their decisions.

90. *M.A.* v. *INS*, 899 F.2d 304, 313 (4th Cir. 1990).
91. Ibid. See also, for example, *INS* v. *Aguirre-Aguirre*, 526 U.S. 415, 425
(1999), stating that "judicial deference to the Executive Branch is especially appropriate in the immigration context where officials 'exercise
especially sensitive political functions that implicate questions of foreign
relations'"; *Elien* v. *Ashcroft*, 364 F.3d 392, 396 (1st Cir. 2004), stating
that "[a]s immigration law frequently implicates some expertise in matters of foreign policy, BIA interpretations of the statutes and regulations it
administers are accorded substantial deference"; and *Kaveh-Haghigy* v.
INS, 783 F.2d 1321, 1323 (9th Cir. 1986), stating that, "[a]bsent exceptional circumstances, it is not the place of the judiciary to evaluate the
political justifications of the actions of foreign governments." For academic treatments of the subject of judicial review in the political asylum
context, see Stephen H. Legomsky, "Political Asylum and the Theory of
Judicial Review," *Minnesota Law Review*, 73 (1989), pp. 1205–16; Rex
D. Khan, "Why Refugee Status Should Be Beyond Judicial Review,"
University of San Francisco Law Review, 35 (2000), p. 57.

3 | *What is "Persecution"?*

The preceding chapters have articulated a political approach to asylum, one that explains why asylum should be reserved for persecuted people. Asylum provides not only protection to the refugee, but also chastises the persecutory state for its misconduct. But to precisely which kinds of harm does the label "persecution" apply? The question is a difficult one. Certain kinds of harm obviously qualify: for example, the murder or torture of political dissidents or ethnic or religious minorities constitute the classic cases of persecution. But beyond this core, which harms does the concept of "persecution" encompass? The UNHCR Handbook, meant to provide interpretive guidance to courts and administrative agencies, begins its discussion of persecution with a striking disclaimer: "There is no universally accepted definition of 'persecution,' and various attempts to formulate such a definition have met with little success."[1] Guy Goodwin-Gill, a prominent commentator, concurs that the definition of persecution has "no coherent or consistent jurisprudence."[2] American law, in particular, is in disarray. The asylum statute leaves "persecution" undefined, and the agency charged with issuing regulations – now the Department of Homeland Security – has offered little regulatory guidance. The federal courts of appeals, meanwhile, have employed a number of definitions which appear similar on their face but, in fact, vary in subtle ways that can have important implications.[3]

The growing acceptance of a humanitarian conception of asylum partly explains the confusion over persecution's meaning. The term "persecution" seems to connote more than just the bare infliction of harm; persecution is a particular kind of harm. Yet from a humanitarian standpoint, the purpose of asylum is to protect refugees regardless of the particular kind of harm to which they are exposed. To give "persecution" its plain meaning would, from a humanitarian perspective, amount to a deviation from asylum's animating purpose. As the humanitarian approach has taken root, this tension has been eased by broadening the definition of "persecution" to encompass a wider array of types of harm. For example, in the United States, "government sanction" was initially regarded as a necessary element of persecution; so too was a punitive intent.[4] By the late 1990s, those prerequisites had been eliminated. The American trend has been in the direction taken more definitively by Canadian, British, and Australian courts: persecution means nothing more than serious harm against which the state is unable, or unwilling, to provide protection.[5]

That gloss on "persecution," however, is problematic for several reasons. First, it cannot account for the requirement in the Convention definition that persecution be "for reasons of race, religion, nationality, membership of a particular social group, or political opinion." From a humanitarian standpoint, that requirement – known as the "nexus clause" – introduces yet another departure from the purpose of asylum to protect. Not only is it arbitrary to focus on persecution to the exclusion of other harms, but it is also arbitrary to focus on certain reasons for persecution to the exclusion of other reasons. While courts have found it possible to gloss "persecution" in a way that promotes humanitarian ends – defining it as the absence of state protection against serious harm – they have had much more difficulty evading the nexus clause.

The humanitarian gloss on "persecution" is problematic in a more fundamental way as well. It fails to recognize that persecution is a distinctive *kind* of harm that warrants a distinctive kind of response: condemnation and (if the persecution is sufficiently widespread) external interference. The gloss I offer is grounded in the political approach to asylum advanced in the preceding chapter. The broad theme is that "persecution" describes state conduct warranting international condemnation and suspending a state's sovereign right against external interference. The persecution requirement, then, rests upon a theory of international legitimacy – a theory that explains when such interference is justified.

I do not offer a comprehensive theory of international legitimacy. Instead, my goal is merely to show how, with the concept of international legitimacy as an anchor point, the persecution requirement (together with the nexus clause) can be given a coherent and focused meaning, and to illustrate that meaning by reference to a number of difficult questions of application.

Persecution and international legitimacy

International law imposes a general rule against interference in the internal affairs of other states. That rule stems from a commitment to the principle of communal self-determination, the idea that a political community with a common way of life should have the freedom to decide for itself how it should be governed. That principle follows from the liberal idea that legitimate government must rest upon the consent of the governed. And it is implemented by what I shall call a "presumption of legitimacy," the assumption that, as a general matter, governments do indeed exercise power with the consent of their citizens. That presumption is reflected in the related doctrines of state sovereignty and territorial integrity. Ordinarily, states have exclusive jurisdiction and control over their territories, and external interference constitutes a wrongful act of aggression.

Of course, except in unusual situations, no "social contract" is ever actually ratified by citizens. Rather, as Michael Walzer explains:

Over a long period of time, shared experiences and cooperative activity of many different kinds shape a common life. "Contract" is a metaphor for that process of association and mutuality, the ongoing character of which the state claims to protect against external encroachment. The protection extends not only to the lives and liberties of individuals, but also to their shared life and liberty, the independent community they have made, for which individuals are sometimes sacrificed.[6]

Not every state acts with the tacit or express authorization of its citizenry. Nonetheless, the presumption of legitimacy reflects a practical judgment that communal self-determination is better served by a rule prohibiting external interference rather than by a rule permitting it. Recall Pufendorf's comment that an international system in which other states constantly "thrust [themselves] forward as a kind of arbitrator of human affairs ... could easily lead to great abuse."[7] Walzer explains:

[T]he recognition of sovereignty is the only way we have of establishing an arena within which freedom can be fought for and (sometimes) won. It is this arena and the activities that go on within it that we want to protect, and we protect them, much as we protect individual integrity, by marking out boundaries that cannot be crossed, rights that cannot be violated. As with individuals, so with sovereign states: there are things that we cannot do to them, even for their own ostensible good.[8]

The effect is to permit states to adopt a wide range of domestic institutions and laws, free of external interference.

The presumption of legitimacy, however, is not absolute. There are situations when "the violation of human rights within a set of boundaries is so terrible that it makes talk of community or self-determination ... seem cynical and irrelevant, that is, in cases of enslavement or massacre."[9] Recall Rawls' concept of outlaw states and Arendt's concept of "rightlessness," discussed in Chapter 2. When such harm is widespread, a broad-gauged response by bystander states is appropriate. As Walzer puts it:

> If the dominant forces within a state are engaged in massive violations of human rights, the appeal to self-determination ... is not very attractive. That appeal has to do with the freedom of the community taken as a whole; it has no force when what is at stake is the bare survival or the minimal liberty of (some substantial number of) its members ... [W]hen a government turns savagely upon its own people, we must doubt the very existence of a political community to which the idea of self-determination might apply.[10]

In such cases, external interference advances rather than impinges on the principle of communal self-determination.

When harm is serious but not so widespread, wholesale intervention and overthrow would be inappropriate. That does not mean, however, that bystander states are without recourse. Asylum is a means to remedy on a retail level state misconduct that, if sufficiently widespread, would justify more intrusive forms of external interference.

The elements of "persecution"

The meaning of "persecution" should be informed by the role of asylum as an international sanction. "Persecution" is conduct so at odds with the principle of communal self-determination that a presumption of legitimacy cannot be justified, and external interference is warranted. Such mistreatment cannot be trivial; it must involve the infliction of serious harm. The mistreatment must also be motivated by "illegitimate reasons" – reasons inconsistent with the theory behind a presumption of legitimacy, namely, that a state acts as the fiduciary of its citizenry. The nexus clause – the requirement that persecution be on account of "race, religion, nationality, membership of a particular social group, or political opinion" – provides examples of such illegitimate reasons. A state that seeks to inflict serious harm on a citizen because he or she is of a different race, religion, nationality, or because of some other ascriptive characteristic, or because he or she possesses a certain political opinion, cannot intelligibly be said to act on behalf of that citizen. "Persecution" thus has three elements: (1) serious harm that is (2) inflicted or tolerated by official agents (3) for illegitimate reasons. In this chapter, I consider in greater detail the first and third element; Chapter 4 will take up the second element.

Serious harm

One element of "persecution" is that it involves *serious* harm of some sort. "Persecution," as one court has put it, is an "extreme concept."[11] It "does not encompass all treatment that our society regards as unfair, unjust, or even unlawful or unconstitutional."[12] The presumption of legitimacy affords states wide latitude to arrange their affairs as they wish. Thus, asylum policy is not designed to remedy every injustice or injury. Minor harms or inconveniences, even if carried out for illegitimate reasons, do not call for international condemnation and interference.

It is easy to think of harms that clearly cross the threshold of requisite seriousness: enslavement, torture, imprisonment, death. We can also (perhaps with somewhat greater difficulty) identify a lower bound: persecution involves "more than a few isolated incidents of verbal harassment or intimidation, unaccompanied by any physical punishment, infliction of harm, or significant deprivation of liberty."[13] The threshold of seriousness lies somewhere between "threats to life or freedom," on the one hand, and "mere harassment and annoyance," on the other hand.[14] Actions that "might cross the line from harassment to persecution include: detention, arrest, interrogation, prosecution, imprisonment, illegal searches, confiscation of property, surveillance, [or] beatings."[15]

Often it is hard to decide whether treatment crosses the threshold of seriousness, and judges can reasonably disagree. This difficulty is largely due to the impossibility of placing on a single spectrum the infinite variety of incommensurable experiences of harm. The case of Li Xu Ming is representative of this difficulty. Li was forcibly subjected by Chinese population control officials to a half-hour long gynecological exam to determine whether she was pregnant.[16] When she tried to resist, she was physically restrained by two nurses and threatened with a sterilization operation.[17]

The majority held that the examination did not constitute persecution, contrasting Li's case with more usual cases of arbitrary detention and physical abuse. In *Prasad*,[18] for example, a Fijian of Indian descent was arrested by ethnic Fijians, placed in a cell for four to six hours, and "hit on his stomach and kicked from behind." The majority held that

Li's forced examination was significantly less serious than Prasad's detention both in the intensity of harm inflicted and the duration of that harm.[19] The dissenting judge, meanwhile, compared Li's forced examination to rape, and rejected the length of detention as a reliable measure by which to judge the seriousness of the harm inflicted.[20]

"Seriousness" is a judgment call, and different judges might reasonably reach very different answers. Precedent serves as a guide to judges in deciding whether harm passes the requisite threshold of seriousness, but cannot constrain them entirely: factual variations are endless – suppose Prasad had only been hit on his stomach? or arrested twice for four hours each, but had never been hit? and so on – and we lack the means for easy comparison. Consequently, as one court has put it, "courts have tended to consider the subject on an ad hoc basis."[21]

Illegitimate reasons

Seriousness is not the only element of persecution. After all, states routinely inflict harm that we might regard as persecutory if done for the wrong reasons, but that we regard as entirely proper when done for the right reasons. Most obviously, states imprison people. Imprisonment is persecutory when used, say, to punish a religious minority for its beliefs; but it is legitimate when used to punish a murderer. States also institutionalize people and force them to undergo medical treatment. Shock treatments might be regarded as legitimate when given to treat the mentally ill, but illegitimate when given to "treat" homosexuals or others regarded as "socially deviant." States also take people's property in the form of taxation and condemnation; those legitimate takings are distinguished from illegitimate confiscation.

Thus, another element (and the more important one, for present purposes) is that the serious harm be inflicted for illegitimate reasons – reasons inconsistent with the usual presumption that a state acts as the fiduciary of its citizenry. As Judge Richard Posner has written, persecution is "punishment or the infliction of harm for political, religious, or other reasons that this country does not recognize as legitimate."[22] The definition of "persecution" is, therefore, undergirded by a political theory that describes which reasons for inflicting official harm are legitimate and which are illegitimate.[23]

The nexus clause – which requires that persecution be "for reasons of race, religion, nationality, membership of a particular social group, or political opinion" – illustrates illegitimate reasons for inflicting serious harm. It reflects a distinctively liberal conception of legitimacy: one that protects pluralism by promoting the values of *equality, religious toleration*, and *political accountability*, while still leaving states with wide latitude to enact policies that respond to local needs or reflect local values and culture. In light of these values, the bases for harm identified by the nexus clause are manifestly at odds with the usual presumption that the state acts for the benefit of its citizenry.

The specification of race and nationality as illegitimate reasons for harm reflect the self-evident proposition that a state that targets sectors of its population for harm on the basis of immutable, ascriptive characteristics cannot possibly be said to act on their behalf. The same is true of harm inflicted on account of religion. Although a state need not be neutral with respect to religion, it must nonetheless tolerate minority faiths by allowing their members to exercise their beliefs freely. The same could also be said about harm inflicted on account of other ascriptive characteristics not explicitly delineated in the nexus clause, such as ethnicity, disability, kinship, sexual orientation, and gender. "Membership in a social group" should be read to encompass such attributes. That reading is consistent with the gloss given by current US law: a "social group" is understood to refer to any group sharing "a common, immutable characteristic," including "an innate one such as sex, color, or kinship ties," as well as "a shared past experience such as former military leadership or land ownership ... [W]hatever the common characteristic that defines the group, it must be one that the members of the group either cannot change, or should not be required to change because it is fundamental to their individual identities or consciences."[24]

Political opinion is an impermissible basis for harm because the freedom to express grievances is necessary if leaders are to be held accountable for official misconduct or errors in judgment. A regime need not be democratic to enjoy freedom from external interference, but it must allow its citizens to assemble for peaceful protest, to publish dissenting opinions in the media, and to hold diverse viewpoints. A regime unwilling to permit criticism does not take seriously its responsibility to act on behalf of its citizenry. As Immanuel Kant put it long ago, "the citizen must ... be entitled to make public his opinion on whatever of the ruler's measures seem to him to constitute an injustice against the commonwealth ... *Freedom of the pen* is the only safeguard of the rights of the people ..."[25]

The idea that political opinion is an illegitimate basis for inflicting harm can explain the doctrine of imputed political opinion, which holds that people can be persecuted on account of a political opinion that they do not actually hold but that is imputed to them by a persecutor. "What justifies refugee protection" in such a case, explains Daniel Steinbock, "is that the political opinion that the persecutors attribute to the victim is an ... improper[ ] ground for punishment," regardless of whether the victim actually espouses that opinion.[26]

In one important way, the nexus clause is too narrow. In focusing on various personal characteristics as illegitimate bases for harm, it fails to capture what I shall call liberalism's anti-brutality norm: the idea, reflected in international human rights law, that some harms are so serious that their infliction for any reason is inconsistent with the presumption of legitimacy. For example, customary international law recognizes as peremptory the rights to be free from genocide, slavery, murder or disappearance of individuals, torture, prolonged arbitrary detention, and apartheid.[27] These harms are always outside the boundaries of permissible state action, no matter what the reason for inflicting them.

People may reasonably disagree about the scope or interpretation of these peremptory human rights – for example, whether capital punishment is simply judicial murder or can sometimes be legitimate – and they may also disagree about whether other rights should be added to this list. For example, the anti-brutality norm may also bar serious violations of international humanitarian law, so that states may never target civilians or carry out military operations that expose them to harm that is disproportionate to the military objective. But bracketing these disputes about interpretation and scope, the notion that there are some absolute constraints on governmental action is well accepted.

"Subsidiary protection" in the European Union can be understood, in part, as implementing the anti-brutality norm. That form of protection effectively extends asylum to people who would, if returned to their country of origin, face the death penalty, torture, or other inhuman or degrading punishment.[28] In the view of the EU, all three categories of treatment can never be justified by a state's legitimate interest in punishment. They are in every case beyond the bounds of legitimate state authority.

Recognizing an anti-brutality norm would require a change to US law. Currently, applicants must show that they have been persecuted because they possess, or have had imputed to them, one of the characteristics listed in the nexus clause: race, religion, nationality, social

group membership, or political opinion. The list of grounds given by the
nexus clause is an exclusive one. This has had unhappy consequences in
many cases, most notoriously those involving police investigations.

Matter of R – is representative of such cases. A 21-year-old Sikh man
was visited by Sikh militant separatists at his home in Punjab and was
asked for money in support of their cause. He declined to give them
money because he advocated separatism only through non-violent
means. He was subsequently arrested by the Indian police and was
brutally tortured while being interrogated about the militants' visit.
He was eventually released without charges, and upon his arrival
home, was confronted again by the militants, who beat him and threatened to kill him and his family unless he joined them. Fearing harm
from both the militants and the police, R fled to the United States.[29]

The US Board of Immigration Appeals (BIA) rejected his asylum
claim on the grounds that neither:

the Sikh militants [nor] the police who confronted the applicant sought to punish
him on account of one of the grounds enumerated in the [nexus clause] … [T]he
Sikh militants were seeking operating resources from the applicant in the form of
material assistance and manpower … Similarly, there is no indication that the
police actions against the applicant extended beyond the investigation of and
reaction against those thought – rightly or wrongly – to be militants seeking the
violent overthrow of the government … While the applicant states he was
subjected to police brutality, which we certainly do not countenance, the record
reflects that the purpose of the mistreatment was to extract information about
Sikh militants, rather than to persecute the applicant "because" of his political
opinions or the mere fact that he was a Sikh.[30]

In other words, R failed to qualify for asylum because the police
tortured him to gain information they believed he possessed; the militants beat him in order to recruit additional manpower; and these are
not protected grounds under the nexus clause. That approach to the
nexus clause has rightly struck many observers as troubling.[31]

One could argue that the BIA mischaracterized the police's reasons
for harming R, and that the torture was at least in part on account of
political opinions they imputed to him. But even assuming that the BIA's
analysis of the facts was correct, and that the police's sole reason for
torturing R was to gain information that they believed he possessed, R
should have been granted asylum. Customary international law would
certainly regard the police torture of R as having violated a peremptory

human rights norm, reflecting the judgment that such treatment can never be justified for any reason. Extending asylum eligibility to people like R follows straightforwardly from a political conception of asylum.*

It is true that people like R are often eligible for protection against deportation under the Convention Against Torture (CAT). For example, in the United States, an alien cannot be removed if he "is more likely than not to be tortured in the country of removal."[32] But that is a more stringent standard than in asylum proceedings: to benefit from CAT, applicants must prove that they are "more likely than not" to be tortured, while asylum applicants must prove only a "well-founded fear" of persecution. A "well-founded fear" may exist even if there is a 10 percent probability of harm.[33] Moreover, protection under CAT is a much less desirable status than asylum. In the United States, it does not entitle one to family reunification or place one on the path to permanent residence and citizenship. Under the EU's directive providing for subsidiary protection, recipients are guaranteed only a renewable one-year grant of protection, as opposed to a renewable three-year grant of protection for those qualifying as Convention refugees.[34]

One approach to incorporating an anti-brutality norm into current law is to add to the Convention refugee definition another set of grounds on which an asylum claim could be based. This is roughly what the EU has done with the device of subsidiary protection (although the EU continues to distinguish between Convention refugees and recipients of subsidiary protection in terms of the relief given). Another approach would be to adopt a statutory presumption that victims of torture and other "brutal" treatment have suffered persecution on account of a Convention reason. The US Board of Immigration Appeals has suggested in passing that "there may be situations in which the severity of the violations of the Geneva Convention may support an inference that the abuse is grounded in one of the protected grounds under the asylum law."[35] Such an inference could be presumed for the violation of peremptory human rights norms, including torture.[36] As we shall see below, the United States has, in effect, adopted such a presumption for victims of China's

---

* One may object that granting asylum to those who suffer torture or abuse during a legitimate police investigation would mean granting refuge to terrorists and criminals who have experienced mistreatment by their states of origin. But there is no such danger. Separate rules under both international and domestic law exclude such persons from asylum. I further discuss these "bar statutes" below.

coercive sterilization program, and a similar statutory presumption was proposed for victims of female genital mutilation.

Constraining adjudicators

Because people can reasonably disagree about whether particular reasons are a legitimate basis for harm and about whether certain treatment is proscribed by a peremptory human rights norm, adjudicators will inevitably need to rely on their own judgment as to the bounds of legitimate state authority. Some might raise the specter of adjudicators deciding cases based on nothing other than their own subjective moral assessments. But, in fact, a variety of mechanisms meaningfully constrains adjudicators and ensures that their decisions reflect collective judgments about legitimacy.

First, adjudicators are constrained by statute, which – as just discussed – outlines the types of reasons that should be regarded as illegitimate bases for harm. Any determination needs to remain anchored to the statute. Second, adjudicators are constrained by precedent. Over time, through the accretion of decisions, interpretive gaps are narrowed and a consensus will emerge on the types of harms regarded as sufficiently serious to constitute persecution and on the reasons for harm regarded as illegitimate. At the same time, this consensus is dynamic, and our notion of what constitutes persecution can shift with changing moral sensibilities. For example, courts have been increasingly open to the idea that sexual orientation and gender should be regarded as "social groups" under the asylum statute, so that harm inflicted on their account can give rise to asylum eligibility.[37]

Third, normative disagreements can be at least partly resolved at the policy-making level through the use of administrative guidelines and legislative presumptions. For example, the Immigration and Naturalization Service (INS) Gender Guidelines, designed to create "uniformity and consistency" in gender-related claims, alerted American adjudicators to a variety of considerations relevant to such claims. The BIA, whose members are appointed by the Attorney General, issues decisions that set binding agency policy. In addition, the legislature always remains free to step in and overrule a policy judgment made by the BIA or the courts that it dislikes.

The law concerning Chinese coercive population control policy provides a good example. The BIA had held that the Chinese program was not persecutory because, as a law of general application, it did not target people for harm on account of any of the characteristics listed in the nexus clause. Congress responded by enacting a statute deeming involuntary abortion and involuntary sterilization to be persecution "on account of political opinion" in all cases – even those lacking any evidence of political opinion. Effectively, the statute treated coercive population control as falling within the anti-brutality norm: as beyond the scope of legitimate government action no matter what the reason for it.[38]

The role for human rights

In Chapter 2, I suggested that asylum can be linked to a human rights-oriented foreign policy, and above I suggested that international human rights law can offer guidance in determining the scope of the anti-brutality principle. Respect for core human rights, that is, those rights recognized by customary international law as peremptory, is a necessary condition for legitimate state conduct, and so treating the violation of those basic rights as giving rise to asylum eligibility is consistent with the political conception of asylum. But, under the approach I have suggested, legitimacy should remain the touchstone for defining "persecution," not human rights.

That approach runs counter to the main trend among refugee scholars in recent years, which has been to couple asylum policy to international human rights law, so that the violation of any of the human rights listed in the Universal Declaration of Human Rights (UDHR) and codified in either the International Covenant on Civil and Political Rights (ICCPR) or the International Covenant on Economic, Social, and Cultural Rights (ICESCR) would constitute persecution. This "human rights approach" (as I shall call it) was pioneered by Professor James Hathaway, has been embraced by other prominent academics and activists, and has been endorsed by courts in Canada, Britain, Australia, and New Zealand.[39]

The rationale is that the human rights listed in the Covenants represent "the minimum duty owed by a state to its nationals," which "[a]ll states are bound to respect as a minimum condition of legitimacy."[40] When a state "ignores or is unable to respond to legitimate expectations as defined in international human rights law [by failing] to comply with its most basic duty," citizens of that state should have the "prospect of legitimate disengagement from that community in favour of surrogate protection elsewhere."[41] Thus, Hathaway concludes, "persecution may be defined as the sustained or systemic violation of human rights demonstrative of a failure of state protection."[42]

Human rights fall into four categories. In the first are rights from which no derogation is ever permitted, including not only the peremptory human rights norms covered by the anti-brutality principle, but also a right against *ex post facto* criminal punishment and rights to legal personhood and freedom of thought, conscience, and religion. The second category includes rights from which derogation is permitted in times of public emergency, including freedom from arbitrary detention, the right to a fair trial in criminal proceedings, privacy rights, rights to political participation, the right to join trade unions, and freedom of opinion, expression, assembly, and association. The third category consists of economic and social rights, such as rights to food, clothing, housing, health care, and social security; states are obligated to "take steps" to achieve these rights to the extent that their resources allow. In the fourth group are rights listed in the UDHR, but not codified in either the ICCPR or ICESCR, such as the right to be free from arbitrary deprivation of property. Hathaway concludes that the violation of rights in this fourth category does not constitute "persecution."[43]

In effect, the human rights approach expands the scope of the anti-brutality principle from the core of basic human rights recognized as binding under customary international law to the full roster of rights listed in international instruments. One consequence of this approach would be radically to de-emphasize the nexus clause. Rather than determining whether harm is inflicted for an illicit reason, the human rights approach identifies a large class of harms that cannot be inflicted for any reason.[44]

The human rights approach is helpful in giving additional texture to the concept of persecution and thereby promoting consistency of decision-making. But "persecution" should not be defined solely through the prism of human rights. Instead, legitimacy must remain the primary conceptual framework. This is so for several reasons.

Overinclusion and underinclusion

First, the human rights approach reifies a list of human rights that was the product of both political compromise and aspirational thinking.

The human rights codified in the ICCPR and ICESCR may in the aggregate be good proxies for legitimacy, but they are not determinative of legitimacy. The list is both overinclusive and underinclusive. As an example of overinclusion, consider the right "[t]o vote and to be elected at genuine periodic elections,"[45] derogable only in cases of national emergency. One might find it implausible that every citizen of a benign and decent monarchy has been persecuted. Perhaps democracy is the most just method of governance; but a decent monarchy is not liable to external intervention or deserving of international condemnation merely due to the nature of its political system. To award asylum to citizens of a monarchy on such a basis is at odds with the political conception. Similarly, one might find implausible the notion that a wealthy state's failure to provide social security[46] violates the "minimum conditions" of its legitimacy, thereby permitting poor would-be pensioners to claim asylum elsewhere. Rectifying this kind of distributive injustice is not what asylum is for.

In light of examples such as these, it is unsurprising that the Commonwealth courts adopting the human rights approach emphasize that eligibility for asylum is limited to applicants who can show a well-founded fear of serious harm *in addition* to a violation of human rights. " 'Being persecuted,' " they have held, "is the construct of two separate but essential elements, namely risk of serious harm *and* a failure of state protection" of human rights.[47] The requirement that human rights violations be accompanied by serious harm dramatically curtails the scope of the human rights approach. Some human rights violations inherently involve serious harm, most notably the peremptory human rights norms encompassed by the anti-brutality principle, like slavery, torture, murder, and prolonged arbitrary detention.

However, for most rights listed in the ICCPR and ICESCR, their violation does not inherently constitute serious harm; and in the case of many, it is hard to see how their violation could *ever* constitute serious harm. In the last category fall rights to political participation and many economic, social, and cultural rights, such as the rights of trade unions, the right to maternal leave, the right to reasonable limitation of working hours, and the right to equal pay for equal work. In sum, the requirement that human rights violations must be accompanied by serious harm in order to constitute persecution effectively acknowledges that the roster of human rights in the ICCPR and ICESCR is overinclusive for purposes of asylum policy, and that the violation of such human rights does not necessarily violate the minimum conditions of a state's legitimacy.

At the same time, the list of human rights in the ICCPR and ICESCR is also underinclusive from the perspective of legitimacy. Limiting asylum to those who have been denied those rights alone would leave unprotected several categories of people who should be eligible for asylum. For example, the "right to own and be free from arbitrary deprivation of property"[48] is not included in either the ICCPR or the ICESCR and, therefore, on Hathaway's scheme, its violation could not constitute persecution. But American courts rightly agree that, in some circumstances, "confiscation of property" can "cross the line from harassment to persecution."[49]

Punishment for "absolute political offenses" – such as a coup or other criminal act directed against the existence of a state or against a head of state[50] – offers another example of underinclusion. Punishing coup-plotters or rebels does not violate their human rights. The ICCPR recognizes a right to political expression, but it is subject to a limitation for "the protection of national security or of public order."[51] Rebellion falls outside the scope of this right on two counts: it is action rather than expression; and even if it were regarded as expression, it would certainly come within the exception for national security and public order. This result is unsurprising, given that the human rights conventions were the result of negotiation among governments which presumably were unwilling to forfeit their power to punish traitors and insurrectionists. But given asylum's historical role of sheltering revolutionaries from punishment – in particular, revolutionaries who have fought against tyrannical regimes – the conclusion that insurrectionists are ineligible for asylum is quite unsatisfying. Later on in this chapter, I shall have more to say about insurrectionists and their eligibility for asylum.

Human rights are not self-defining

The second reason that legitimacy, rather than human rights, must be the touchstone for asylum is that human rights are not self-defining. They require interpretation. What does it mean to be "treated with humanity and respect for the inherent dignity of the human person"? What constitutes "arbitrary" arrest or detention? How extensive is the right to "freedom of expression" or "freedom of association" or "freedom of conscience"? Similar interpretive problems arise concerning socio-economic rights, which are violated only when a state fails to "take steps" to secure them to the extent that their resources allow. But what constitutes an adequate "step"? Resources are scarce; how much latitude should states have in allocating them as they deem appropriate? In sum, we must look beyond the ICCPR and ICESCR to fill out the content of human rights. In defining their scope, we are necessarily thrown back on an underlying theory of legitimacy. This should be unsurprising. After all, the list of human rights in the ICCPR and ICESCR did not drop from the sky, but instead were themselves distilled from widely shared notions of legitimacy.

To take just one of many possible examples, how should one regard laws enforcing Islamic dress, for example, Iran's law requiring women to wear chadors, or hair coverings, when in public? Saideh Hassib-Tehrani, a native of Iran, entered the United States in 1984 and applied for asylum shortly thereafter. She claimed that she had been questioned and briefly detained on a couple of occasions for having violated various Islamic morals regulations. One time, she had attended a party at a male friend's house and had seen him in a bathing suit. She was later detained by the authorities for several hours with other female guests and was instructed that "being present with a man in a bathing suit was incorrect." Another time, she was stopped on the street by four government officials because she "had a few pieces of hair hanging out of her [chador] by mistake," was forced into their car at gunpoint, admonished "not to appear on the street like that again," and returned home. Hassib-Tehrani testified that she had been so greatly distressed by these events that she became ill, missed several months of work, and fled Iran.[52] Her asylum application argued that the enforcement of the chador law constituted persecution.

How would her case be analyzed from the standpoint of the human rights approach? One possibility would be to invoke the "right to free-dom of expression."[53] In fact, that label ill fits Hassib-Tehrani's case. She objected to the chador law, but she did not express her objections pub-licly. The one time she was detained for having violated the law, it was because she had left some hair exposed "by mistake." Nor did she testify that, if she returned to Iran, she would openly defy the law in protest. But, counterfactually, we can imagine an activist who would openly violate the law upon returning to Iran to express her opposition to it.

The right to freedom of expression can be limited, says the ICCPR, "[f]or the protection of national security or of public order ... or of public health or morals."[54] One could view the chador law as a morals regulation akin to Western laws forbidding public indecency. Morals regulations of this sort enforce culturally-based views about what should remain hidden from public scrutiny. Such views differ from society to society – even within the West. For instance, German women visiting American beaches are sometimes surprised to discover that removing their tops is against the law.[55] Few would think that nudists are persecuted when they are punished for venturing outside without any clothes – even if nudism has some expressive significance. Governments may legitimately enforce general criminal prohibitions, even against political activists who violate them in order to express their opposition.[56] Otherwise, as Steinbock has noted, a bank robber could claim that his robbery expressed the political opinion that "capital is theft" and that his punishment would, therefore, be persecutory.[57]

A better argument is that the chador law amounts to sex discrimination – indeed, it is just one facet of a social system that severely discriminates on the basis of sex – and that the "public morals" account neglects this social reality. Requiring women to wear a chador when in public is a means of controlling them. And the ICCPR guarantees "equal protection of the law" and enumerates a right against "any discrimination" on the basis of sex.[58]

But the "public morals" account has some force in the face of this objection as well. Even in the West, stricter standards of decency apply to women than to men; yet public decency laws are nonetheless regarded as laws of general application. Iranian laws regulating public decency are certainly more invasive of personal freedom than Western ones, and the gap between what is forbidden for women and for men is greater, but perhaps that should be regarded as a difference in degree rather than in kind. Along these lines, the court concluded in Hassib-Tehrani's case that she "merely ... faces a possibility of prosecution for an act deemed criminal in Iranian society, which is made applicable to all [women] in that country," and that "prosecution for general crimes" should be distinguished from persecution.[59]

Whether the chador law should be regarded as a public morals regulation or as sex discrimination cannot be answered from the text of the ICCPR alone. Rather, any answer will turn on an underlying conception of legitimacy that gives texture to those rights. Surely there are limits to what can be imposed on women in the name of public morals. Imagine, for example, a society which regarded painful and disfiguring foot-binding as essential to decency. A law requiring women to undergo foot-binding would rightly be regarded as persecutory. Or, less hypothetically, imagine a society which required women, either as a matter of law or as a legally condoned cultural practice, to undergo the painful and disfiguring removal of part of their genitalia.

The court's depiction of the chador law in Hassib-Tehrani's case – as a law of general application – is therefore parasitic on an implicit judgment that Iran is within its latitude to impose such burdens on women in pursuit of a communal interest in regulating morals. On that view, the chador law is more like Western laws proscribing topless sunbathing than like foot-binding or female genital mutilation. The court's conclusion also reflects the likelihood that many Iranian women support the chador law.

Where exactly one should draw the line between a ban on topless sunbathing and foot-binding – at chadors? at burkas? somewhere else? – is not self-evident. We might conclude that while a chador law passes muster, a law requiring women to wear burkas – which interfere with vision – does not, and is better described as illegitimate sex discrimination than as a legitimate regulation of public morals. The answer will inevitably draw upon one's own culturally influenced intuitions as to when the burdens imposed upon women in the name of public decency are so severe that the presumption of legitimacy is overcome. Nothing in the ICCPR compels an answer one way or another, and in cases like Hassib-Tehrani's, reasonable people may well have very different intuitions.[60]

Human rights in conflict

The third reason that legitimacy rather than human rights must be the touchstone in defining persecution is that human rights can come into conflict. As Michael Ignatieff has noted, politics is rife with tragic choices.[61] The case *Matter of Chang*, concerning Chinese coercive population control measures, offers a useful example of such a conflict.[62] Chang claimed that he was afraid to return to China because he believed that he would be subjected to forced sterilization for having had a second child with his wife, in contravention of China's "one couple, one child" policy.[63] The couple had already been forced to leave their commune after they were given no work to do, and both Chang and his wife had been ordered to report to a sterilization clinic. His wife had been able to postpone her visit because of an illness, but Chang decided to flee the country.[64]

The BIA rejected Chang's application. The population control law, it reasoned, was one of general application; in the absence of any evidence that the policy was "a subterfuge for some other persecutive purpose," Chang was not eligible for asylum.[65] The BIA's decision was heavily criticized by human rights activists, who endorse a Canadian decision as a template for such cases.[66] The Canadian court described forced sterilization as a "serious and totally unacceptable violation of [one's] security as a person. Forced sterilization ... is such an extreme violation of their basic human rights as to be persecutory, even though this was thought to advance the modernization of China." The court concluded, "Brutality in furtherance of a legitimate end is still brutality."[67]

While the Canadian court may have reached the right outcome, its analysis skates over the complexity of the situation. China adopted coercive population control measures because it judged them to be the lesser of two very unpleasant options. As the BIA explained:

China has adopted a policy whose stated objective is to discourage births through economic incentives, economic sanctions, peer pressure, education, availability of sterilization and other birth control measures, and use of propaganda. Chinese policymakers are faced with the difficulty of providing for China's vast population in good years and in bad. The Government is concerned not only with the ability of its citizens to survive, but also with their housing, education, medical services, and the other benefits of life that persons in many other societies take for granted. For China to fail to take steps to prevent births might well mean that many millions of people would be condemned to, at best, the most marginal existence.[68]

On the Board's telling, China believed that it faced a stark and tragic choice. Either it adopted extreme measures, or it would, before long, be unable to satisfy the basic subsistence needs of its population.[69] China's solution may have been the wrong one, but human rights lie on both sides of the balance. An analysis of Chang's case must look beyond the roster of human rights to an underlying conception of legitimacy that explains why some rights should be given priority over others.

***

To sum up: in arguing against the human rights approach to defining persecution, I have sounded a number of variations on a theme. In deciding whether a government measure constitutes persecution, the roster of human rights given by the international covenants is an unreliable guide, and one must often fall back on an underlying theory that describes the limits of legitimate government authority. The roster of human rights is both over and underinclusive as a proxy for legitimacy; human rights themselves are not self-defining but require interpretation in light of underlying principles; and human rights often conflict, requiring a decision-maker to rely on a theory that explains why some rights should be prioritized over others. For these reasons, legitimacy rather than human rights must remain the touchstone in determining what constitutes "persecution."

Hard cases

In many, indeed, most cases, it will be clear whether a state's reason for inflicting harm should be presumed legitimate or should be regarded as inconsistent with that presumption. But other cases are less obvious. Below, I discuss a few of these hard cases.

The case of rebels and other political offenders

How should asylum law treat coup plotters, insurrectionists, and others who commit quintessentially political offenses, directed at the security of the state and its leaders? Should their punishment be regarded as legitimate prosecution for treason or instead as political persecution?

Consider two straightforward, but mistaken, answers to the question. The first is that governments always have the legitimate right to punish rebellion. The case *Matter of Maldonado-Cruz* offers an example of this erroneous approach. The applicant in that case was a Salvadoran who had been kidnapped by guerrillas in 1983 and impressed into their army. A few days later, he managed to escape and flee to the United States. He was afraid that, were he returned to El Salvador, he would be killed by the government for being a guerrilla. The BIA denied his claim to asylum, reasoning that because "the Government of El Salvador is ... a duly constituted and functioning government of that country, it has the internationally-recognized right to protect itself against the guerrillas who seek to overthrow it."[70]

That analysis confused a *de facto* exercise of power with a legitimate exercise of power.[71] A government can be "duly constituted and functioning" but still conduct itself in ways that make it liable to justified resistance and overthrow. Indeed, a limited right to revolution lies at the core of the liberal tradition. Sovereign authority is not absolute, and one of asylum's core historic purposes was to facilitate the right to revolt by sheltering revolutionaries who had waged unsuccessful rebellions against autocratic regimes.[72]

The second straightforward but mistaken answer is to say that, because *all* rebellions are political, punishment for rebellion should always be regarded as harm inflicted on account of political opinion, giving rise to eligibility for asylum. But condemnation is not always an appropriate response to the suppression of rebellion. Some governments do have a "legitimate right" to defend themselves against rebels. What we need are criteria for identifying such governments.

One possibility is that democracies may legitimately punish rebels, but non-democracies may not. Rebellion, the argument goes, is a legitimate vehicle for political expression when a country lacks "elections to governing organs." In such countries, "a coup is the only means through which a change in the political regime can be effected … In this context, [a coup plotter's] political expression is embodied in his political act."[73] Applying this criterion, an American court in *Dwomoh* v. *Sava* ruled that a Ghanaian coup plotter was eligible for asylum.

The democracy–nondemocracy distinction reflects a misguided notion of international legitimacy. For example, a decent monarchy – one that respects the rule of law, protects liberty, and is willing to accept criticism and advice from the populace – should enjoy freedom from external interference and international condemnation. States should have latitude to choose institutional arrangements that resonate with their particular traditions and customs. Conversely, an illiberal democracy – one that persecutes its minorities – should not enjoy any such entitlement.

A better approach would look to whether the state tolerates peaceful expression of dissenting viewpoints. If so, then it may legitimately punish those dissenters who choose to use force. Applying this principle, another American court denied asylum to a Filipino military officer charged with attempting a coup against Aquino in 1987. In ruling that his punishment constituted legitimate prosecution rather than political persecution, the court emphasized that "diverse political views are tolerated in the Philippines." It concluded that "prosecution for participation in a coup does not constitute persecution on account of political opinion when peaceful means of protest are available for which the alien would not face punishment."[74] A coup is defensible only when normal avenues of political protest are blocked.

***

Even if rebels do have a legitimate right to rebellion, they must still conduct their rebellion using legitimate tactics. The distinction familiar from the law of war – between *jus ad bellum* and *jus in bello* – has application in this context. Recall from Chapter 1 the case of the "wretch Fieschi," who killed eighteen bystanders in his unsuccessful attempt on the life of King Louis-Philippe of France in 1835.[75] Even if Fieschi had a legitimate right to rebel, he could nonetheless be legitimately punished by France: not for the mere act of rebellion, but instead for the carnage he inflicted in the process. Asylum should not protect him from such punishment. Accordingly, people who commit serious non-political crimes, even if those crimes were politically motivated, are ineligible for asylum.[76]

At the same time, however, a state's legitimate right to investigate and punish people like Fieschi does not give it a blank check to use extreme tactics. Consider *Matter of R –*, the case involving the Sikh man who was tortured for information regarding separatist Sikh militants. It is true, as Board member Heilman argued in concurrence, that "the political program of the Sikh extremists" – "the violent separation of Punjab from India through a program of murder and terrorism" – could be punished legitimately.[77] The Indian state permitted peaceful dissent and, in fact, engaged in negotiations with non-violent Sikh activists; and moreover, the tactics of the Sikh extremists were in the same class as those of Fieschi. But R himself was not a militant, and the inhuman treatment to which he was subjected as a non-belligerent "was disproportionate to any measured government reaction that could be expected as a response to anti-government activity."[78] A government's general right to repress uprisings does not justify *all* action taken toward that end. The anti-brutality principle constrains what a state may legitimately do in self-defense.

But what happens when an illegitimate rebellion is met by illegitimate investigatory tactics? Suppose, for example, that one of the Sikh militants – clearly deserving of punishment not only for rebelling against a state that permits lawful dissent but also for committing atrocities in the process – is likely to be brutally tortured if he is returned to India. Should he be granted asylum? It is true that he faces treatment (torture) deserving of condemnation. But are his own deeds so odious that he forfeits any claim to asylum's benefits? A similar question arises concerning terrorists who are justly sought for punishment by their states, but who are likely to be tortured if returned there. Should the policy concerns that drive asylum, that is, the promotion of rule of law and respect for basic human rights, give way to other policy concerns, like ensuring that particularly dangerous criminals are punished, even if excessively or inhumanely so?

The political conception of asylum points both ways. On the one hand, asylum is intended (as Grotius wrote) "for the benefit of those who suffer from undeserved enmity, not those who have done something that is injurious to human society or to other men."[79] This suggests that asylum should not be available to those deserving of punishment for their deeds – even if the punishment is excessive. That view echoes not only Grotius, but also Vattel, who argued that criminals "who by the character and frequency of their crimes are a menace to public security everywhere"[80] ought to be extradited and punished, not granted asylum. On the other hand, excessive or cruel punishment is never deserved; and a state whose justice system endorses such punishment is deserving of the condemnation that asylum expresses. Recall the English tradition, which extended asylum to any fugitive from a despotic state – including not only innocent victims but also (as Jefferson put it) "the most atrocious offenders ... who have been able to get there."[81]

Although theory pulls in both directions, as a practical matter states cannot be expected to shelter asylum seekers who pose a danger to the community of refuge. The American regulations governing both asylum and CAT reflect this view. Neither form of relief is available to aliens who have "ordered, incited, assisted, or otherwise participated" in the persecution of others; who have committed a "serious nonpolitical crime outside the United States"; or who pose a "danger to the security of the United States"[82]; or, in the case of asylum, who have "engaged in terrorist activity."[83] Other states have similar provisions, as does the UN Convention.[84]

Such exclusions, however, should be applied carefully so as not to sweep in the innocent. For example, a person has not "participated in the persecution of others" merely because his actions had the effect of furthering persecution. The term "persecution" implies a culpable mental state on the part of the persecutor. Thus, the "bus driver who unwittingly ferries a killer to the site of a massacre can hardly be labeled a 'persecutor,' even if the objective effect of his actions was to aid the killer's secret plans."[85] Nor has one engaged in persecution if one's actions were carried out under duress.[86]

In this respect, American law is problematic in its expansive definition of "engaging in terrorist activity," which includes committing any "act that the actor knows, or reasonably should know, affords material support" to a terrorist organization or to any individual who the actor has reason to know has committed or plans to commit terrorist activity.[87] "Material support," in turn, is defined broadly, and includes such acts as providing food, shelter, or transportation. There is no exception for acts undertaken in duress. The consequence has been the denial of asylum to a nurse from Colombia who was kidnapped and forced to provide medical treatment to members of the FARC, a terrorist group; a fisherman from Sri Lanka who was abducted by the Tamil Tigers and forced to pay his own ransom; and a journalist from Nepal who was beaten and forced to pay money to Maoist terrorists.[88] The material support bar has also been used as the basis for rejecting asylum seekers from Iraq who had paid ransoms to free family members kidnapped by Shiite or Sunni militias. The Department of Homeland Security has subsequently determined that material support provided under duress should not disqualify an asylum seeker – but only if the material support was provided to terrorist groups not specifically designated as such by the Secretary of State.[89] This concession will do little to help victims of groups like the FARC, the Tamil Tigers, and al-Qaeda in Iraq, all of which have been designated "foreign terrorist organizations" by the State Department.

Laws of general application

Laws that apply generally to the entire population enjoy a very strong presumption of legitimacy; they are assumed to reflect the will of the community that is bound by them. There are narrow exceptions to this rule. For example, I have argued that particularly brutal policies – like torture or other violations of peremptory human rights – are illegitimate even if they are generally applied. These norms form side constraints on states' freedom of action. General laws can also sometimes be a subterfuge for discrimination; imagine, for example, a ban on male circumcision in a society generally repressive toward Jews. One might infer that the ban, though phrased in general terms, is in substance a measure directed at Jews. One can also imagine a general law that is enforced discriminatorily. But notwithstanding these narrow exceptions, the usual rule is that communal self-determination is advanced by out-siders' respect for laws of general application.

Not infrequently, general laws have an unintended adverse impact – sometimes quite a severe one – on minority populations. For example, a law regulating animal slaughter might interfere with the sacrificial practices of a religious minority; similarly, a law proscribing psychede-lic drugs may interfere with a religion's ritual practices. How should asylum law address situations like these? To avoid persecuting religious minorities, must a state accommodate their practices by exempting them from laws of general application?

The case of the Canas brothers, Jehovah's Witnesses from El Salvador, provides a concrete example. The Canas brothers' religion forbade them from participating in military service. But El Salvador did not exempt conscientious objectors from its mandatory military draft, nor did it make available to conscientious objectors any other form of national service. Violators of the draft faced between six months and fifteen years in prison. The BIA denied the Canas brothers asylum on the ground that the conscription law "applies equally to all Salvadorans."[90]

In one sense, that was true: the draft law was generally applicable. But Jehovah's Witnesses were differently situated than other Salvadoran citizens who had no conscientious objection to military service; the Jehovah's Witnesses needed either to violate their religious beliefs by serving or face jail time for draft evasion. That was not a choice that other Salvadorans needed to face. In that sense, the law did not apply equally to all Salvadorans: it burdened some citizens much more severely than others on account of their religion. Did El Salvador's failure to exempt the Canas brothers constitute religious persecution? Or was El Salvador entitled "simply [to] insist[ ] on universal military service for all citizens" without any such exemption?[91]

One approach would be to say that the presumption of legitimacy that attaches to generally applicable laws can be overcome only by evidence showing that the law is a pretext to inflict harm for an illegi-timate reason. The burden of producing that evidence would lie on the asylum applicant. For example, a general law that disparately impacts a religious minority might be regarded as pretextual if the religious minority otherwise faces discrimination or oppression, or if there are no possible legitimate reasons for the general law. Under this approach, the Canas brothers would certainly lose. A general conscription law is not a pretext for religious persecution; rather, the state needs to raise an army.

A second approach holds that a state must exempt disparately affected minorities from a general law unless it has some legitimate reason for not doing so. The burden of producing such a reason would lie on the immigration service. This approach is somewhat more favorable to asylum seekers, but the Canas brothers would lose under it as well. There are several good reasons why a state may decline to exempt Jehovah's Witnesses from conscription laws: an exemption would open a loophole that could be exploited by those simply unwilling to fight; it can be costly to administer especially at a time of national emergency; and it is at odds with the republican principle that all those who enjoy the benefits of citizenship should also bear its burdens.

A final approach, significantly more protective of religious minorities, would require states to exempt disparately affected minorities from general laws whenever the affected group is "unduly burdened" by the law. The Ninth Circuit Court of Appeals initially took roughly this approach in the Canas brothers' case.[92] It would require courts to engage in substantially more fact-finding than either of the first two approaches. An adjudicator would need to consider, for example, how costly an exemption would be to administer and the degree to which an exemption would subvert the state's regulatory scheme. Those interests would then need to be weighed against those of the religious minority's. On that side of the scale, one would need to consider how central a given practice is – for example, non-violence or psychedelic drug use – to the religion.

When the problem is viewed through the prism of legitimacy, one is guided toward the first or second approach rather than the third. The concept of legitimacy affords states wide latitude to make policy decisions, and even unjust policies are not illegitimate if they are enacted in good faith. Here, there are several good faith reasons for a generally applicable draft law that makes no exception for conscientious objectors. Unless there is countervailing evidence to support an inference of animus, the Jehovah's Witnesses should lose. And, indeed, in similar cases, many American courts have so decided.[93] Perhaps a perfectly just society would make special efforts to accommodate its religious minorities' special needs, but international legitimacy does not demand perfect justice. It only requires the decency of reasons, offered in good faith, connected to the promotion of the common good.

Military service continued

While courts have repeatedly held that "it is not persecution for a country to require military service of its citizens"[94] – even when that law burdens religious minorities like the Canas brothers – they have at the same time carved out two exceptions. The first exception involves cases where punishment is imposed on a particular objector on account of an illegitimate reason. For example, if a state selectively subjected Jehovah's Witnesses to especially severe punishment for failure to serve, the punishment would be regarded as persecutory.

The second exception encompasses cases where "the alien would necessarily be required to engage in inhuman conduct as a result of military service required by the government."[95] Thus, one court has granted asylum to a Salvadoran who was "ordered by a military officer, under threat of death, to participate in the paid killing of two men."[96] This second exception is rooted in the anti-brutality principle: international humanitarian law places limits on what states may do, and order their soldiers to do, during battle.*

---

* It is important to distinguish between violations of *jus in bello* – the law governing conduct *in* war – and violations of *jus ad bellum* – the law governing the conditions under which a state may resort to war. While courts have been open to an asylum seeker's claim that he would be forced to engage in violations of *jus in bello*, they have generally rejected claims that an asylum seeker would be forced to participate in an unjust war. Just as states have the authority to draft their citizens into military service, they also have the authority to order those citizens to fight, even if the war is unjust. There is nothing "inhuman" about fighting an unjust war in accordance with the rules of international humanitarian law. But states cannot order their soldiers to carry out atrocities – even if there are just reasons for going to war. Applying that distinction, a Canadian court rejected an asylum claim by an American soldier who objected to being forced to serve in Iraq. *Hinzman* v. *Minister of Citizenship and Immigration* [2006] F.C. 420, at 188. (On appeal, the court declined to address that issue, instead finding that the applicant had not exhausted the protection available to him under the American exemption for conscientious objectors. *Hinzman* v. *Canada*, [2007] F.C.A. 171.)

The soldier's liability as a war criminal tracks the distinction between *jus ad bellum* and *jus in bello*: one can become a war criminal by virtue of illegal acts committed as a foot soldier, that is, for violations of *jus in bello*; one cannot become a war criminal merely by having participated in an illegal war. For a general discussion, see Cecilia M. Bailliet, "Assessing Jus ad Bellum and Jus in Bello Within the Refugee Status Determination Process: Contemplations on Conscientious Objectors Seeking Asylum," *Georgetown Immigration Law Journal*, 20 (2006), pp. 337–84.

Courts emphasize, however, that to qualify for this second exception, the inhuman conduct must be ordered as an official policy. "[M]isconduct by renegade military units is almost inevitable during times of war,"[97] and does not constitute official action. That caveat also follows from asylum's expressive dimension. Condemnation is misplaced if atrocities are carried out by renegades against official orders. Of course, when "renegade" units are common, and the military appears to condone their operation, then the atrocities they carry out do reflect official state policy.

What constitutes the kind of "inhuman conduct" in the course of military service that can give rise to eligibility for asylum? The UNHCR Handbook, a guide to the interpretation of the Refugee Convention, suggests that the conduct must be "condemned by the international community as contrary to basic rules of human conduct."[98] One court has read this to mean that "recognized international governmental bodies" (such as the United Nations or the Organization of American States) must have *actually* condemned the conduct.[99] Under this standard, a court could not rely on news clippings or reports by groups like Human Rights Watch or Amnesty International to establish that conduct was "inhuman."

That is misguided. An asylum seeker's claim should not depend on whether the United Nations or some other intergovernmental organization has decided to issue a resolution labeling his state's military policies to be "inhuman." International organizations may fail to take such action for many reasons entirely unrelated to the barbarity of the state's conduct. To defer to the judgment of such organizations is an abdication of the judicial role. "[T]he basic rules of humanitarian conduct are well documented and readily available to guide [courts] in discerning what types of actions are considered unacceptable by the world community,"[100] and courts are expert at assessing the strength of documentary evidence submitted to them in order to determine whether a legal standard has been met.

One court has expressed concern that "[t]his responsibility would require [courts] to make immigration decisions based on our own implicit approval or disapproval of U.S. foreign policy and the acts of other nations. Courts could be put in the position of ruling, as a matter of law, that a government whose actions have not been condemned by international governmental bodies engages in persecution against its citizens."[101] But, I have argued throughout, that is precisely what asylum law asks adjudicators to do. And, as I suggested in Chapter 2, concern about judicial meddling in politics is to some degree mitigated by the fact that administrative law judges – who are part of the executive branch – determine asylum eligibility in the first instance. Although their determinations are reviewed by the courts, review is deferential to both the agency's factfinding and its policy judgments.

Civil war

Alexander Aleinikoff has referred to the case of "persons caught in the crossfire of a civil war" as "the hypothetical case that is always present in discussions of the definition of refugee."[102] Civil wars often affect entire populations, and fear of opening the floodgates has long led US courts to bar asylum claims for non-combatants on the theory that war is different: "activities directly related to civil war are not persecution,"[103] even if they involve atrocities that would constitute persecution during peacetime. An exception has been made for asylum seekers fleeing ethnic or religious conflicts. Victims of ethnic violence are harmed on account of a Convention reason, and so fall squarely within the Convention definition.[104] Canadian courts have been more open to applicants fleeing civil wars, extending asylum so long as applicants could establish that their "fear [was] not that felt indiscriminately by all citizens as a consequence of the civil war,"[105] but instead was especially acute due to a Convention reason.*

Some have attacked current law as being too narrow, contending that asylum law should recognize that "aerial bombardments of villages, 'scorched-earth' tactics, and pitched battles in urban neighbourhoods constitute persecution of innocent victims" regardless of the attackers' motivations and regardless of whether the same risk is generally shared by others.[106] They suggest that the nexus clause should be expanded to include all individuals fleeing civil strife, and propose that in the

---

* Many states offer protection on a basis other than asylum to civil war victims who do not qualify under the Convention definition. In the EU, applicants fleeing a civil war can qualify for subsidiary protection even when a civil war is not ethnically based, so long as they can show a "serious and individual threat to life or person by reason of indiscriminate violence." EU Qualifications Directive, Council Directive 2004/83/EC of April 29, 2004, art. 15. In Canada, such applicants are regarded as "person[s] in need of protection" who are eligible for asylum if they can show that they would face a risk to their life "in every part of [their] country" and that the risk "is not faced generally by other individuals in or from that country," regardless whether that risk is due to a Convention reason. Immigration and Refugee Protection Act (2001, c. 27) section 97(1)(b).

meantime, flight from civil strife should give rise to a presumption that the nexus clause has been met.[107]

How does the political approach to asylum respond to the situation of civil war? It depends. A distinction must be drawn between, on the one hand, civil wars that are primarily battles for power between a government and rebel group, each of which claims to represent the entire community; and on the other hand, civil wars fought along ethnic, racial, national, or religious lines.

In the first type of civil war, civilians are aptly described as cross-fire victims. When villages become the settings for battles, villagers are deprived of physical security, but their insecurity is a side effect, not the intention, of the combatants' operations. When states use force to defend themselves against insurrection, the tragic and unavoidable consequence is that some innocent civilians will lose their lives. Frequently, though, civilians can remove themselves from the battlefield and reside temporarily in another part of the country. Once even a fragile peace takes hold, or the lines of battle shift, they will be able to return to their homes to rebuild their lives free from harm. In that situation, asylum would be inappropriate. If civilians need international protection for the duration of the conflict, it can be provided through refugee policy tools other than asylum.

A different scenario is presented if civilians are directly targeted by the combatants for harm. Clearly, asylum is appropriate in cases of ethnic conflict and genocide. The deliberate targeting of civilians for harm on account of their race, religion, or nationality belies any notion that the responsible combatant acts on behalf of the entire citizenry. Indeed, asylum is appropriate when combatants target civilians for harm even absent any Convention reason. For example, combatants may seek to depopulate villages as a military tactic, without regard to the racial, ethnic, religious, or political make-up of the villages. In the 1980s, for example, the Salvadoran government depopulated areas of possible guerrilla resistance through "the use of murder, torture, rape, the burning of crops in order to create starvation conditions, and a programme of general terrorism and harassment."[108] When a government turns on its citizens in such a manner, its conduct enjoys no presumption of legitimacy; rather, such conduct constitutes a clear violation of international humanitarian law, and should be regarded as persecution under the rubric of the anti-brutality principle. That conclusion could be accommodated within the present law by presuming that any violation of international humanitarian law is for a Convention reason.[109]

Kleptocracy and negligence

Another hard case involves "kleptocracy" – government by thievery – characterized by the extortion of citizens by security forces. The case of Fritz Desir, an asylum applicant from Haiti, presents this problem with clarity. On several occasions over the period of a few years, Desir was arrested and beaten by the Ton Ton Macoutes, the Haitian security forces under the Duvalier regime, for having failed to pay "protection money" to the Macoutes and for having competed with Macoutes-approved businesses. The BIA denied his application for asylum, concluding that the Macoutes "harassed Desir not because of his ... political opinion" or any other ground protected by the nexus clause, but instead "because they wished to extort money from him for personal reasons."[110]

On appeal, the Ninth Circuit Court of Appeals reversed the BIA. Its reasoning was framed to satisfy the nexus requirement. It noted that Haiti operated as a "kleptocracy" in which the security forces were unpaid and depended for their livelihood on corruption and the extortion of their fellow citizens. The reprisals inflicted on those who refused to pay up were "tactics whereby the Duvalier regime systematically exercised its authority by way of terror and intimidation." In light of this political context, it reasoned, Desir's "[r]efusal to accede to extortion resulted in his classification and treatment as a [political] subversive." He was "perceived as disloyal and subversive and the machinery of the state, enforced by the Macoutes, was violently engaged against him." Thus, the court concluded, he was persecuted on account of political opinion.[111]

The court's decision is defensible from the standpoint of legitimacy. In the interest of promoting the rule of law, states are increasingly imposing sanctions on members of foreign governments who are responsible for kleptocracy and corruption. Such sanctions range from the withholding of aid to the freezing of assets. When a citizen is subjected to serious harm for refusing to capitulate to extralegal extortion, international protection and international condemnation are both warranted. Asylum is an appropriate response.

But what about the indirect victims of kleptocracy, the people reduced to a marginal existence due to economic policies that are designed to enrich and entrench those in power? Can they too claim asylum? This presents a much closer case. At least one observer has argued that "where the political system serves only to perpetuate economic disparity and widespread impoverishment," courts should recognize the existence of "structural economic persecution"[112] and award asylum to those fleeing impoverished conditions. Much can be said for that position. Kleptocratic economic policies are deserving of condemnation, and if the impoverishment and suffering they cause (albeit indirectly) rise to the level of "serious harm," asylum would seem to be a fitting response.

On the other hand, however, describing indirect harm as "persecution" seems to stretch the concept beyond its language. The term connotes targeting or selecting particular individuals, or a particular class of individuals, for harm. Dictionary definitions of the term "persecution" employ synonyms like "pursue," "torment," "harass," "punish," and "exterminate." The word "persecution" does not describe accurately capture the situation of people impoverished by kleptocratic states. Their suffering may be traceable to illegitimate policies, but it is not the *intention* of those policies.

In the end, a concern for practical consequences points against granting asylum to victims of "structural economic" harm. Much of the world could arguably be described as falling into that category. Furthermore, the line between confiscatory policies worthy of condemnation and inept policies deserving of international assistance can often be hard to draw. Developing nations often seek to promote the rule of law, but find that embedded interests make success difficult to achieve.

For similar reasons, asylum is an inappropriate response to the threat of harm caused by official negligence – for example, a state's failure to take adequate steps to protect citizens against environmental catastrophe. The condemnation expressed by asylum is more appropriate when harm is intended than when it is the unintended consequence of negligence. Also, it may be quite difficult for adjudicators to determine whether a state has been negligent. The concept of negligence is dependent on some notion of a reasonable standard of care; but what is reasonable will vary widely across societies, depending on the available economic resources, competing priorities which lay claim to those scarce resources, and practical challenges – such as a lack of human capital, poor infrastructure, and barriers to communication, command, and control – that make it difficult to execute even a well-conceived policy. Moreover, technical experts may often disagree about whether, for example, a particular economic policy is wise or so foolish as to be negligent. By contrast, in the garden variety asylum case involving a citizen targeted for harm, these problems do not arise.

"Persecution" also does not generally describe the situation of famine victims, even though, as Amartya Sen has famously argued, famine is the consequence of a political and economic failure, that is, the lack of an *entitlement* to food, not a lack of available food.[113] In the usual case of famine, no one intended for the victims to starve; their situation is the result of inept governance, not malice. The appropriate posture toward the victims' state is assistance, not condemnation.

Of course, there are exceptions. An entitlement to food can some-times be withheld for an illegitimate reason. For example, in Zimbabwe in 2005, limited grain supplies were funneled to areas expected to be "swing" areas in upcoming elections. Those regions which were either solidly behind the ZANU-PF ruling party or the opposition Movement for Democratic Change thus bore the brunt of the famine caused by the mismanaged land reform of the 1990s. Furthermore, even in swing areas, the state-controlled Grain Marketing Board would not sell corn to rural families without a ZANU-PF membership card. And President Robert Mugabe refused to allow the World Food Program to deliver food to these areas, because to allow international assistance would belie his claim that the land reform had resulted in a bumper harvest.[114] In cases like that of Zimbabwe, asylum is an appropriate response to famine.

Conclusion

I have argued that "persecution" should be defined as serious harm inflicted or condoned by official agents for illegitimate reasons. The "serious harm" requirement recognizes that asylum is not meant to remedy every wrong or injustice committed by a state against a citizen; harm must reach a certain threshold of seriousness before it warrants international condemnation and external interference. The reference to "illegitimate reasons" refers to reasons that belie the principle of com-munal self-determination that justifies the ordinary presumption of legitimacy given to state policies. Asylum policy involves a series of judgments about what reasons fall within that category and thus warrant international condemnation and external interference. The nexus clause provides some guidance, but it is not exclusive. Indeed, certain types of harm – such as torture and other violations of peremptory international human rights norms – are always beyond the pale, no matter why they have been inflicted.

Asylum law is therefore an ongoing normative enterprise – one in which adjudicators draw and articulate the bounds of legitimate state conduct in light of concrete cases and scenarios. Some might object that adjudicators will rely too much on personal, idiosyncratic views about what states may and may not do to their citizens. But that concern is overstated. A number of mechanisms exist to channel adjudicators' discretion. In addition to the Convention definition itself, hard calls can be made collectively through legislation or regulations that govern an entire class of cases; other times, an adjudicator's decision is controlled by the accretion of legal precedent reflecting a consensus borne of experience. But sometimes, an adjudicator will face novel issues and will need to consult his or her own judgment.

Some have suggested that international human rights law should provide the measure of legitimacy, and that the term "persecution" should be interpreted in light of the rights delineated in the international human rights covenants. Such an approach has been endorsed by some of the Commonwealth countries. But, for a number of reasons, that approach masks difficult normative determinations. First, not all violations of human rights constitute persecution; second, human rights themselves must be interpreted and applied to concrete factual situations in light of underlying, and too often unarticulated, notions of legitimacy; third, human rights can conflict, requiring an adjudicator to resort to a higher order principle, namely, legitimacy. In sum, while the roster of human rights can offer some guidance, in the end asylum adjudicators and policymakers will need to engage directly with underlying first principles of legitimacy.

Some may object that the approach to asylum advanced here leaves too many needy people unprotected. But that humanitarian objection misunderstands asylum's role in the refugee policy toolkit. Asylum is not the one-size-fits-all solution for all of the world's refugees. It has a more targeted focus, connected to its expressive character. At the same time, however, states should also take seriously their humanitarian obligation to assist refugees who are excluded by asylum, using refugee policy tools like relief aid, development assistance, and humanitarian protection abroad (typically on a temporary basis). A targeted asylum policy does not justify a stingy refugee policy.

Notes

1. UNHCR, *Handbook on Procedures and Criteria for Determining Refugee Status Under the 1951 Convention and the 1967 Protocol Relating to the Status of Refugees*, UN Document HCR/PRO/4 (1979), revised 1992, paragraph 51.
2. Guy Goodwin-Gill, *The Refugee in International Law*, 2nd edn. (New York: Oxford University Press, 1996), p. 67.
3. The US courts of appeals have employed a number of definitions of persecution which, if carefully parsed, have very different implications for certain kinds of cases. One widely cited definition treats persecution as "the infliction of suffering or harm, under government sanction, upon persons who differ in a way regarded as offensive ... in a manner condemned by civilized governments." *Kovac v. INS*, 407 F.2d 102, 107 (9th Cir. 1969). This definition would exclude harm committed by non-state actors without government sanction. Another widely cited definition states that persecution is "harm or suffering ... inflicted upon an individual in order to punish him for possessing a belief or characteristic a persecutor sought to overcome." *Matter of Acosta*, 19 I. & N. Dec. 211, 223 (BIA 1985). This definition suggests that, to be classified as persecution, harm must be inflicted with a punitive intent. That would exclude, for example, the victim of female genital mutilation or a lesbian who was subjected to forced institutionalization to "cure" her of her lesbianism. Cf. *Pitcherskaia v. INS*, 118 F.3d 641 (9th Cir. 1997). Another widely cited definition states that persecution is "oppression which is inflicted on groups or individuals because of a difference that the persecutor will not tolerate." *Hernandez-Ortiz v. INS*, 777 F.2d 509, 516 (9th Cir. 1985). That definition suggests that persecution could result from the state's failure to exempt, say, a religious group from a generally applicable law that severely burdens the religious group. The failure to accommodate could be regarded as a refusal to "tolerate" a "difference." The BIA has more recently defined persecution as "the infliction of harm or suffering by a government, or persons a government is unwilling or unable to control, to overcome a characteristic of the victim." *Matter of Kasinga*, 21 I. & N. Dec. 357, 365 (BIA 1996). But the older definitions just reviewed nonetheless continue to be cited by courts.
4. See note 3, above.
5. *R. v. Secretary for the Home Department, ex parte Shah* [1999] 2 A.C. 653; *Minister for Immigration and Multicultural Affairs v. Khawar* [2002] 210 C.L.R. 1, at 120; New Zealand Refugee Appeal No. 74665/03 (July 7, 2004), paragraph 53.
6. Michael Walzer, *Just and Unjust Wars* (New York: Basic Books, 1977), p. 54.

7. Samuel Pufendorf, *De Jure Naturae et Gentium Libri Octo* (1672), trans. C. H. Oldfather and W. A. Oldfather (Oxford: Clarendon Press, 1934), VIII.6.14.

8. Walzer, *Just and Unjust Wars*, p. 89.

9. Ibid., p. 90.

10. Ibid., p. 101.

11. *Ghaly* v. *INS*, 58 F.3d 1425, 1431 (9th Cir. 1995).

12. *Fatin* v. *INS*, 12 F.3d 1233, 1240 (3rd Cir. 1993).

13. *Mikhailevitch* v. *INS*, 146 F.3d 384, 390 (6th Cir. 1998).

14. *Aguilar-Solis* v. *INS*, 168 F.3d 565, 570 (1st Cir. 1999).

15. *Begzatowski* v. *INS*, 278 F.3d 665, 669 (7th Cir. 2002), quoting *Mitev* v. *INS*, 67 F.3d 1325, 1330 (7th Cir. 1995).

16. *Li* v. *Ashcroft*, 312 F.3d 1094 (9th Cir. 2002), vacated and rev'd, *Li* v. *Ashcroft*, 356 F.3d 1153 (9th Cir. 2004) (en banc).

17. Ibid., p. 1098.

18. *Prasad* v. *INS*, 47 F.3d 336 (9th Cir. 1995).

19. *Li*, 312 F.3d at 1101.

20. Ibid., p. 1105.

21. *Aguilar-Solis*, 168 F.3d at 570.

22. *Diallo* v. *Ashcroft*, 381 F.3d 687, 697 (7th Cir. 2004); *Osaghae* v. *INS*, 942 F.2d 1160, 1163 (7th Cir. 1991).

23. See, for example, *Matter of Izatula*, 20 I. & N. Dec. 149 (BIA 1990); *Dwomoh* v. *Sava*, 696 F. Supp. 970 (S.D.N.Y. 1988); Carolyn Patty Blum, "License to Kill: Asylum Law and the Principle of Legitimate Government Authority to 'Investigate its Enemies,'" *Willamette Law Review*, 28 (1992), p. 719; Carolyn Patty Blum, "Political Assumptions in Asylum Decision-Making: The Example of Refugees from Armed Conflict" in Howard Adelman (ed.), *Refugee Policy: Canada and the United States* (Toronto: York Lanes Press, 1991), pp. 282–91; Note, "Political Legitimacy in the Law of Political Asylum," *Harvard Law Review*, 99 (1985), p. 450.

24. *Matter of Acosta*, 19 I. & N. 211, 233 (BIA 1985).

25. Immanuel Kant, "On the Common Saying, 'This May Be True in Theory, But It Does Not Apply in Practice'" in Immanuel Kant, *Political Writings*, trans. and ed. Hans Reiss (Cambridge University Press, 1991), pp. 84–5 (emphasis in original).

26. Daniel J. Steinbock, "Interpreting the Refugee Definition," *UCLA Law Review*, 45 (1998), p. 794.

27. American Law Institute, *Restatement of the Law, Third: The Foreign Relations Law of the United States* (St. Paul, MN: American Law Institute Publishers, 1987 & Supp. 2007), section 702(a)–(f) and cmt.n.

28. EU Qualifications Directive, Council Directive 2004/83/EC of April 29, 2004 on minimum standards for the qualification and status of third

country nationals or stateless persons as refugees or as persons who otherwise need international protection and the content of the protection granted, art. 15.

29. *Matter of R –*, 20 I. & N. Dec. 621, 622 (BIA 1992).

30. Ibid., pp. 623–5.

31. See, for example, T. Alexander Aleinikoff, "The Meaning of 'Persecution' in U.S. Asylum Law" in Adelman (ed.), *Refugee Policy: Canada and the United States* (Toronto: York Lanes Press, 1991), pp. 309–13; Michelle Foster, "Causation in Context: Interpreting the Nexus Clause in the Refugee Convention," *Michigan Journal of International Law*, 23 (2002), p. 338.

32. 8 C.F.R. section 208.16.

33. *INS v. Cardoza-Fonseca*, 480 U.S. 421, 431 (1987).

34. EU Qualifications Directive, art. 24.

35. *In re S – P –* , 21 I. & N. Dec. 486, 494 n. 3 (BIA 1996).

36. Aleinikoff, "The Meaning of 'Persecution,'" p. 309.

37. For discussion, see Deborah E. Anker, "Refugee Law, Gender, and the Human Rights Paradigm," *Harvard Human Rights Journal*, 15 (2002), pp. 133–54; Karen Musalo and Stephen Knight, "Steps Forward and Steps Back," *International Journal of Refugee Law*, 13 (2001), pp. 51–70; and Erik D. Ramanthan, "Queer Cases: A Comparative Analysis of Global Sexual Orientation-Based Asylum Jurisprudence," *Georgetown Immigration Law Journal*, 11 (1996), pp. 1–44.

38. 8 U.S.C. section 1101(a)(42).

39. James Hathaway has been the most influential advocate of a tight linkage between refugee law and international human rights law. See James C. Hathaway, *Law of Refugee Status* (Toronto: Butterworths, 1991); James C. Hathaway, "Reconceiving Refugee Law as Human Rights Protection," *Journal of Refugee Studies*, 4 (1991), p. 113. Courts in Canada and New Zealand have adopted his analysis in order to determine eligibility for asylum in their respective countries. See *Canada (Attorney General) v. Ward* [1993] S.C.R. 689; New Zealand Refugee Status Appeals Authority, Refugee Appeal No. 71427/99 [2000] N.Z.A.R. 545. He is quoted approvingly in British and Australian asylum decisions as well. See, for example, *Horvath v. Secretary of State for the Home Department* [2001] 1 A.C. 489 (UK); and *Minister for Immigration and Multicultural Affairs v. Khawar* [2002] H.C.A. 14 (Australia). The linkage between international human rights law and asylum law is less developed in the United States.

40. Hathaway, *Law of Refugee Status*, p. 106.

41. Hathaway, "Reconceiving Refugee Law," p. 123.

42. Hathaway, *Law of Refugee Status*, pp. 104–5.

43. Ibid., pp. 109–11.
44. Hathaway states, for example, that "[u]nder current interpretations, refugee status requires a risk to basic human rights ... *in addition* to some differential impact based on civil or political status [i.e. a Convention reason] ... The proposal here is that refugee status become the entitlement of all persons whose basic human rights are at risk." Hathaway, "Reconceiving Refugee Law," p. 121 (emphasis in original).
45. International Covenant on Civil and Political Rights, December 16, 1966, 999 U.N.T.S. 171 (entered into force March 23, 1976), art. 25 [ICCPR].
46. International Covenant on Economic, Social and Cultural Rights, December 16, 1966, 933 U.N.T.S. 3, art. 9.
47. Refugee Appeal No. 74665/03 (July 7, 2004) (New Zealand), paragraph 53, available at www.nzrefugeeappeals.govt.nz. The formula quoted above was originally expressed in the UK decision *ex parte Shah* [1999] 2 A.C. at 653; it was also approved of by the Australian High Court in *Khawar* [2002] HCA 14, at 120.
48. Universal Declaration of Human Rights, G. A. Res. 217A, U.N. GAOR, 3rd Sess., Supp. No. 3, at 71, U.N. Doc. A/810 (1948), art. 17.
49. See, for example, *Begzatowski*, 278 F.3d at 669.
50. German Extradition Law of December 23, 1929, art. 3(2), quoted in *Dwomoh*, 696 F. Supp. at 976 n. 8.
51. ICCPR, art. 19(2)–(3).
52. *Fisher* v. *INS*, 79 F.3d 955, 959–60 (9th Cir. 1996) (en banc).
53. ICCPR, art. 19(2).
54. Ibid., art. 19(3)(b).
55. Thanks to Inken Wiese for this example.
56. This argument assumes that the punishment for violating the chador law is appropriate for the violation of a morals offense. Evidence in some chador cases suggests that activists who violate the law are sentenced to up to one year in prison and subjected to public corporal punishment in the form of lashings. The harshness of that sentence – especially if it is only imposed on activists – raises an inference that although the formal charge is for violating the chador law, the punishment is inflicted on account of political opinion.
57. Steinbock, "Interpreting the Refugee Definition," p. 755.
58. ICCPR, art. 26.
59. *Fisher*, 79 F.3d at 961–2 (alterations in original).
60. The chador case also offers another example of the way in which a human rights approach can be overinclusive. Even if one were to conclude that the chador law was discriminatory and therefore in violation of the ICCPR, one might still conclude that the discrimination was not

sufficiently serious to rise to the level of persecution. The chador law may be "inconvenient, irritating, mildly objectionable, or highly offensive," but it does not mandate the infliction of physical pain or harm (unlike, say, the hypothetical foot-binding law or like female genital mutilation), and courts generally conclude that discrimination or minor harassment is not sufficiently serious to constitute persecution – even though such discrimination or harassment can cause mental trauma, as in Hassib-Tehrani's case. *Fisher*, 79 F.3d at 962. See also *Yadegar-Sargis v. INS*, 297 F.3d 596 (7th Cir. 2002); *Fatin*, 12 F.3d 1233; *Safaie v. INS*, 25 F.3d 636 (8th Cir. 1994).

61. "Liberty and equality, freedom and security, private property and distributive justice ... conflict, and, because they do, the rights that define them as entitlements are also in conflict ..." Michael Ignatieff, *Human Rights as Politics and Idolatry* (Princeton, NJ: Princeton University Press, 2001), pp. 20–1.

62. *Matter of Chang*, 20 I. & N. Dec. 38 (1989). Currently, the Immigration and Nationality Act provides that "a person who has been forced to abort a pregnancy or to undergo involuntary sterilization, or who has been persecuted for failure or refusal to undergo such a procedure or for other resistance to a coercive population control program, shall be deemed to have been persecuted on account of political opinion, and a person who has a well founded fear that he or she will be forced to undergo such a procedure or subject to persecution for such failure, refusal, or resistance shall be deemed to have a well founded fear of persecution on account of political opinion." 8 U.S.C. section 1101(a)(42)(B).

63. While "one couple, one child" was the general rule, exceptions were made in limited circumstances, for instance if the first child was disabled and so unable to work. *Matter of Chang*, 20 I. & N. Dec. at 40.

64. Ibid., p. 39.

65. Ibid., p. 47.

66. See, for example, Jacqueline Bhabha, "Embodied Rights: Gender Persecution, State Sovereignty, and Refugees," *Public Culture*, 9 (1996), p. 11.

67. *Cheung v. Canada (Minister of Employment and Immigration)* [1993] 102 D.L.R. (4th) 214, 221–22 (Fed. Ct. App.).

68. *Matter of Chang*, 20 I. & N. Dec. at 43–4.

69. One might offer the following rejoinder: "Socio-economic human rights are abrogated only where a state either neglects their realization in the face of adequate resources, or implements them in a discriminatory way; ... the existence of generalized hardship is [not] a sufficient ... factor in defining the existence of socio-economic persecution." Hathaway, *Law of Refugee Status*, p. 119. Thus, China faces no conflict of rights.

Although it might be unable to provide for a larger population, this inability arises from neither neglect nor discrimination. That response is unconvincing. Subsistence is certainly a critical component of human dignity and an interest of such fundamental importance that China should seek to remedy the situation with the same urgency as it should seek to remedy violations of civil and political rights.

70. *Matter of Maldonado-Cruz*, 19 I. & N. Dec. 509, 518 (BIA 1988). The BIA's decision was overturned by the Ninth Circuit on the ground that Maldonado-Cruz's neutrality amounted to a political opinion. *Maldonado-Cruz* v. *U.S. I.N.S.*, 883 F.2d 788 (9th Cir. 1989). However, other circuits declined to follow the Ninth Circuit in holding that political neutrality is a political opinion. See, for example, *Perlera-Escobar* v. *Executive Office for Immigration*, 894 F.2d 1292, 1297 n. 4 (11th Cir. 1990).

71. Blum, "Political Assumptions," offers a similar argument.

72. The BIA made a second mistake in the quote above as well: it confused the legitimacy of an end with the legitimacy of the means. Even if the Salvadoran government did have a right to defend itself against rebellion, it would not follow that the government's legitimate right to investigate and detain its enemies extended to the treatment feared by Maldonado-Cruz. A government's general right to repress uprisings does not justify *any* action taken toward that end. The anti-brutality principle places a substantive limit on the steps a state may take to defend itself.

Another example of this second mistake was provided by another Board decision, involving Indian counter-terror operations. In *In Re Jagraj Singh*, the BIA denied eligibility for asylum to an Indian Sikh who was harassed and tortured by police after providing food to Sikh militants who had threatened his life if he refused to help them. The police "beat [Singh] repeatedly with a rifle, and asked him about the militants. When Singh did not reveal the militants' names, the police shot him in the leg." On another occasion, the police beat Singh so severely that he could not walk for two weeks, and he was only released when his mother gave a $25,000 bribe. Unpublished opinion cited and overturned in *Singh* v. *Ilchert*, 801 F. Supp. 313, 316 (N.D. Cal. 1992). The BIA ruled that Singh was beaten as part of a criminal investigation falling under Indian anti-terrorism laws, and that the police were interested in gaining information about Sikh militants, not in punishing Singh for his political views. The police, the Board said, have a "legitimate right to investigate to determine whether [Singh] could provide information about these people." Ibid., p. 317. For other examples of the BIA's endorsement of a "legitimate right" to self-defense, see Blum, "License to Kill," pp. 729 et seq. Asylum adjudication should consider not only whether a government may legitimately defend itself, but also whether the means employed in pursuit of that end are legitimate. See Blum, "Political Assumptions" and Note, "Political Legitimacy" for a similar point.

73. *Dwomoh*, 696 F. Supp. at 979 and n. 11. Even assuming *arguendo* that Ghana did have a legitimate right to punish Dwomoh, the court continued, it needed to do so in accordance with due process. Ibid., p. 978. See also *Izatula*, 20 I. & N. Dec. 149.

74. *Chanco* v. *INS*, 82 F.3d 298 (9th Cir. 1996).

75. Sir James Fitzjames Stephens, *History of the Criminal Law of England*, vol. 2 (London: Macmillan, 1883), p. 70.

76. See, for example, *INS* v. *Aguirre-Aguirre*, 526 U.S. 415, 421–2 (1999); 8 U.S.C. section 1231(b)(3)(B); UN Convention Relating to the Status of Refugees, July 28, 1951, 189 U.N.T.S. 137, art. 1(F)(b).

77. *Matter of R–*, 20 I. & N. Dec. at 635 (Heilman, Board member, concurring).

78. Ibid., p. 629 (majority opinion).

79. Hugo Grotius, *De Jure Belli ac Pacis Libri Tres* (1625), trans. Francis W. Kelsey (Oxford: Clarendon Press, 1925), II.21.5.

80. Emer de Vattel, *The Law of Nations or the Principles of Natural Law* (1758), trans. Charles G. Fenwick (Geneva: Slatkine Reprints – Henry Dunant Institute, 1983), I.19.232.

81. Thomas Jefferson, "Letter to Washington, Nov. 7, 1791," in Thomas Jefferson Randolph (ed.), *Memoir, Correspondence, and Miscellanies from the Papers of Thomas Jefferson*, vol. 3, 2nd edn. (Boston, MA: Gray and Bowen, 1830), p. 131.

82. 8 C.F.R. section 1208.16; 8 U.S.C. section 1231(b)(3)(B).

83. 8 U.S.C. section 1158(b)(2)(A).

84. EU Qualifications Directive, art. 12; Immigration and Refugee Protection Act (2001, c. 27), section 98 (Canada); UN Convention, art. 1(F).

85. *Castaneda-Castillo* v. *Gonzales*, 488 F.3d 17, 20 (1st Cir. 2007) (en banc).

86. *Hernandez* v. *Ashcroft*, 345 F.3d 824 (9th Cir. 2003).

87. 8 U.S.C. section 1182(a)(3)(B), (F).

88. Human Rights First, "Abandoning the Persecuted: Victims of Terrorism and Oppression Barred From Asylum" (2006), www.humanrightsfirst. info/pdf/06925-asy-abandon-persecuted.pdf (last visited February 27, 2008).

89. Department of Homeland Security, "Exercise of Authority Under Sec. 212(d)(3)(B)(i) of the Immigration and Nationality Act," 72 Fed. Reg. 9958 (March 6, 2007).

90. *Canas-Segovia* v. *INS*, 902 F.2d 717, 723 (9th Cir. 1990). After the Ninth Circuit reversed, holding that the Canas brothers had been persecuted on account of religion, 902 F.2d at 725–6, the US Supreme Court vacated

the decision, 502 U.S. 1086 (1992), based on the rule that, for harm to constitute persecution on account of religion, the persecutor must have been motivated to inflict the harm on account of the victim's religion. There had been no evidence before the court that the Salvadoran government had refused to allow an exemption for Jehovah's Witnesses because it sought to harm them. Rather, the government was likely simply indifferent to the fact that some religious minorities might be severely burdened by compulsory conscription. On remand in the Canas brothers' case, the Ninth Circuit found persecution on grounds of imputed political opinion. *Canas-Segovia* v. *INS*, 970 F.2d 599, 602 (9th Cir. 1992).

91. *Foroglou* v. *INS*, 170 F.3d 68, 71 (1st Cir. 1999).

92. *Canas-Segovia*, 902 F.2d at 723.

93. *Zehatye* v. *Gonzales*, 453 F.3d 1182 (9th Cir. 2006); *Foroglou*, 170 F.3d 68.

94. *Matter of A – G –*, 19 I. & N. Dec. 502, 506 (BIA 1987).

95. Ibid.

96. *Barraza Rivera* v. *INS*, 913 F.2d 1443, 1450 (9th Cir. 1990).

97. *M.A.* v. *INS*, 899 F.2d 304, 312 (4th Cir. 1990).

98. UNHCR, *Handbook*, section 171.

99. *M.A.*, 899 F.2d at 313.

100. Ibid., p. 323 (Winter, J., dissenting).

101. Ibid., p. 313 (majority opinion).

102. Aleinikoff, "The Meaning of 'Persecution,'" p. 312.

103. *Matter of Rodriguez-Majano*, 19 I. & N. Dec. 811 (BIA 1988). See also UNHCR, *Handbook*, paragraph 164, stating that "[p]ersons compelled to leave their country of origin as a result of international or national armed conflicts are not normally considered refugees under the 1951 Convention or 1967 Protocol."

104. See, for example, *In re H –*, 21 I. & N. Dec. 337 (BIA 1996); *Minister for Immigration & Multicultural Affairs* v. *Abdi* [1999] 162 A.L.R. 105 (Fed. Ct. Aust.); New Zealand Refugee App. No. 71462/99 (September 27, 1999).

105. *Salibian* v. *Minister of Employment & Immigration* [1990] 3 F.C. 250, 258 (Canada). See also *Adan* v. *Secretary of State for the Home Department* [1999] 1 A.C. 293 (UK).

106. Aleinikoff, "The Meaning of 'Persecution,'" p. 313.

107. Ibid., p. 309.

108. Mark R. von Sternberg, "The Plight of the Non-Combatant in Civil War and the New Criteria for Refugee Status," *International Journal of Refugee Law*, 9 (1997), p. 188 (internal quotation marks omitted).

109. See ibid., p. 195, and Hugo Storey and Rebecca Wallace, "War and Peace in Refugee Law Jurisprudence," *American Journal of International Law*,

95 (2001), p. 349. See also: *In re S – P –*, 21 I. & N. Dec. 486, 494 n. 3 (BIA 1996), stating that "the severity of the violations of the Geneva Convention may support an inference that the abuse is grounded in one of the protected grounds under the asylum law."

110. *Desir* v. *Ilchert*, 840 F.2d 723, 725 (9th Cir. 1988).
111. Ibid., pp. 727–9.
112. Note, "Political Legitimacy," p. 463.
113. Amartya Sen, *Poverty and Famines: An Essay on Entitlement and Deprivation* (Oxford: Clarendon Press, 1981).
114. Michael Wines, "Zimbabwe Extends Crackdown on Dissent as Election Looms," *New York Times*, December 24, 2004.

4 | *Persecution by Private Parties*

Traditionally, forced migration has been caused by state-sponsored violence, and until now, I have exclusively considered "persecution" carried out by agents of the state. But increasingly, refugees seek protection from violence perpetrated by non-state agents, such as death squads, criminal gangs, rebel armies, and clans.[1] How ought asylum law respond to this reality? Under what circumstances should asylum be extended to those fleeing harm inflicted by non-state agents?

At the outset, one can distinguish between two types of situations. In the first, the state is *unable*, owing to limited resources, poor organization, or weak institutions, to provide effective protection against violence inflicted by non-state agents. In the second, the state tacitly condones or is complicit in such violence and is therefore *unwilling* to provide protection against it. I conclude that asylum law should treat these two scenarios differently. In the first, I argue, asylum is not an appropriate response; instead, those fleeing violence carried out by non-state agents should be able to receive temporary protection while their states build the capacity necessary to offer effective protection. In the second, by contrast, asylum is entirely fitting: a state can and should be held to account for violence by non-state agents that it condones, tolerates, or encourages.

That conclusion is controversial. Increasingly, courts in Europe, North America, Australia, and New Zealand decline to distinguish between an inability to protect and an unwillingness to do so. An applicant is eligible for asylum, these courts say, when his state is unwilling *or* unable to provide him with effective protection against violence by non-state agents inflicted for a Convention reason (race, religion, nationality, social group membership, or political opinion). I argue that this approach – called the "protection approach" – expands eligibility for asylum in a manner that is inconsistent with the political conception of asylum.

146

The "accountability approach"

A distinction between a state's unwillingness to protect and its inability to protect is endorsed by what is known as the "accountability approach."[2] Under this approach, the state is obligated to "take reasonable steps to prevent [the infliction of serious harm] and to use the means at its disposal to carry out a serious investigation of violations committed within its jurisdiction, to identify those responsible, impose the appropriate punishment, and ensure the victims adequate compensation"[3] without discrimination.

Private violence should be regarded as persecution when the state, for illegitimate reasons, is unwilling to make a good faith effort to provide its citizens with protection from violence inflicted by non-state actors. When state agents facilitate, condone, tolerate, or are otherwise complicit in private violence by failing for illegitimate reasons to use the means at their disposal to provide protection, that private violence is transformed into state-sanctioned persecution. Conversely, where the state has tried but failed to ensure protection against violence by non-state actors, the accountability approach would not grant asylum. For example, asylum would not be available to individuals fleeing Islamic extremist violence in Algeria because the Algerian state is trying to combat that violence and does not tolerate or condone it.[4]

Until recently, the accountability approach was employed by France and Germany, and in a limited form by the Netherlands, but those countries have since changed their policies in response to an EU Directive.[5] The waning popularity of the accountability approach is due in part to the growing acceptance of a humanitarian conception of asylum. From that perspective, it is asylum seekers' need for protection that justifies asylum, whether or not the state of origin is culpable for the harm they face. The accountability approach's emphasis on state involvement appears, from a humanitarian perspective, to be arbitrary, and is typically explained as an historical anachronism[6] or a quirk of German legal theory.[7]

But the accountability approach bears an obvious affinity to the political conception of asylum. A state deserves condemnation for being unwilling to protect its citizens; it does not deserve condemnation for being unable to do so. Instead, outsiders should offer aid and assistance to help build the state's capacity to enforce its laws. In the meantime, those exposed to violence by non-state actors have a claim to temporary protection abroad.

One question presented by the accountability approach concerns the definition of a "state." The term should be defined functionally. Non-state actors, such as clans or insurgent groups, can exercise effective authority over a swath of territory, and when they do, they should be treated as states for purposes of asylum law. For example, the Taliban certainly enjoyed effective state authority over much of Afghanistan prior to the NATO invasion in 2001, as do the Tamil Tigers in northern Sri Lanka and Hamas in Gaza following its defeat of Fatah. Similarly, Hezbollah arguably exercises effective state authority over southern Lebanon, as do the Kurdish authorities in Northern Iraq.[8] These quasi-states have largely ousted the internationally recognized governments that nominally lay claim to the territories they control, and they act as the guarantors of security and order in those territories. They should be held accountable for an unwillingness to use their authority to protect citizens against private violence. Non-state actors can also be employed as state agents, and in such cases, harm inflicted by the non-state actors is accountable to the state. The Janjaweed, who act on behalf of the Sudanese government, are an example.

Another question presented by the accountability approach is whether adjudicators can feasibly distinguish between a state's inability to protect and an unwillingness to protect. After all, police resources are limited in every society, but especially so in weak states, and enforcement priorities must be set. How can an adjudicator determine whether a state's failure to protect a citizen from private violence was due to inadequate resources (a legitimate reason for a failure to protect) or instead due to an unwillingness to recognize the citizen as deserving of the state's protection (an illegitimate reason for a failure to protect)?

The standard is one of deliberate official indifference to harm threatened by non-state agents. Determining whether the state has been deliberately indifferent will not always be easy, but it is a task that courts are accustomed to undertaking. For example, adjudicators already must ascertain the motivations of state actors for the purpose of determining whether harm is inflicted for a "Convention reason" (race, religion, nationality, social group membership, or political opinion). Key factors to be considered by an adjudicator when determining whether a state was deliberately indifferent to a citizen's need for protection, that is, unwilling to protect, include whether citizens similarly situated to the applicant, for example, those who share his or her race, religion, nationality, social group membership, or political opinion, are systematically denied state protection; whether the applicant actually sought state protection to no avail and the manner in which protection was refused; whether it would have been reasonable for the applicant to have sought state protection if he or she failed to do so; and data regarding the efforts undertaken by the state to protect citizens against the kind of private violence to which the applicant was exposed.

A final question concerns the applicability of the accountability approach in a situation of state breakdown or anarchy, where effective authority has ceased to exist. In that situation, the political conception of asylum has no application. It is premised on the existence of an "effective state authority over the territory"[9] that can be held accountable for an unwillingness to protect. If there is no government at all, then there is no authority to hold accountable. Thus, states employing the accountability approach have refused asylum to Afghani and Somali applicants on the ground that neither Afghanistan nor Somalia had functioning governments at the time that the applicant suffered harm.[10] That may seem disturbingly restrictive from the standpoint of victims, but any harshness is mitigated by the availability of other refugee policy tools, such as temporary protection, which should remain available to individuals fleeing violent anarchy.

The "protection approach"

States have increasingly rejected the accountability approach in favor of what is called the "protection approach." Versions of the protection approach are currently practiced by the United States, the UK, Canada, Australia, New Zealand, Belgium, and Sweden;[11] additionally, Germany and France recently shifted from the accountability to the protection approach in response to EU guidelines. The protection approach is also favored by the UNHCR, refugee advocates, and most academic commentators.[12]

The protection approach grants asylum not only to those refugees whose states are unwilling to protect them from private violence, but also to those whose states are unable to protect them from such violence when it is inflicted on account of a Convention reason.[13] For example, applying the protection approach, the US Board of Immigration Appeals (BIA) awarded asylum to H, a Somali national and member of the Marehan subclan who claimed to fear persecution by the United

Somali Congress on account of his subclan membership, in revenge for the favoritism that former ruler Mohammed Siad Barre had shown to Marehan subclan members. The applicant's father was murdered in Mogadishu and his brother shot by members of the Congress, and his brother was then murdered in the hospital to which he had been taken for treatment. The applicant himself was detained and beaten along with other subclan members.[14] The immigration judge (IJ) who first heard the applicant's case denied him asylum because "there is no evidence there is a government in Somalia."[15] However, the BIA held that the IJ's decision was in error, and concluded that persecution could take place even amidst a background of civil strife in a failed state with "no functioning judicial system."[16]

The protection approach follows from the view that the purpose of asylum is to provide surrogate protection to those exposed to violence. "The intention of the [Convention]," writes Walter Kälin:

was ... to protect persons ... [in] situations in which there was a risk of a type of injury that would be inconsistent with the basic duty of protection owed by a state to its own population. *A state fails to fulfill this basic duty* not only where its authorities are unwilling to provide protection against persecution by non-state actors, but *also where it is so disorganized that it is no longer in a position to provide security to some of its citizens against acts of violence by other citizens* ... [T]his idea is deeply rooted in Western political thinking: According to Hobbes, to defend the citizen not only "from the invasion of foreigners," but also from "the injuries of one another," is the very foundation of the political commonwealth.[17]

On this view, the absence of state protection transforms private violence into persecution. An asylum inquiry is thus focused on the fact of the victim's vulnerability, not on the state's culpability. It makes no difference to victims whether the state is unwilling or unable to prevent violence against them. They experience the same insecurity in either case, and it is this insecurity that creates their need for protection abroad.[18]

The logic of the protection approach would have dramatic consequences for asylum policy if followed to the hilt. The "injuries of one another" against which one may need surrogate protection include violence of all sorts, not only persecution inflicted for Convention reasons. A citizen of a crime-ridden society in which brigandry, rape, and kidnapping are widespread and victimization highly likely is no less in need of protection than a member of a racial minority who is targeted for hate crimes. From the victim's standpoint, to focus on the attacker's motivations is to miss the point. The logic of the protection approach thus points toward a humanitarian conception of asylum: one focused on offering protection against harm of all types, not just persecution inflicted for a Convention reason.

Hemming in the protection approach: the nexus clause

Courts implementing the protection approach have been sensitive to its expansive logic and have limited its impact in two ways. First, they have relied upon the nexus clause, which limits the set of harms against which one can claim surrogate protection to those inflicted for a Convention reason. For example, courts have used the nexus clause to deny asylum to individuals who lack protection against forcible guerrilla recruitment; the guerrillas, courts have reasoned, are motivated by an interest in gaining manpower, and so any persecution suffered by the applicant is not on account of a Convention reason.[19]

So too with the sexual violence that often accompanies civil war. The British Law Lords reasoned:

Assume that during a time of civil unrest, women are particularly vulnerable to attack by marauding men, because the attacks are sexually motivated or because they are thought weaker and less able to defend themselves. The government is unable to protect them, not because of any discrimination but simply because its writ does not run in that part of the country. It is unable to protect men either ... I do not think that they would be regarded as subject to persecution within the meaning of the Convention. The necessary element of discrimination is lacking.[20]

Along similar lines, courts in the United States, Australia, and elsewhere have used the nexus clause to derail asylum claims made by victims of domestic violence. Such violence has been regarded as "personally motivated,"[21] not motivated by a Convention reason, and so victims are ineligible for asylum even if their states are unable to protect them.

But the nexus clause lies in deep tension with the protection approach. From the victim's standpoint, there is no principled basis for distinguishing among types of harm (persecution versus other types of harm) or

reasons for harm (Convention reasons versus other reasons).* But even
though the nexus clause is (on the humanitarian view) an ad hoc limitation on asylum's scope, it is one that courts have felt constrained by. As
the Law Lords have stated, "It would ... be wrong to depart from the
demands of language and context by invoking the humanitarian objectives of the Convention without appreciating the limits which the
Convention itself places on the achievement of them."[22]

Hemming in the protection approach: what constitutes "adequate" protection?

A second limitation on the reach of the protection approach, adopted by
British courts, turns on the standard for "adequate state protection."
No state can entirely eliminate threats of harm; but, adopting the
victim's standpoint, one might sensibly conclude that state protection
is "adequate" only when it reduces the risk of harm to an acceptably
low level, for example, to the point where potential victims no longer
have a well-founded fear of being harmed. After all, it would be odd
indeed to say that victims enjoy adequate protection from their state

---

* In an attempt to rationalize the nexus clause, Hathaway suggests that harm
  inflicted on account of a Convention reason is worthy of special concern because
  "persons affected by these forms of fundamental socio-political
  disenfranchisement [a]re less likely to be in a position to seek effective redress from
  the state." Hathaway, *Law of Refugee Status*, pp. 135–6. In other words,
  Convention reasons for harm serve as a proxy for the victim's inability to obtain
  protection.
  That is not a persuasive explanation. The victim's inability to obtain protection
  is already built into Hathaway's definition of persecution on the protection
  approach: a violation of human rights demonstrative of a failure of state
  protection. There is no need to use the nexus clause as a proxy when the
  phenomenon with which Hathaway is concerned – an absence of state
  protection – is accounted for already.
  Moreover, the nexus clause is underinclusive from the victim's standpoint
  because it excludes people who lack effective redress from their state but who are
  harmed for non-Convention reasons. So, from the standpoint of protection, the
  nexus clause is not only an unnecessary proxy, but also an imperfect one. It is
  perhaps unsurprising that Hathaway has elsewhere argued for the elimination of
  the nexus clause: "Under current interpretations, refugee status requires a risk to
  basic human rights ... *in addition* to some differential impact based on civil or
  political status [i.e. a Convention reason] ... The proposal here is that refugee
  status become the entitlement of all persons whose basic human rights are at risk."
  James C. Hathaway, "Reconceiving Refugee Law as Human Rights Protection,"
  Journal of Refugee Studies, 4 (1991), p. 121.

when they still possess a well-founded fear of serious harm from non-state actors. What else could "effective protection" mean other than that potential victims are more or less secure from attack?

The UNHCR has reasoned along exactly these lines:

Inability is a result-driven determination, i.e. does the protection exist or not. The efforts of the State to provide protection are largely irrelevant. A government may take numerous "reasonable steps," indeed it may take "extraordinary steps," to protect its nationals ... Yet, if despite these best efforts, its nationals continue to have a well-founded fear of persecution, protection should be afforded.[23]

The New Zealand Refugee Appeals Board has similarly stated:

[T]he refugee inquiry is not an inquiry into blame. Rather the purpose of refugee law is to identify those who have a well-founded fear of persecution for a Convention reason. If the net result of a state's "reasonable willingness" to operate a system for the protection of the citizen is that it is incapable of preventing a real chance of persecution of a particular individual, refugee status cannot be denied that individual.[24]

But the implications of that approach are striking: it would extend asylum to many people whom we do not ordinarily regard as refugees. Consider, for example, the case of Jessica Dolamore, a New Zealand woman who was beaten nearly to death by her husband on repeated occasions. Although she moved out and tried to hide from him, he was able to locate her and made calls and sent letters in which he threatened to kill her. The police were responsive to her requests for help, but Dolamore feared that they would be unable to protect her should her husband decide to act on his threats.[25] She sought asylum in Canada.

Or recall from the Introduction the case of Angela, a Jamaican whose 13-year old daughter was killed after a quarrel with a gang member. Angela reported the murder to the police and provided them with the name of the gang member responsible. As a result, she was labeled an "informer," her son was murdered and her brother shot, and she began to receive death threats from the gang. Evidence suggested that Angela's relocation elsewhere in Jamaica would be futile because the gangs had developed island-wide networks to punish informers. While the Jamaican police had undertaken major efforts to control the gang problem, they had largely failed. Angela fled to Britain and sought asylum there.[26]

Similar questions are raised by, for example, the asylum applications of a Honduran man who feared retaliation by gang members when he refused to join their gang; a Honduran "street child" who was threatened and physically abused by Honduran street gangs who pressured him to rob and steal for them; and a wealthy Guatemalan family whose members had been kidnapped by a criminal gang for ransom.[27] According to the protection approach, should such applicants be eligible for asylum?

Without doubt, inadequate protection for battered women, police informants, and citizens exposed to gang violence are serious social problems in virtually every society. But one might wonder whether asylum is the right vehicle for addressing these kinds of problems. Certainly, extending asylum to Dolamore, Angela, and others like them takes us a long way from asylum's historical heartland. Nonetheless, assuming such applicants face harm for a Convention reason – for example, Dolamore on account of gender (as some courts have held and many advocates have urged) and Angela on account of her membership in the social group of witnesses to crime who have cooperated with the police – it would appear that they would be eligible according to the protection approach. Although New Zealand and Jamaica have made efforts at protection, Dolamore and Angela continued to have a well-founded fear of serious harm.

British courts have been leery about following the protection approach down this road, and they struck a different path in *Horvath*, a case involving a Slovakian Roma who had been beaten and threatened by skinheads. Horvath claimed that the Slovakian police had failed to offer adequate protection against skinhead violence. The Law Lords denied Horvath's asylum claim, finding that the protection afforded him by the Slovakian authorities had been adequate. "The standard to be applied," reasoned Lord Hope of Craighead, "is ... not that which would eliminate all risk and would thus amount to a guarantee of protection in the home state." After all, he continued, "we live in an imperfect world. Certain levels of ill-treatment may still occur even if steps to prevent this are taken by the state to which we look for our protection." Indeed, Lord Lloyd of Berwick noted, "there are parts of London or New York where one may ... have a well-founded fear of being attacked in the street."[28]

The standard for adequate protection, concluded Lord Hope, "is a practical standard, which takes proper account of the duty which the state owes to all its own citizens," namely, "to establish and to operate a system of protection against the persecution of its own nationals." In the case of skinhead attacks against Roma in Slovakia, Lord Hope acknowledged that "[t]he police do not conduct proper investigation in all cases and there may have been cases where their investigation has been very slow." Nonetheless, "[t]he institutions of government are effective and operating in the Republic of Slovakia. The state provides protection to its nationals by respecting the rule of law and it enforces its authority through the provision of a police force."[29]

In other words, protection can be adequate even if the applicant continues to be at serious risk of harm. As Lord Clyde put it, "The sufficiency of state protection is not measured by the existence of a real risk of an abuse of rights but by the availability of a system for the protection of the citizen and a reasonable willingness by the state to operate it."[30]

This standard hems in the protection approach at the cost of abandoning its underlying logic. It incorporates into protection analysis an element of the accountability approach: whether protection is adequate depends not on the victim's viewpoint, but instead on the state's efforts. Good faith efforts at protection are "adequate" even if they fail to reduce the risk of harm faced by the applicant.

***

In sum, judicial efforts to limit the protection approach do not yield appealing results. The nexus clause substantially limits the kinds of harm that can give rise to an asylum claim; but, from the standpoint of the victim's need for protection, its limits are arbitrary and ad hoc. The same is true of the Law Lords' efforts to define "adequate protection" in terms of the state's good faith efforts at protection rather than in terms of the risk of harm faced by the applicant. They short-circuit the protection approach's slide toward humanitarianism, but only by changing the subject from the state's efficacy in protecting the victim to the diligence of its efforts in attempting to do so.

The accountability approach also focuses on the diligence of the state's efforts, but it is grounded in a theory that explains why this is the appropriate inquiry. On the political view of asylum I have defended, asylum policy should reflect the distinction between a state's inability to protect and its unwillingness to do so. Only the latter is worthy of condemnation.

Whose motivations matter? The case of battered women

I have so far argued that harm inflicted by non-state actors should give rise to asylum only when it is condoned, tolerated, or endorsed by the state, as evidenced through the state's unwillingness to protect. When the state is not complicit in private violence, but is unable to prevent it, other refugee policy tools, such as temporary protection, are appropriate.

There is one more wrinkle to iron out. In cases where the state is unwilling to protect, what role should the nexus clause play? Should one look to the *private actor's* reason for inflicting harm? Or instead to the *state's* reason for failing to protect against that harm? American courts have opted for the former approach, holding that the private agent must inflict harm for a Convention reason. That is a mistake. One should instead look at the state's reason for withholding protection: when a state is unwilling to protect for illegitimate reasons, asylum is the appropriate response. Private violence carried out for "personal," non-Convention reasons is transformed into "persecution" when the state is unwilling to provide protection against it on account of the victim's race, religion, nationality, social group membership, or political opinion (or for some other illegitimate reason).

The shortcomings of the American approach are highlighted in cases involving asylum claims by battered women like Rodi Alvarado Peña, a Guatemalan woman whose story of abuse by her husband Francisco Osorio was recounted in the Introduction.[31] "Good lawyering" in these cases has been a game of trying to shoehorn women's claims into the categories established by the nexus clause to establish a link between the husband's violence and a Convention reason. Two main strategies have been attempted.

The first is to claim that husbands batter their wives on account of their wives' political opinions.[32] For example, Alvarado Peña argued that her attempts to flee her husband and her filing of complaints against him with the police expressed a political opinion "opposing his male dominance," and that Osorio harmed her on account of this political opinion of hers.[33] The majority of the BIA was not persuaded. It noted Alvarado Peña's testimony that Osorio beat her "for no reason at all" and "whenever he felt like it." Even acquiescence did not spare her. The seeming pointlessness of the beatings led the majority to conclude that Osorio not only had no "understanding of [Alvarado Peña's] perspective," but also that he did not "even care ... what [that] perspective may have been."[34] The BIA also rejected Alvarado Peña's attempt to cast her resistance to Osorio as reflecting a political opinion. On that analysis, said the BIA, "virtually any victim of repeated violence who offers some resistance could qualify for asylum," a result that would dilute substantially the meaning of "political opinion."[35]

A second way that battered women have tried to meet the nexus requirement is to argue that they have been persecuted on account of their membership in the social group of women. But, said the BIA, if Osorio was indeed motivated to harm Alvarado Peña because she was a woman, then one should expect him to pose a risk to other members of that social group. "The record," however, "indicates that [Osorio] has ... not shown an interest in any member of this group other than [Alvarado Peña] herself. [Alvarado Peña] fails to show how other members of the group may be at risk of harm from him."[36] In sum, the majority concluded that Osorio's violence toward Alvarado Peña was motivated by personal reasons. While the BIA acknowledged that the abuse suffered by Alvarado Peña was "more than sufficient ... to constitute 'persecution,'"[37] her claim foundered on the nexus issue.

The reasons for state inaction

The BIA's decision in Alvarado Peña's case is deeply unsatisfying. The nexus analysis should be focused not on Osorio's motivations for abusing her, but rather on the state's reasons for failing to protect her. As the Immigration Judge (IJ) found, Guatemala systematically refuses to protect women from domestic abuse. When the analysis is refocused in this way, the case is easy: Alvarado Peña is being tortured by her husband,[38] never mind why, and her government is unwilling to do anything to protect her because it regards women as undeserving of protection against violence inflicted by their husbands. The state's complicity in violence against women transforms Osorio's beatings into state persecution on account of gender.

In a British domestic violence case, Lord Hoffmann offered a helpful analogy. Suppose that in the early 1930s – when the Nazis refused to protect Jews from violence directed against them, but before anti-Semitic violence was officially organized – a German Jewish shopkeeper was attacked by an Aryan business competitor "motivated by business rivalry and a desire to settle old personal scores."[39] The shopkeeper, said Lord Hoffmann, had been persecuted on account of his religion, even though the competitor was motivated by "personal" reasons. The government's unwillingness to protect Jews made the shopkeeper vulnerable to such attacks, and this unwillingness transformed an act of private violence into an act of persecution.

Accordingly, the Law Lords have granted asylum to Pakistani women who were falsely accused of adultery by their respective husbands and who would be stoned to death if forced to return to Pakistan.[40] Lord Hoffmann acknowledged that the "threat of violence" to the applicants by their respective husbands "is a personal affair, directed against them as individuals." But, he continued, "there is the inability or unwillingness of the State to do anything to protect them. There is nothing personal about this. The evidence was that the State would not assist them because they were women. It denied them a protection against violence which it would have given to men."[41] The discriminatory enforcement of the state's criminal laws – leaving women unprotected on account of their gender – makes the state accountable for the husbands' "personal" threats of violence.

The Law Lords' approach also explains why Dolamore, the New Zealander victimized by domestic violence, would not qualify for asylum even though New Zealand may be unable to guarantee her safety. As the Australian High Court explained in yet another domestic violence case, "[M]aladministration, incompetence, or ineptitude, by the local police ... would not convert personally motivated domestic violence into persecution."[42]

The BIA in Alvarado Peña's case had ample evidence before it to conclude that she had been persecuted on account of her gender. Alvarado Peña's entreaties to the state for help were entirely ignored on six occasions: three times the police declined to respond to her call; twice they declined to enforce a court summons of her husband; and once a judge declined to intervene in what he classified as a domestic dispute.[43] Nor was the state's unwillingness to assist Alvarado Peña an isolated occurrence. While the state generally was able to maintain law and order, it systematically declined to use its power to protect women in abusive relationships because those in charge viewed such abuse as a "private" matter, beyond the purview of the state. The IJ found the existence of an "institutional bias" against spousal abuse claims "stem[ming] from a pervasive belief, common in patriarchal societies, that a man should be able to control a wife or female companion by any means he sees fit: including rape, torture, and beatings."[44] For these reasons, responsibility for the violence suffered by Alvarado Peña lies not only with her husband, but with her state as well. Accordingly, she should have been granted asylum.

Conclusion

The prevalence of private violence, and the inability of weak states to protect against it, presents urgent questions for refugee policy. From a humanitarian perspective, the purpose of asylum is to offer protection to those exposed to serious harm. The identity of the person inflicting harm – husband, father, or gang leader; or police officer, soldier, or intelligence agent – is irrelevant to the asylum seeker's need for protection, and so should be irrelevant to the asylum seeker's eligibility for asylum. Thus, although the protection approach purports to interpret the meaning of the term "persecution" – which it defines as "Serious Harm + The Failure of State Protection"[45] – in fact the logic of the protection approach would extend eligibility for asylum far beyond the persecuted. Indeed, one can need protection – and thus be eligible for asylum – for harm that is inflicted by no one at all: for example, one might need shelter from a natural disaster, or from severe poverty caused by an economic system that has no identifiable author. It is not surprising that courts applying the protection approach, faced with such sweeping logic, have looked for ways to limit its reach – even at the expense of abandoning its underlying rationale.

The protection approach reflects a mistaken view about asylum's role within refugee policy. Without doubt, refugee policy should assist those who lack state protection against serious harm. But asylum is just one refugee policy tool among many, and it is not the best one for this job. The protection approach jeopardizes asylum's expressive character by collapsing the distinction between a state's inability to protect and its unwillingness to do so. An inability to protect typifies burdened societies, who ought to be assisted, not condemned. Refugees from such states can be assisted in some cases by relief aid, and in other cases by humanitarian protection abroad, while their states strengthen their capacity to provide protection at home.

Asylum should be focused on remedying state malfeasance, namely, state-directed persecution or a state's unwillingness (not mere inability) to protect against non-official violence for illegitimate reasons. The accountability approach reflects this focus, while remaining sensitive to the serious harm that private actors can inflict on others when the state ignores victims' entreaties to act.

Notes

1. Jennifer Moore, "From Nation State to Failed State: International Protection from Human Rights Abuses by Non-State Agents," *Columbia Human Rights Law Review*, 31 (1999), p. 83.
2. See *R* v. *Secretary of State for the Home Department, ex parte Adan* [2001] 2 A.C. 477.
3. Reinhard Marx, "The Notion of Persecution by Non-State Agents in German Jurisprudence," *Georgetown Immigration Law Journal*, 15 (2001), p. 451.
4. France took this position until 2003 and Germany until 1994. See *ex parte Adan*. Reasoning along these lines, Germany denied asylum to Sri Lankan Tamils fleeing violence at the hands of the Tamil Tigers, because the Sri Lankan state did not tolerate Tamil violence. BVerfGE 80, 315 (July 10, 1988). A 1994 Federal Administrative Court decision, however, reversed this position, leaving the German position unclear. See Ben Vermeulen *et al.*, "Persecution by Third Parties" (Nijmegen, Netherlands: Research and Documentation Centre of the Ministry of Justice of the Netherlands, May 1998), p. 21.
5. A new German Immigration Act, which came into force on January 1, 2005, for the first time recognized that non-state actors can be responsible for persecution. The German law implemented the EU Qualifications Directive issued April 29, 2004, see Council Directive 2004/83/EC, art. 6. In France, the 2003 Asylum Act introduced into French law for the first time the concept of persecution by non-state actors. For more on the accountability approach in Germany prior to 2005, see Marx, "The Notion of Persecution," pp. 457 *et seq.*; on France, see Vermeulen *et al.*, "Persecution by Third Parties," pp. 29–30.
6. Vermeulen *et al.*, "Persecution by Third Parties," p. 15.
7. Walter Kälin, "Non-State Agents of Persecution and the Inability of the State to Protect," *Georgetown Immigration Law Journal*, 15 (2001), pp. 421–2.
8. Thus, German courts (prior to 2005) recognized anti-Lebanese actions of the Syrian army in Lebanon as persecution because the Syrian army exercised effective authority in Lebanon. Moore, "From Nation State to Failed State," p. 107 n. 68.
9. Jean-Yves Carlier *et al.* (eds.), *Who is a Refugee?* (The Hague: Kluwer Law, 1997), p. 271.
10. Moore, "From Nation States to Failed States," p. 108. The German Federal Administrative Court, for example, ruled that Somali "clans and clan-leaders who fight each other over influence do not exercise 'state-like' power in their respective areas of influence." Ibid.

11. Ibid., p. 108 n. 70; Vermeulen, *et al.*, "Persecution by Third Parties." On France and Germany, see note 4, above.

12. See, for example, UNHCR, *Handbook on Procedures and Criteria for Determining Refugee Status Under the 1951 Convention and the 1967 Protocol Relating to the Status of Refugees*, UN Doc. HCR/PRO/4 (1979), revised 1992, paragraph 65; Guy Goodwin-Gill, *The Refugee in International Law*, 2nd edn. (New York: Oxford University Press, 1996), pp. 70–4; Atle Grahl-Madsen, *The Status of Refugees in International Law*, vol. 1 (Leiden: A. W. Sijthoff, 1966), p. 191; James C. Hathaway, *Law of Refugee Status* (Toronto: Butterworths, 1991), pp. 124 *et seq.*; Kälin, "Non-State Agents"; Moore, "From Nation States to Failed States"; Jennifer Moore, "Whither the Accountability Theory," *International Journal of Refugee Law*, 13 (2001), p. 32; Vermeulen *et al.*, "Persecution by Third Parties"; Steven Edminster, "Recklessly Risking Lives: Restrictive Interpretations of 'Agents of Persecution' in Germany and France," in US Committee for Refugees, *World Refugee Survey, 1999* (Washington, DC: US Committee for Refugees, 1999).

13. The seminal case for this proposition is *Canada* v. *Ward* [1993] 2 S.C.R. 689.

14. *In re H –*, 21 I. & N. Dec. 337, 340–1 (BIA 1996). This decision follows an earlier Canadian decision in which the court ruled that a "situation of civil war in a given country is not an obstacle to a claim provided the fear felt is not that felt indiscriminately by all citizens as a consequence of the civil war, but that felt by the applicant himself, by a group with which he is associated, or, even, by all citizens on account of a risk of persecution based on one of the reasons stated in the definition." *Salibian* v. *Canada* [1990] 3 F.C. 250, 258.

15. *In re H –*, 21 I. & N. Dec. at 338.

16. Ibid., pp. 343–4.

17. Kälin, "Non-State Agents," p. 430 (emphasis added). See also Vermeulen *et al.*, "Persecution by Third Parties," p. 11, stating that, "[i]n the protection view, the only relevant issue is whether the persons involved are not effectively protected against human rights violations, regardless of the source of these violations" (emphasis added). It would seem to follow that effective protection is the only relevant issue regardless of the *motivation* of these violations as well.

18. Reinhard Marx writes: "Perpetrators of serious human rights violations in the context of civil wars and internal strife range from traditional agents of the State to militia, paramilitary groups, war-lords, and alike. However, the victims remain largely the same people. A protection-based approach of the Convention ... follows the assessment of a well-founded fear regardless of [who] are the perpetrators." Marx, "Notion of Persecution," p. 454.

19. *Elias-Zacarias* v. *INS*, 502 U.S. 478 (1992).
20. *Secretary of State for the Home Department, ex parte Shah* [1999] 2 A.C. 629 (Lord Hoffmann).
21. *Minister for Immigration and Multicultural Affairs* v. *Khawar* [2002] H.C.A. 14.
22. *Horvath* v. *Secretary of State for the Home Department* [2001] 1 A.C. 489.
23. Quoted in Karen Musalo and Stephen Knight, "Steps Forward and Steps Back," *International Journal of Refugee Law*, 13 (2001), pp. 62–3.
24. New Zealand Refugee Appeal No. 71427/99 (August 16, 2000), paragraphs 63, 66.
25. See *MCI* v. *Jessica Robyn Dolamore* [2001] F.T.C. 421. Initially, in 2000, the Refugee Board granted Dolamore asylum, but upon appeal, the Federal Trial Court found that the Board had not adequately addressed the issue of whether she was able to receive protection in New Zealand. Upon remand in July 2002, the Board denied Dolamore's asylum application. Andrea Sands and Raquel Exner, "Burn Victim's Refugee Claim Rejected," *Edmonton Sun*, January 15, 2003, p. 3.
26. *A* v. *Secretary of State for the Home Department* [2003] EWCA Civ. 175 (CA).
27. See, respectively, *Valdiviezo-Galdamez* v. *Attorney General*, 502 F.3d 285 (3d Cir. 2007); *Escobar* v. *Gonzales*, 417 F.3d 363 (3d Cir. 2005); and *Ucelo-Gomez* v. *Gonzales*, 464 F.3d 163 (2d Cir. 2006).
28. *Horvath* [2001] 1 A.C. 489. For criticism of *Horvath*, see Helene Lambert, "The Conceptualisation of 'Persecution' by the House of Lords: *Horvath* v. *Secretary of State for the Home Department*," *International Journal of Refugee Law*, 13 (2001), pp. 16–31.
29. *Horvath* [2001] 1 A.C. 489.
30. Ibid.
31. *In re R – A –*, 22 I. & N. Dec. 906 (BIA 1999), vacated by order of the Attorney General, January 19, 2001. There is a large literature on asylum claims by battered women. Good articles include Deborah E. Anker, "Refugee Status and Violence Against Women in the 'Domestic' Sphere: The Non-State Actor Question," *Georgetown Immigration Law Journal*, 15 (2001), p. 391; Deborah E. Anker *et al.*, "Women Whose Governments are Unable or Unwilling to Provide Reasonable Protection from Domestic Violence May Qualify as Refugees Under United States Asylum Law," *Georgetown Immigration Law Journal*, 11 (1997), p. 709; Pamela Goldberg, "Anyplace but Home," *Cornell International Law Journal*, 26 (1993), p. 565; Nancy Kelly, "Gender-Related Persecution: Assessing the Asylum Claims of Women," *Cornell International Law Journal*, 26 (1993), p. 625.

32. This approach had been successful in the past – see: *Lazo-Majano* v. *INS*, 813 F.2d 1432 (9th Cir. 1987) – but the decision in *Elias-Zacarias*, 502 U.S. 478, undermined the reasoning used in *Lazo-Majano*.

33. *In re R – A –*, 22 I. & N. Dec. at 942 (dissenting opinion).

34. Ibid., p. 915 (majority opinion).

35. Ibid., p. 916.

36. Ibid., p. 921.

37. Ibid., p. 914.

38. Rhonda Copelon, "Recognizing the Egregious in the Everyday: Domestic Violence as Torture," *Columbia Human Rights Law Review*, 25 (1994), p. 291.

39. *Shah* [1999] 2 A.C. 629 (Lord Hoffmann).

40. Ibid.

41. Ibid.

42. *Khawar* [2002] HCA 14.

43. *In re R – A –*, 22 I. & N. Dec. at 909.

44. Ibid., p. 930 (dissenting opinion).

45. New Zealand Refugee Appeal No. 74665/03 (July 7, 2004), paragraph 53; *Shah* [1999] 2 A.C. at 653; *Khawar* [2002] 210 C.L.R. 1, at 120.

5 | Asylum, Temporary Protection, and the Refugee Policy Toolkit

I have so far argued that asylum is a distinctive mode of refugee relief because it is expressive rather than merely palliative. That sets it apart from other refugee policy tools, such as humanitarian protection and *in situ* relief aid. This chapter further explores asylum's place in the refugee policy toolkit. In particular, I address two questions.

First, what is the nature of the remedy that asylum offers to persecuted people? Should they be entitled to remain indefinitely in the state of refuge? Should they be eligible to become citizens? Or should asylum instead be granted for a presumptively temporary period? I argue that persecuted people should receive membership in the state of refuge, and that the necessity of that remedy further distinguishes asylum from other refugee policy tools. I also explore the proper scope of humanitarian protection available to non-persecuted refugees.

Second, how should states, which have limited resources to devote to refugee policy, allocate them among various refugee policy tools? If the ultimate goal of refugee policy is to save the most lives possible, one might question whether resources expended on asylum are well spent. First, asylum has a "proximity bias": it is available only to refugees who manage to enter the territory of the state of refuge. But those refugees might not be the most in need of help. To eliminate proximity bias, should states replace their asylum programs with overseas refugee resettlement programs, which select refugees located in their states or regions of origin for resettlement abroad? Second, asylum has an "expatriate bias": it helps people by giving them assistance abroad, rather than in their states of origin. But that is a very expensive way to lend assistance. Given the reality of limited budgets, other refugee policy tools (for example, *in situ* aid) may be a more cost-effective means of advancing refugee policy's ultimate aim. Should states move away from asylum (and other forms of international protection, like humanitarian protection and overseas refugee resettlement) in favor of aid designed to help refugees in their states of origin? In answering these questions, I argue that there are strong institutional reasons to maintain asylum. It is an uncapped, judicially enforceable form of protection that is rooted in an international legal obligation; other refugee aid, by contrast, is susceptible to downward budgetary pressures and political manipulation. Refugees on the whole may be better off with asylum, despite its proximity bias and expatriate bias.

The membership principle

Traditionally, asylum has been a distinctive refugee policy tool not only because of its expressive dimension, but also because of the remedy it offers to its recipients: not merely protection abroad, but also surrogate membership in the state of refuge. Thus, in the United States, Convention refugees may become legal permanent residents after one year, and citizens five years after that.[1] In Canada, Convention refugees immediately receive permanent residence and can become citizens roughly three years later.[2] In Australia, Convention refugees who receive a "permanent protection visa" – available to those who entered Australia with authorization and who did not spend more than seven days in any other country that could have offered effective protection – immediately become permanent residents, and can become citizens four years later.[3]

That has set asylum apart from the protection given to non-Convention refugees, which, in many states, is presumptively temporary rather than permanent. In the United States, for example, Temporary Protected Status (TPS) is available for certain non-Convention refugees for a fixed time period of six, twelve, or eighteen months. When the time period has expired, the Attorney General can decide whether to renew TPS for an additional fixed time period. TPS does not permit recipients to adjust their status to permanent residence, no matter how long protection has lasted, absent very rare circumstances or special legislation that must pass the Senate by a supermajority.[4]

Under the temporary protection regime put into place by the European Union – designed to handle situations of mass influx in which the ordinary asylum system would be overwhelmed – recipients receive temporary protection for one year, extendable for two more years in six-month increments.[5] (The EU directives outline the minimum that member states must offer, leaving member states free to enact legislation more favorable to refugees, which many have.) In other states, certain non-Convention refugees receive an initial temporary grant of protection, but protection can become permanent with the passage of time. For example, the United Kingdom sometimes offers "discretionary leave to remain" to non-Convention refugees, with an initial grant usually lasting for no more than three years, though it can be extended if conditions require it. Recipients can sometimes apply for permanent residence after six years (other times after ten years).[6]

The result has been, by and large, a two-tiered scheme of refugee protection. Convention refugees, that is, persecuted people, receive surrogate membership through asylum. Some non-Convention refugees – those in need of protection for reasons other than persecution – are eligible for protection abroad on a presumptively temporary basis.

Questioning the two tiers

At first blush, it may seem odd to provide persecuted people with surrogate membership in a state of refuge, but other refugees with only temporary protection. After all, from the refugee's standpoint, the harm faced by a persecuted person might be neither worse nor longer lasting than the harm faced by a non-Convention refugee, such as someone fleeing from civil war or violence of some other kind. Why should two groups, similarly situated with respect to their need of protection, be treated differently by a state of refuge? Why should persecuted people receive VIP treatment while other refugees receive merely temporary sanctuary? From a humanitarian point of view, the two-tiered structure seems arbitrary.

Several states have accordingly collapsed the two tiers into one. Canada has elected to offer surrogate membership not only to Convention refugees, but also to other "persons in need of protection." Many states, however, have moved in the other direction, giving temporary protection to Convention and non-Convention refugees alike. The UK, for example, provides both Convention refugees and certain non-Convention refugees (those eligible for "humanitarian protection") an initial five-year period of temporary protection, after which the refugees must re-prove their need for ongoing refuge. If they can do so, they may then become permanent residents. The EU's "qualifications directive" – which sets minimum standards for member states in the area of asylum eligibility – guarantees Convention refugees longer-lasting protection than non-Convention refugees, but for both groups refuge is presumptively temporary: Convention refugees receive a three-year period of temporary protection, which can be renewed for additional three-year periods if protection continues to be needed, while certain non-Convention refugees (those eligible for "subsidiary protection") are given only a one-year, renewable period of temporary protection.

Temporary protection is appealing to states for a number of reasons. First, it allows them to maintain some control over their borders even as they admit large numbers of refugees. Skeptical publics are more likely to support refugee admissions premised on eventual repatriation, and temporary protection also removes the possibility of chain migrations that can have long-term effects on the demography of the host state. Second, temporary protection is cheaper than asylum: because temporary protection is framed as an emergency accommodation due to exigent circumstances, states are led to "contest[ ]" the "boundaries of ... humane treatment,"[7] offering recipients only the bare minimum in terms of public benefits and social services.

Several prominent scholars have even suggested that states largely replace their asylum programs with temporary protection located in refugees' regions of origin. Western states could provide services like food, shelter, and health care more cheaply there; they would retain control over their borders; and they could more readily share the burden of protecting refugees by splitting the cost.[8]

Why recipients of asylum should receive surrogate membership

The trend toward temporary protection for persecuted people misunderstands the distinctive nature of the harm they have suffered. As I argued in Chapter 2, persecution is not just another type of harm against which protection is needed. It is a *political* harm that effectively expels victims from their political communities, and it calls for a political response. Condemnation is one element of such a response; providing the victim with surrogate membership abroad – a political remedy to a political harm – is a second element.

Providing surrogate membership to persecuted people also reflects the attitude of condemnation and sanction that outsiders ought to take toward an outlaw state. When a state of refuge welcomes persecuted people as members, it gives effect to the condemnation expressed by asylum by treating them as political orphans in need of adoption by a new political community. Thus, offering surrogate membership to recipients of asylum is intertwined with the expressive dimension of asylum. It dramatizes the judgment that the state of origin has engaged in conduct so despicable that the political relationship between it and the refugee has been sundered.

The upshot is that recipients of asylum should receive surrogate membership, and not only protection, in the state of refuge. Call this the **membership principle**. By contrast, non-persecuted people retain standing as members in their home states even when they are exposed to serious harm. While a state may choose (as Canada has) to offer such people permanent protection, the membership principle does not require it; their needs can be met through presumptively temporary protection, renewable if conditions of insecurity persist.[9]

Applying the membership principle

The membership principle suggests that recent Australian policy was deeply problematic. Until July 2008, Australia granted only temporary protection to Convention refugees who either (1) entered its territory without documentation or authorization, or (2) resided, prior to entering Australia, for more than seven days in a country where they could have received effective protection. Temporary protection was valid for three years; after thirty months of that period, the former group could become permanent residents if they could show that they still had a well-founded fear of persecution. The latter group, however, remained forever ineligible for the surrogate membership that asylum should provide.[10]

The UK's policy is also at odds with the membership principle insofar as it provides even persecuted people with an initial five-year period of temporary protection rather than surrogate membership. On that score, the EU's minimum requirements for member states in this area are even more problematic: member states need offer Convention refugees only a three-year period of temporary protection, which can be renewed for additional three-year periods if protection continues to be needed.[11] Persecuted people, who have been expelled from their own political communities, should not be forced to spend years in limbo before being welcomed into another one as permanent residents on the path toward citizenship. Such delay fails to recognize both the distinctive, political harm faced by persecuted people, as well as the expressive significance of granting them surrogate membership rather than merely protection.

Until very recently, American law governing asylees' adjustment of status was sorely deficient in this respect as well. Before the REAL ID

Act was passed in May 2005, the number of asylees who could adjust their status to permanent residence in any given year was capped at 10,000.[12] As a result, there was, as of January 2005, a waiting list for legal permanent residence approximately twelve years long: an asylee who filed for an adjustment of status in winter 2005 would have had to wait until 2016 to receive a green card. This made a mockery of the type of relief that asylum should offer. The REAL ID Act removed the 10,000-person annual cap so that all asylees could adjust their status to legal permanent residence in a timely fashion.[13]

Implications: the doctrine of past persecution

The membership principle can help to explain a doctrine in asylum law known as "past persecution." Under current US law, the fact that an applicant has suffered past persecution is relevant to his or her claim in two ways.

First, a showing of past persecution creates a presumption that the applicant has a well-founded fear of future persecution. Once this presumption is created, the burden shifts to the immigration service to demonstrate by a preponderance of the evidence that "[t]here has been a fundamental change in circumstances [in the country of origin] such that the applicant no longer has a well-founded fear of persecution" or that "[t]he applicant could avoid future persecution by relocating to another part of the applicant's country of nationality."[14]

Second, and more importantly for present purposes, even if conditions have changed or internal relocation is possible, an applicant is still eligible for asylum if he or she "has demonstrated compelling reasons for being unwilling to return to the country [of origin] arising out of the severity of the past persecution."[15] That is, the applicant may still be eligible for asylum even if he faces no future risk of persecution whatsoever in his country of origin. For example, in *Matter of Chen*, the US Board of Immigration Appeals (BIA) granted asylum to a Chinese Christian who had suffered unspeakable abuse during the Cultural Revolution, notwithstanding the fact that "conditions in China have changed significantly" since the 1970s – indeed, so much so that the applicant no longer had a well-founded fear of persecution were he to return to China.[16] The BIA similarly granted asylum to a supporter of the Afghan mujahidin who had suffered ten months of detention and torture by the KHAD, the Afghani secret police under the

Communist regime. Although political conditions had changed since the applicant's initial hearing – the mujahidin "finally deposed the Communist government in Afghanistan and set up an interim government of their own" – and the applicant consequently no longer had a well-founded fear of persecution, the BIA nonetheless found that "the past persecution suffered by the applicant was so severe that his asylum application should be granted notwithstanding the change of circumstances."[17]

This second aspect of the past persecution doctrine is ordinarily defended in humanitarian terms. The UNHCR Handbook, for example, refers to the "general humanitarian principle" that:

a person who – or whose family – has suffered under atrocious forms of persecution should not be expected to repatriate. Even though there may have been a change of regime in his country, this may not always produce a complete change in the attitude of the population, nor, in view of his past experiences, in the mind of the refugee.[18]

Yet the doctrine may nonetheless appear puzzling on the humanitarian conception of asylum. That conception, after all, views the purpose of refugee law as providing *protection* against the denial of basic rights. But in cases involving purely past persecution, there is no prospective risk of persecution whatsoever, and therefore no need for protection. Current law responds to this problem by stressing the psychological hardship that victims of severe past persecution would undergo were they to return to their country of origin. As one court has put it, "[t]he experience of persecution may so sear a person with distressing associations with his native country that it would be inhumane to force him to return there even though he is in no danger of further persecution."[19]

The membership principle offers an alternative justification for the doctrine. That may at first seem surprising. After all, people who face no prospective risk of harm might be said to have had their standing as members restored to them. Also, the regime that persecuted them may no longer be in power, making the expressive sanction of asylum inappropriate. Nonetheless, asylum might still be warranted. Sometimes, persecution can *irredeemably* repudiate one's standing as a member, so that reintegration as a member – even after a political transition – is impossible. The atrociousness of harm may be one factor to consider in identifying such cases, but more important are the circumstances in which the severe harm was inflicted.

The case for granting asylum purely on grounds of past persecution is strongest when severe persecution was carried out by society at large (condoned or facilitated by the state) rather than by the government alone or by a sector of society. For although a political transition may bring to power a new regime that respects its citizens' civic standing, a social transition is much more difficult to accomplish: the population itself cannot be so easily replaced. To the extent that one believes Daniel Goldhagen's thesis that "ordinary Germans" were enthusiastic participants in the Holocaust,[20] the case of a Holocaust survivor offers a prime example of the affinity between the membership principle and the past persecution doctrine. When an entire populace is complicit in the repudiation of a victim's membership, much more than a regime change is needed to restore that person's civic standing. Application of the doctrine thus seems appropriate in the case of Chen, the Chinese Christian persecuted during the Cultural Revolution, but less so in the case of the Afghan mujahid who had been tortured by the Communist secret police.

Objections to the membership principle and responses

Consider two possible objections to my exposition of the membership principle. First, one might contend that to lack protection of one's basic rights *is* to be denied membership. It would follow that refugees fleeing burdened societies and outlaw states (see Chapter 2) are equally in need of the remedy that asylum offers. Second, one might argue that the membership principle, as I've framed it, trades on an ambiguity in the word "membership." To be deprived of membership is to be exposed to serious harm for illegitimate reasons; but to receive membership as an asylee is to be granted not only civic standing in the most rudimentary sense, but also rights to political participation and, in some societies, welfare and advanced health care. To truly match the remedy to the problem, the objection continues, the persecuted would be entitled only to recognition as rights-bearing individuals; but such recognition can be granted in Western legal systems without providing full membership. I address these objections in turn.

A distinction with a difference?

The most fundamental objection to the membership principle is that it is premised on a misunderstanding of what membership entails: those fleeing burdened societies and those fleeing outlaw states equally lack membership and should, therefore, equally enjoy access to asylum. Refugee scholar Andrew Shacknove has argued in an influential article that the "bond of trust, loyalty, protection, and assistance" between state and citizen – upon which membership is premised – is "ruptured" whenever the citizen's basic needs are unmet. Because the "political commonwealth is formed on the premise that people experience a generalized condition of insecurity when outside the protective confines of society," it is "the absence of state protection of the citizen's basic needs ... which constitutes the full and complete negation of society."[21] On this account, the persecuted are similarly situated to other individuals whose basic needs – for physical security as well as "unpolluted air and water, adequate food, clothing, and shelter, and minimal preventative health care"[22] – are unmet. They have an equal need for, and thus an equal claim to, membership through asylum.[23]

The hard case for Shacknove is one in which basic needs are unmet due to a natural disaster such as a typhoon, earthquake, or drought. A government's response to such a disaster can, of course, be more or less competent, but even a generally well-organized, well-intentioned state may have trouble immediately meeting the basic needs of all those affected. Consider the 2004 Asian tsunami. The logic of Shacknove's argument would commit him to the view that these victims – if they cannot be helped in their state of origin – are similarly situated to persecuted people with respect to their civic standing, and so should be eligible for asylum abroad.[24] The "bond of loyalty" between citizen and state, it may be argued, is dissolved *whenever* the state is unable to protect a citizen's basic needs, no matter what the reason.

But that strong humanitarian view errs in equating "the absence of state protection of the citizen's basic needs" with "the full and complete negation of society."[25] To equate the victim of state-perpetrated torture with the victim of an earthquake because they are equally in need of assistance is to miss the special horror of violence organized and exploited for political ends. Rony Brauman of Médecins Sans Frontières has said that he fears that, if Auschwitz were taking place today, humanitarians would describe it as a humanitarian crisis.[26] That chilling remark exactly captures the importance of preserving the distinction between persecution and other types of harm. Hitler's victims did not simply die; they were murdered.

Recall from Chapter 2 Rawls' distinction between burdened states and outlaw states, and Arendt's distinction between a deprivation of rights and a position of rightlessness. People whose state is temporarily unable to provide them with security are differently situated than those whose state denies them entitlement to security altogether. In the former case, a social contract continues to exist, though the state may be in default. By contrast, in the latter case, the law is nothing more than "a scheme of commands imposed by force" that "lacks the idea of social cooperation."[27]

Multiple meanings of membership

A second objection to the membership principle runs as follows: a critic may concede that persecuted people have a stronger claim to membership abroad than anyone else does, but argue that even persecuted people do not have a very strong claim. While they have been deprived of "membership" in their countries of origin, "membership" in that sense is very different from the surrogate membership they would receive in a state of refuge. The "membership" of which they have been deprived consists of civic standing in the most minimal sense: freedom from persecution. The "membership" they would receive consists of much more: rights of political participation; access to social insurance; and in some countries, access to advanced health care. One might argue that the logic of matching a remedy to the problem does not justify providing "full membership" to remedy the absence of "minimal membership." Instead, the objection continues, persecuted people should receive what they lack: legal and physical protection that ensures their freedom from persecution. And Western states extend that status to *all* persons within their territory, whether they are members or not.

There are several responses. First, the objection misses the expressive significance of granting full membership to persecuted people. Doing so dramatizes the host state's judgment that the state of origin's conduct toward the asylum seeker has been so reprehensible that the political relationship between the two has been sundered. Having been orphaned, the persecuted refugee now needs a new society that he or she can call home. Providing that person with only minimal membership would express that message much less clearly.

A second response, inspired by Arendt, is that we can safely count on the continued recognition of our entitlement to rights only as members of states.[28] And, in Western societies, membership means *full* membership, not a second-class status. Although "the Rights of Man ... had been defined as 'inalienable' because they were supposed to be independent of all governments ... it turned out that the moment human beings lacked their own government and had to fall back upon their minimum rights, no authority was left to protect them and no institution was willing to guarantee them."[29] The importance of full membership is especially visible today in the context of the war on terror, which governments have waged in part by subjecting aliens to scrutiny and regulation that, in some cases, would likely be illegal if applied to citizens.[30] Its importance is also evident when one considers that non-members are always liable to the revocation of permanent residence and deportation – even for the commission of minor offenses.[31] But asylees have no society to which they can be deported. The commission of a minor offense can thus render them effectively stateless.

A third response appeals to the liberal democratic norms of states of refuge, which cannot tolerate a permanent under-caste. The last twenty years have seen the steady erosion of political statuses other than full citizenship.[32] While the distinction between citizens and aliens still has legal force, it can be sustained intellectually only because an alien's presence is assumed to be temporary. For example, consider the fate of Germany's guest-worker program.[33] Once it became clear that guest workers had no intention of returning home, contrary to the terms of their invitation, the program became insupportable. A liberal democracy like Germany could not abide the creation of a permanent, disenfranchised laboring caste. The importation of guest workers was discontinued, and naturalization laws were revised to facilitate the political incorporation of guest workers already present. The same point could be made about the periodic amnesty of illegal immigrants in the United States. In light of Western political values, the creation of a permanent caste of non-citizen asylum recipients would be a retrograde step.

Humanitarian protection: its duration and scope

Should non-persecuted refugees also receive permanent protection?

The membership principle explains why asylum, the mode of refugee relief aimed at helping persecuted people, has traditionally given its recipients surrogate membership and not merely protection. That remedy matches the distinctive nature of the harm suffered by persecuted people, and it follows from the judgment of condemnation that

asylum expresses. But, notwithstanding the distinction between persecution and other types of harm, should states also grant surrogate
membership to non-Convention refugees who are given humanitarian
protection? Or does the membership principle require that membership
be given *only* to persecuted people? As mentioned above, Canada
provides surrogate membership not only to Convention refugees, but
also to other "persons in need of protection" – including people who
face a substantial risk of torture or an individualized risk to their lives
against which the state of origin is unable or unwilling to provide
protection (unless that risk is due to inadequate medical care).[34]

Canada deserves accolades for its generosity in offering surrogate
membership to non-persecuted refugees as well, but such generosity
goes beyond what the membership principle requires. Surrogate membership is costly: it entails a permanent commitment to the recipient, the
full integration of the recipient into the host society, and, accordingly,
entitles him or her to a more robust set of rights and benefits than
recipients of temporary protection. In a world with over 9 million
refugees and 5.5 million internally displaced persons, every refugee
policy dollar spent integrating refugees as members is a dollar not
spent helping refugees left behind. States are justified in choosing to
spread scarce resources broadly by offering remedies less costly than
membership to non-persecuted refugees who, after all, retain standing
as members in their states of origin and need only surrogate protection,
not surrogate membership.

If a state does choose, like Canada, to grant membership to both
persecuted people and to non-Convention refugees, it should be sure to
preserve a policy distinction between asylum, on the one hand, and
"humanitarian protection" given to non-Convention refugees, on the
other hand. Asylum would no longer clearly express an attitude of
criticism and condemnation toward the recipient's country of origin if
eligibility for asylum were extended beyond persecuted people. After all,
condemnation would be inappropriate for many of the harms remedied
by humanitarian protection. It is important for states to maintain
asylum as a distinctive, expressive mode of refugee assistance, and to
do so, it must be limited to persecuted people.

In practice, Canada's generosity is unusual. For the reasons discussed
above, states generally prefer temporary to permanent protection.
Although temporary protection is usually adequate to address the
needs of non-persecuted refugees, that principle has one caveat. At

some point, recipients of temporary protection should be able to overcome the presumption that they need protection only temporarily. The case of the tiny Caribbean island of Montserrat provides a good example. In 1995, the island's volcano erupted, forcing about 7,000 people – two-thirds of the island's inhabitants – to flee, and leaving two-thirds of the 77-square-mile island under ash. Most fled to Britain or other Caribbean islands, but 292 came to the United States, where they were granted temporary protected status that was extended year after year. Recent scientific estimates, however, indicate that volcanic activity in Montserrat is likely to continue for at least twenty more years, and possibly for centuries, making it impossible for Montserratians to safely return.[35] Surely temporary protection is an unsatisfactory solution for them. Their need for protection is anything but temporary. The same could be said of refugees from countries like Somalia, where civil war and chaos have ruled for nearly two decades, with no end in sight.

When refugees from burdened societies are unable to return home after years of "temporary" protection abroad, they should be able to adjust their status and receive permanent residence, lest the notion of temporary protection become a cruel fiction. The law might therefore allow (as the UK's does) adjustment to permanent residence after five years of temporary protection (particularly for families with children), if refugees from burdened societies can establish that repatriation continues to be unsafe.* Such a policy would recognize the importance of social connections that recipients of temporary protection develop in their place of refuge over many years, so that it would be unfair to ask them to leave. Perhaps even more importantly, the liberal democratic norms of Western host countries also demand that the possibility of adjustment be made available. Such norms are inconsistent with the continuing disenfranchisement of a group of people who, practically speaking, have become permanent residents.

This is an area in which current American law needs to be revised. Recipients of temporary protection in the United States currently may adjust their status to legal permanent residence only if they meet a series of onerous requirements. First, they must be continuously present in the

---

* Granting permanent residence to recipients of temporary protection who have been resident for five years will not dilute the expressive meaning of asylum, because the adjustment of status stems from an internal commitment to an anti-caste norm, not from a critical judgment about another state's practices.

United States for a period of ten years; second, they must have demonstrated "good moral character" during that time, and must not have been convicted of any designated crimes; and third, they must show that their removal would cause "exceptional and extremely unusual hardship" to a US citizen or permanent resident spouse, parent, or child.[36] The temporary protection statute also forbids the Senate from considering any bill that would allow recipients of temporary protection to become permanent residents without the support of a three-fifths supermajority.[37]

The Montserratians provide a good example of the pitfalls of this current approach. In July 2004, after they had spent seven years in the United States with temporary protected status,[38] the Department of Homeland Security told citizens of Montserrat to pack their bags: their temporary protected status was terminated, even though their island remained uninhabitable.[39] The Department of Homeland Security justified the termination with the following logic:

The volcanic activity causing the environmental disaster in Montserrat is not likely to cease in the foreseeable future. Therefore it no longer constitutes a temporary disruption of living conditions that temporarily prevents Montserrat from adequately handling the return of its nationals.[40]

In other words, temporary protection was revoked because the need for protection was no longer temporary. That is a travesty. A better approach would have replaced temporary protection with permanent residence, in recognition of the fact that Montserratians were unlikely to be able ever to return home and had already been in the United States seven years.[41] Somalis offer another example. They first received temporary protection in the United States in 1991. Since then, it has been extended fifteen times, each time for twelve- or eighteen-month periods.[42] Long ago, the United States should have offered the Somalis the chance to adjust their status to permanent residence in recognition of the social connections they have formed with their host society.

The scope of protection for non-Convention refugees

Finally, a word must be said about the breadth and mechanics of humanitarian protection for non-persecuted refugees, whether on a presumptively temporary basis (as in most countries) or on a permanent basis (as in Canada). In many countries, the scope of such humanitarian protection is surprisingly narrow. For example, the UK, in accordance with EU guidelines,[43] offers humanitarian protection to asylum seekers who face a "real risk" of torture, inhuman or degrading punishment, the death penalty, extralegal killing, or a "serious and individual threat to a civilian's life or person by reason of indiscriminate violence in situations of international or internal armed conflict."[44] These categories overlap to some extent with the persecution requirement; for example, victims of torture may often also be victims of persecution (and, according to the argument I offered in Chapter 3, they should *always* be so regarded). The main contribution of the UK's humanitarian protection is to offer shelter to non-persecuted victims of civil conflicts. But that leaves unprotected people who are exposed to other forms of violence (other than persecution) or displaced by environmental catastrophe or famine. From a humanitarian standpoint, the UK's "humanitarian protection" is far too narrow.

Some European states have additional refugee assistance programs to fill these gaps, but not all. The UK, for example, offers something called "discretionary leave to remain"; but, as the name suggests, it is entirely discretionary – there are no criteria laid out by statute or regulation – and it is invoked only in exceptional circumstances. Before 2003, the UK offered a form of relief called "exceptional leave to remain" which had a wider scope than "humanitarian protection," but it was eliminated when UK law was revised in accordance with EU guidelines. The Home Office explained that its elimination and replacement with "humanitarian protection" was intended to make Britain's refugee policy "more focussed."[45]

The narrow scope of humanitarian protection has placed expansive pressure on the meaning of "persecution." The term has been stretched to cover violence inflicted by private parties against which the state is unable to ensure protection. The result is that applicants are granted asylum even when there is no reason to condemn the state of origin. That expansion of the meaning of "persecution" muddies the expressive dimension of asylum.

By contrast to humanitarian protection in the UK, temporary protected status (TPS) in the United States is quite broad in scope. The Attorney General is authorized to grant TPS to aliens from a country or region experiencing "ongoing armed conflict" so that "requiring the return of aliens" to that area "would pose a serious threat to their personal safety"; to aliens for whom an "earthquake, flood, drought, epidemic, or other environmental disaster" has resulted in a "substantial, but temporary, disruption of living conditions"; and to aliens who are unable to "return[ ] to [their] state in safety" due to other "extraordinary and temporary conditions."[46]

However, TPS is narrower than the UK's humanitarian protection in two important respects. First, humanitarian protection can be claimed as an alternative to asylum by asylum seekers who arrive at a port of entry. By contrast, TPS is only available to people who were already present in the United States prior to a designated cut-off date. The purpose of the cut-off date is to prevent TPS from becoming an immigration magnet; but the effect is to make a refugee's claim to protection dependent on whether, and when, he or she managed to enter the United States. Otherwise qualified refugees who arrive after the cut-off date have no defense to removal, and, for those who have not yet arrived, TPS gives them no claim to admission.

Second, the UK's humanitarian protection involves an assessment of the specific harm to which a particular applicant is exposed. TPS, on the other hand, does not involve any individualized adjudication. Consequently, it is available only to refugees fleeing conditions that affect a large portion of a country's population. The Attorney General is authorized to designate entire countries or regions of countries as unsafe, and anyone from that area is eligible, provided that they were present in the United States before the cut-off date. The American approach is designed to address situations of mass influx, in which it would be either infeasible or inefficient to perform an individualized review. (The EU has a separate regime to govern situations of mass influx as well.[47]) But the consequence is to leave non-Convention refugees without any recourse when they are fleeing an individualized harm that would not warrant a state-wide designation. For example, recall from the Introduction the story of Angela, who was forced to flee Jamaica because the state could not effectively protect her from criminal gangs who sought to harm her. She would not be eligible for TPS in the United States. Her only hope would be to try to spin her case as an asylum claim – a phenomenon that, again, places expansive pressure on the definition of "persecution."

Canada's equivalent to "humanitarian protection" avoids the defects of both the American approach and the European approach. It is even broader in scope than TPS, covering applicants who face any individualized risk to their lives (other than disease) against which the state of origin is unable or unwilling to provide protection; and it can be claimed upon entry. At the same time, however, Canada's policy has a defect of its own: it does not distinguish clearly between asylum and humanitarian protection as different modes of refugee relief, one expressive and one palliative, designed to remedy different kinds of harm.

There is one limiting principle to the scope of humanitarian protection. Anyone who can receive help in his or her state of origin, or in camps along the border, ought to be helped there rather than abroad. Those caught in the cross-fire of armed conflict can sometimes remove themselves from battle areas without great risk of physical harm; and humanitarian relief aid is often (though certainly not always) made available to victims of famine or natural disaster. Call this the *in situ* principle: assistance abroad is reserved for those who cannot find help at home.[48] (The *in situ* principle applies to persecuted people as well, and explains the widely followed legal doctrine that one is ineligible for asylum if one could safely relocate within one's country of origin.[49] For example, people persecuted by regional or local authorities may find safety elsewhere in the state of origin.)

The *in situ* principle is appealing for several reasons. First, it is best for refugees themselves not to be forced abroad and thereby severed from their communities. In recognition of refugees' strong interest in minimizing their displacement, the UNHCR has recently stressed their "right to return." Second, preferring that refugees receive assistance at home recognizes that the state of origin is the primary guardian of its citizens. People have a strong claim for admission abroad only when their state (even with external assistance) is unable or unwilling to perform the role of guardian, much as public foster care is available only to children whose parents are unable or unwilling to provide for them.[50] Third, treating assistance abroad as a second-best, stop-gap measure recognizes the interest that other states have in controlling admission to their territories. The presumption in favor of such control should be overcome only when those seeking admission have no other reasonable option. Finally, it is often cheaper to provide *in situ* humanitarian relief than it is to support refugees in Western states; and, given limited budgets, we ought on balance to prefer more cost-effective forms of relief.

One important implication of the *in situ* principle is that bystander states must take seriously their duties to provide foreign aid and emergency relief to those whose basic rights are threatened and who are capable of receiving *in situ* assistance. If bystander states fail to do so, they become liable to those refugees' claims for admission.

Rights of integration

I have argued that, according to the membership principle, persecuted people are differently situated than victims of other sorts of harms. The former should be entitled to permanent residence and citizenship soon after arriving in a state of refuge; the latter need not be. Because asylum recipients are presumptively on the path to membership, they should be entitled to a wider array of rights and benefits than recipients of temporary protection. That is true for two reasons, one philosophical and one pragmatic. First, to deny basic rights of citizens – such as free movement and the right to earn[51] – to asylees who are to become citizens both offends liberal egalitarianism and frustrates a key function of asylum, which is to provide persecuted people with surrogate membership. Second, to deny asylees basic rights that foster their civic and social integration is foolish, because, as Joseph Carens has put it, "many of the rights and programs provided for refugees are simply wise economic investments that pay off in reduced social costs and higher social benefits down the road."[52]

Providing a lesser package of rights and benefits to those with temporary protection does not offend principles of liberal equality, because their civic standing is not at stake – they remain members elsewhere. Also, if their stay is expected to be temporary, the up-front costs of social welfare programs may be a poor investment. Thus, Carens is wrong to conclude that "[t]he question of what rights refugees deserve or need to live decent lives in the receiving country would appear to be independent of the relative strength of their eligibility for refugee status."[53] What is decent when given to a presumptive temporary sojourner may be offensive or unjust when given to a prospective member. The question of what rights refugees deserve or need to live decent lives must be answered relative to the kind of relief they can claim from their state of refuge.

The practice of many states reflects that principle: recipients of temporary protection have traditionally been eligible for fewer public benefits than asylees. In Denmark, Germany, the Netherlands, and Sweden, the former receive only a small allowance;[54] and the European Union directive on temporary protection (intended for situations of emergency mass influx) requires that member states ensure only "access to suitable accommodation," emergency medical care and "essential treatment of illness," and "necessary assistance in terms of social welfare and means of subsistence."[55] By contrast, EU member states must provide recipients of asylum (and subsidiary protection) with public benefits and medical care at the same level as that provided to nationals.[56] In the United States, recipients of TPS are ineligible for income support programs, while asylees have greater access to those programs than ordinary immigrants.[57] And in Australia, recipients of temporary protection visas have been given access only to emergency medical care.[58]

At the same time, the gap between the rights accorded to asylees and recipients of temporary protection should diminish as time passes and as the presumption of "temporariness" weakens. The policy in place in the Netherlands until 2002 offered an example of how integration rights can be phased in over a period of years. For the first two years, the Netherlands provided recipients of temporary protection only limited work authorization and limited eligibility for public relief, and it did not recognize a right to family reunification. In the third year, recipients of temporary protection were given full work authorization, and at the beginning of the fourth year, they could apply for family reunification.[59] (One might think that family reunification should have come earlier.) This "ascending scale of rights" recognizes that, "as the alien's tie grows stronger, so does the strength of his claim to an equal share" of the host state's resources.[60]

The optimal mix of refugee policy tools

I have argued that asylum plays a unique role among refugee policy tools by expressing condemnation toward persecuting regimes while also offering refugees a safe haven; and that, because of the nature of the harm that persecuted people suffer, asylum should offer its recipients not only protection but also surrogate membership. But, one might object, why should states continue to rely upon asylum in favor of other refugee policy tools that can help refugees in a more equitable or cost-effective manner?

Asylum is vulnerable to this objection on two fronts. First, asylum has a "proximity bias." It is available in Western states only to those who can make it out of their own country and travel to the West – often by traversing great distances at considerable risk and expense. This group is only a small subset of all those who are in need of membership abroad,[61] and may not be the most in need. States could instead replace asylum with overseas refugee resettlement programs, which identify needy refugees in the states or regions of origin and then transport them to states of refuge abroad. These programs are currently operated in significant numbers by the United States, Canada, and Australia.[62] In the United States, the basic eligibility requirements for this program are related to the requirements for asylum: applicants (typically referred to the program by a US Embassy, the UNHCR, or an NGO) must demonstrate a well-founded fear of persecution on account of race, religion, nationality, social group membership, or political opinion.[63] Alternatively, applicants can demonstrate that they are members of a group identified by the government as of "special humanitarian concern" due to the persecution of its members,[64] or, if from one of seventeen countries,[65] that they are the spouse, parent, or unmarried minor child of someone who has already received asylum or been admitted as a refugee.

Second, asylum has an "expatriate bias." Its locus of relief is within Western states of refuge rather than in refugees' states or regions of origin. But that is an extremely costly way to offer refuge. In 2007, the US Department of Health and Human Services spent close to $500 million to assist refugees in their transition to a new life in America; this sum does not include Medicaid, Transitional Assistance to Needy Families, or Supplementary Security Income.[66] In 2003, Britain spent more than $1.5 billion to support 93,000 asylum seekers.[67]

These sums could have been used to aid far more people if less were provided to each recipient. One can imagine, for instance, government-run camps that maintained conditions barely better than those to which refugees from the developing world were accustomed. Or, as some have suggested, one could imagine outsourcing asylum or temporary protection to developing countries where basic subsistence and physical security could be provided more cheaply than in the West.[68] If the ultimate goal of refugee policy is to save the most lives possible, how can asylum and humanitarian protection programs possibly be defended as against more cost-effective alternatives? I consider each of these objections in turn.

Proximity bias

Australia's refugee policy in recent years has been shaped in response to the problem of "proximity bias." The government has noted that asylum seekers often enter Australia without authorization and with the aid of people smugglers, and it describes such people as queue-jumpers who take away scarce refugee protection slots from more needy people who remain offshore. In response, Australia decided (until July 2008) to provide only temporary protection to refugees who arrived without authorization; by contrast, it provided immediate permanent protection to refugees it resettled from overseas. The bulk of its refugees fell into the latter category, and Australia adopted stringent measures – including the excision of certain islands from its "migration zone" and mandatory detention – to discourage onshore applications. As Philip Ruddock, the Australian Minister for Immigration in 2000, put it, "Every time someone who has the resources to pay people smugglers arrives unlawfully in Australia and is granted refugee status, a place is denied to someone else languishing in the most undesirable circumstances."[69] Accordingly, while "[s]ome countries choose to focus only on people who seek asylum in their territory," Australia (says a government report) "assist[s] people through resettlement" and "places great importance on the delivery of orderly durable solutions."[70]

While Australia's program was roundly criticized by observers,[71] it nonetheless poses a challenge: what can justify asylum's proximity bias? As Michael Walzer asks: "Why be concerned only with men and women actually on our territory who ask to remain, and not with men and women oppressed in their own countries who ask to come in? Why mark off the lucky or the aggressive, who have somehow managed to make their way across our borders, from all the others?"[72] Proximity seems to be "a morally arbitrary criterion for determining the responsibilities of states" with regard to refugees.[73] And a proximity bias infects not only asylum, but also humanitarian protection (whether temporary or permanent), which is also limited to those who manage to find their way abroad.

Two responses are possible. One can show that, although asylum's proximity bias introduces an element of moral arbitrariness, this arbitrariness is *not unfair*; or one can show that bias toward refugees at our border is *not morally arbitrary*.

Consider first an argument that asylum's proximity bias, though arbitrary, is not unfair. One could analogize the proximity bias to a lottery. Only some fraction of those who could claim asylum will win the lottery by making it across international borders to a country of asylum; but assuming that all have the same ex-ante expectation of winning, the proximity lottery would not systematically discriminate against any particular group of refugees.

But the premise of that argument is flawed: studies show that women, children, and the poor are systematically disadvantaged by the requirement that they leave their country in order to gain protection abroad.[74] Women and children are less mobile than men, and the poor are unable to afford smugglers whose services are increasingly necessary if one is to evade ever more stringent border controls in the West.

Next consider an argument that asylum's proximity bias is not morally arbitrary. To refuse protection to those at our borders, one could contend, "would require us to use force against helpless and desperate people."[75] We are thus differently situated with respect to refugees at our borders than we are with respect to refugees who remain a continent away. To deny admission to refugees at our border, and force them to return to countries to face serious harm, violates the injunction to "do no harm" and thus implicates us in having caused their plight.

That argument, however, trades on a distinction between actions and omissions, a controversial position in the philosophical literature.[76] It depends on thinking that turning away refugees at the border is morally worse than failing to come to their aid when they are further away, even though we could easily do the latter. Those who argue in favor of distinguishing between acts and omissions say that collapsing the distinction produces a moral theory that is impossibly burdensome: every person would be responsible for "the consequences of every possible course of action that we do not pursue."[77] Extending moral responsibility so far would not only be paralyzing, but also is at odds with common-sense intuitions regarding the scope of our duties to others. Those who argue against distinguishing between acts and omissions say in this context that "[i]f we take satisfaction in being too humane to deport someone seeking asylum while we continue to reject all applications from those in similar situations who have not made it to our shores, we are being hypocritical."[78] Their need for assistance is the same, and assuming that both groups can be helped at a similar cost, the duty to assist would be equally strong in both cases.

Even if asylum's proximity bias does unfairly benefit refugees who are strong enough, mobile enough, and rich enough to travel successfully to the West, there are nonetheless good practical reasons for maintaining asylum – provided that it is supplemented by other refugee assistance programs that help those refugees who are left behind. These reasons rest on the premise that any overseas resettlement program must have a numerical limit. The sheer number of refugees in the world – 9.2 million at the beginning of 2005, in addition to 5.4 million more internally displaced persons in need of humanitarian assistance[79] – requires rationing of some sort.

Proximity is the rationing device employed by asylum, and it sufficiently limits the number of asylum seekers so that states are able to make asylum available to all who qualify, without any numerical limitation. Overseas refugee resettlement programs would need to employ some other rationing device to limit the number of claimants to a manageable number, and numerical caps are likely to be an element of any such scheme. Currently, for example, the United States caps its program at 70,000 recipients annually. (One could imagine an uncapped overseas refugee resettlement program that rationed access by, say, wealth. If "processing fees" were set high enough, the program could be open to all who qualify. But the disadvantages of such an approach are obvious.)

Relying on proximity as a rationing device certainly has its disadvantages. States may give lip service to the principle while setting up barriers designed to prevent refugees from entering the state's territory where they could file an asylum claim; and refugees are encouraged to risk everything – their lives as well as their resources – to evade such barriers. But there are also significant dangers in relying solely on a capped admission program for refugee assistance.

First, politicians attempting to curry favor with domestic constituencies may reserve scarce slots for ethnic groups who do not have objectively strong claims for admission, let alone membership. Historically, this sort of hijacking has clearly marked US refugee policy. Of the 70,000 available slots in 2006, 15,000 were reserved for applicants from Europe and central Asia. Many of these were Jews, evangelical Christians, and Ukrainian Catholics from former Soviet republics. While these groups are still selected for overseas resettlement in numbers out of proportion to their need for membership abroad, only a decade ago the numbers were even more skewed. In 1998, out of a total of 83,000 worldwide refugee admissions slots, over 51,000 were reserved for people from Europe, many of them Jews from the former Soviet Union. Only 7,000 were reserved for Africans, by comparison.[80]

Because Jews from former Soviet republics typically would not meet the statutory requirements for eligibility as refugees, Congress passed the Lautenberg amendment to benefit them.[81] Initially adopted in 1989 and subsequently extended every year or two, the Lautenberg amendment was enacted in response to pressure from American Jewish groups concerned about an increase in denial rates from 16 percent to 37.2 percent between January and March 1989 for overseas refugee applications from Soviet Jews.[82] The amendment states that for purposes of eligibility for the overseas refugee program, Jews as well as evangelical Christians still resident in the former Soviet Union are presumed to face persecution on account of religion, and thus are eligible for overseas refugee visas. A similar presumption exists for active members of the Ukrainian Catholic Church or the Ukrainian Orthodox Church who reside in the former Soviet Union, as well as Iranian religious minorities and specified Vietnamese, Laotian, and Cambodian groups. An amendment that overwhelmingly passed the House in 1989 would have extended this presumption to Polish nationals as well.[83] Over 35 percent of those who received refugee visas between 1989 and 2004 benefited from the Lautenberg presumption,[84] and the religious minorities favored by that presumption still "constitute a significant portion of the caseload" from Europe and central Asia.[85]

Second, politicians may try to reduce the caps or pressure refugee programs to let slots go unfilled for reasons of domestic politics. For example, the United States has reduced its refugee admissions cap from 231,700 in 1980 to 142,000 in 1992 to just 70,000 in 2007.[86] And concerns over security since September 2001 have dramatically increased the time required to process refugee applications abroad. As a result, only 28,422 refugees actually arrived in the United States in 2003, substantially below the ceiling.[87] This number has increased only slightly in the last several years; in 2006, 41,277 refugees actually arrived, still well below the ceiling of 70,000.[88]

Asylum, by contrast, has traditionally been open-ended, and, outside Australia, has remained so. It is a striking fact that, despite the increase in asylum applications over the past twenty years, states generally have not considered placing a cap on asylum.[89] All those who manage to reach the borders of a country of refuge can apply, and they can remain in that country while their applications are being processed (albeit sometimes in detention). In part, that is because states have an international legal obligation (called "non-refoulement") not to return persecuted people to territories where their lives or freedom would be threatened for reasons of race, religion, nationality, membership of a particular social group, or political opinion.[90] That legal obligation has no numerical limit. States have thus chosen to reduce the number of asylum applications in other ways, such as off-shore interdiction, carrier sanctions, and visa requirements, that less obviously run afoul of their rhetorical commitment to the concept of asylum and the legal duty of non-refoulement. There is no corresponding legal obligation to admit refugees who remain overseas.

Asylum thus remains an important refugee policy tool despite its proximity bias. The unfairness of favoring those who manage to make it to the borders of a country of refuge is mitigated by the importance of maintaining a form of refugee relief that is available to all who qualify. The possibility of asylum serves as a guarantee to refugees that there will always be a place in the world to which they can flee.

However, asylum should not be the only avenue through which refugees can gain admittance; an overseas refugee resettlement program also makes an important contribution to refugee policy. States could cap their overseas resettlement programs so that the number admitted under the cap, combined with the expected number of recipients of asylum and humanitarian protection, would fall within the state's absorptive capacity. Australia has done something like this: since 1996, it has linked its asylum program with its overseas refugee resettlement program, so that every asylum admission fills a spot that otherwise would have been allocated to overseas resettlement.[91]

The total number of refugees that a state can reasonably absorb is, of course, difficult to fix with any certainty, but among the factors to consider are: the density of population in the receiving state; the level of unemployment; the sectoral dislocation expected from refugee admissions; the availability of natural resources in the receiving state; the number of needy foreigners it has already absorbed; the expected cultural and environmental impact of admissions; the fiscal impact of providing for the subsistence needs of admitted refugees; the likelihood of integration of a given group of admitted refugees; and the fragility of political support for admission, as well as for other forms of foreign assistance. The costs of refugee admission and integration are also rarely diffused evenly across an entire population. More often, particular localities bear the brunt of the burden, as refugees tend to settle in geographic proximity to compatriots or in areas more welcoming to foreigners.[92]

The variables just outlined will obviously fluctuate over time and across refugee groups. For example, some groups of refugees will be better able to integrate, or will impose less of an economic hardship, because their skill profile better complements the national economy. Some refugee groups may also enjoy greater political support than others. Matthew Gibney has written, for instance, of the remarkable support among Europeans for assistance to Bosnian and Kosovar refugees. Over 100,000 refugees from Macedonia were resettled in Europe, and many Europeans even offered to take Kosovars into their homes.[93] When greater than usual political support for refugee assistance exists, the duty to provide assistance becomes more demanding.

Secondary costs of refugee admission must also be considered. The admission of refugees today can generate even greater demand for admission tomorrow by opening up new channels of chain migration, multiplying the ultimate number of newcomers who result from a single admission. States must be aware that once immigration flows begin, they are often hard to control. As a result, Matthew Gibney has written, "[f]aced with the real and unremitting uncertainties of practice, no state should risk going right up to the brink of social disharmony, for instance. The poor record of states in controlling entrance flows once they have started suggests that few states can be confident of their ability to halt refugee flows just at the edge of imminent disaster."[94]

Still, international comparison can serve as a valuable guide in determining a state's absorptive capacity. For example, the United States can certainly afford to take in more than 120,000 refugees and asylees each year. The total number of refugees and asylum seekers in the United States at the end of 2004 was 684,564, according to the UNHCR. (There were 420,854 refugees and 263,710 asylum seekers.) This number is high compared to other countries in absolute terms, but relative to the size of the US population, it is quite low. The United States hosted only about one refugee or asylum seeker per 432 residents, compared to ratios of 1:89 in Sweden, 1:86 in Germany, and 1:82 in Denmark. Developing countries shoulder an even greater burden, despite their limited resources. For example, Iran and Zambia each hosted one refugee for every sixty-five residents, and in Tanzania, the ratio is 1:61.[95]

Expatriate bias

Perhaps the harder question is why states should continue to offer refuge within their borders – whether in the form of asylum, humanitarian protection, or overseas refugee resettlement – instead of devoting greater resources to temporary protection in the developing world, relief aid to refugees who remain in or near their states of origin, and development assistance to ameliorate the root causes of refugee flows.

In 2003, Western states spent more than $10 billion administering their asylum programs.[96] By contrast, the UNHCR's entire 2003 budget, meant to provide assistance to over 20 million refugees and internally displaced persons, was only $1.17 billion.[97] Imagine what the UNHCR could have accomplished with a budget ten times as large.

Along these lines, scholars James Hathaway, Alexander Neve, and Peter Schuck have argued for replacing asylum programs in Western states with "solution-oriented" temporary protection programs located in refugees' regions of origin.[98] The programs would be funded and monitored by Western states to ensure that refugees have adequate living standards and receive the protection they need; but these goods could be provided much more cheaply in, say, Libya than in London. Much can be said in favor of these proposals. From the standpoint of policymakers, who must decide how to allocate scarce refugee policy resources among the various tools in the refugee policy toolkit in a way that will maximize lives saved, asylum's expatriate bias seems perverse.

Ultimately, the response to this objection – like the response to the "proximity bias" objection – is practical in nature. It may be that refugees on the whole are better off with a numerically unlimited asylum program, supplemented by other refugee programs, than they would be with other refugee policies alone. In part, this is because of the like-lihood of political manipulation and the reality of downward budgetary pressures. In the United States, for example, foreign aid is perpetually unpopular; its recipients, after all, have no electoral influence. It is dangerous to place refugees at the mercy of politicians who like to cut costs without offending their constituents and can do so without violat-ing any international legal obligation; better to leave undisturbed the settled norm of a right to asylum for persecuted people. As Carens has observed: "It is easier to dismantle institutions than to create them ... In seeking to advance the interests of refugees and other needy people, we should be careful not to undermine the legitimacy of one of the few institutions that offer them any sort of protection and hope, however limited and inadequate it may be in many respects."[99] For that reason, asylum has ongoing importance despite its expatriate bias.

Conclusion

Appreciating the role of asylum in refugee policy requires understand-ing its place in the refugee policy toolkit. Unlike other refugee policy tools, it is expressive rather than palliative: it directs condemnation at the state responsible for persecution. That posture of condemnation reflects the distinctive nature of the harm suffered by persecuted people. By virtue of officially-sanctioned harm, they have been effectively expelled from membership in their states of origin. Surrogate membership, the remedy traditionally provided by asylum, matches the political harm suffered by persecuted people, and it dramatizes the judgment that the conduct of the state of origin is so reprehensible as to have broken the political bonds between that state and its victim. The needs of non-persecuted refugees, who remain members in their states of origin, can be addressed through other refugee policy tools, such as humanitarian protection (either on a temporary or permanent basis), which are palliative rather than expressive.

One might fairly question whether states should continue to offer asylum in lieu of other, more cost-effective forms of refugee protection – despite asylum's expressive significance. Because asylum is much more expensive than *in situ* humanitarian aid, due to the cost of individuated determination hearings and the provision of social services in an industrialized economy, a policymaker seeking to maximize the number of lives saved might sensibly advocate a blend of refugee policy tools tilted away from asylum and toward humanitarian relief and protection in refugees' regions of origin. For states in which asylum is the primary commitment to refugee relief, that would amount to a radical shift in priorities.

But even though asylum is an imperfect solution to the problems of refugees, it may nonetheless be the best solution in what is, after all, an imperfect world. Refugees on the whole may be better served in the long run by the institution of asylum, which at least guarantees refuge to persecuted people, than by discarding asylum in favor of greater spending on foreign aid. The latter may be more cost-effective, but budgets may be slowly chipped away over time, leaving refugees with nothing in the end.

In all events, the argument for changing priorities within *refugee* policy – away from asylum and toward *in situ* aid – should not be confused with an argument for changing priorities within *asylum* policy. Humanitarians who contend that the West ought to provide relief to a wider group of refugees than the persecution requirement permits should argue for a renewed commitment to policy tools other than asylum, like humanitarian protection and *in situ* aid, not for expanding asylum's scope to encompass non-persecuted people.

Notes

1. 8 U.S.C. section 1159(b).
2. Immigration and Refugee Protection Act (2001, c. 27), section 21(2); Citizenship Act (R.S., 1985, c. C-29), section 5(1).
3. Australian Citizenship Act of 2007 (Act No. 20 of 2007), sections 5(1), 22(1).
4. 8 U.S.C. section 1254a(a)–(c), (h); 8 U.S.C. section 1229b(b)(1).
5. EU Temporary Protection Directive, Council Directive 2001/55/EC of July 20, 2001 on minimum standards for giving temporary protection in the event of a mass influx of displaced persons and on measures promoting a balance of efforts between member states in receiving such persons and bearing the consequences thereof, arts. 4, 6.
6. Home Office, "Leave to Remain," www.bia.homeoffice.gov.uk/asylum/outcomes/successfulapplications/leavetoremain/ (last visited April 2, 2008).
7. Matthew J. Gibney, "Between Control and Humanitarianism: Temporary Protection in Contemporary Europe," *Georgetown Immigration Law Journal*, 14 (2000), p. 690.
8. James C. Hathaway and R. Alexander Neve, "Making International Refugee Law Relevant Again: A Proposal for Collectivized and Solution-Oriented Protection," *Harvard Human Rights Journal*, 10 (1997), p. 115; Peter Schuck, "Refugee Burden-Sharing: A Modest Proposal," in Schuck (ed.), *Citizens, Strangers, and In-Betweens* (Boulder, CO: Westview Press, 1996), pp. 285, 297. For a response, see Deborah E. Anker *et al.*, "Crisis and Cure: A Reply to Hathaway/Neve and Schuck," *Harvard Human Rights Journal*, 11 (1997), p. 295.
9. This statement of the membership principle differs in an important way from the membership principle proposed by Michael Walzer in *Spheres of Justice* (New York: Basic Books, 1983), pp. 48–9. Walzer recognized that a need for membership can give rise to a claim for admission, but he failed to recognize that a need for protection might as well. He therefore missed the distinction between asylum – which addresses the former need – and other forms of refugee protection, such as temporary protection, which address the latter need.
10. Australian Government, Dept. of Immigration and Citizenship, Fact Sheet 64, "Temporary Protection Visas."
11. EU Qualifications Directive, Council Directive 2004/83/EC of April 29, 2004 on minimum standards for the qualification and status of third country nationals or stateless persons as refugees or as persons who otherwise need international protection and the content of the protection granted, art. 24.

12. Immigration and Nationality Act section 209(b), 8 U.S.C. section 1159 (b) (2000).
13. REAL ID Act, Pub. L. 109-13, Div. B, Title I, sections 101(g)(1)(B)(i), 119 Stat. 305 (May 11, 2005), codified at 8 U.S.C. section 1159(b).
14. 8 C.F.R. section 1208.13(b)(1).
15. 8 C.F.R. section 1208.13(b)(1)(iii)(A).
16. *Matter of Chen*, 20 I. & N. Dec. 16, 20 (BIA 1989).
17. *Matter of B –*, 21 I. & N. Dec. 66, 71–2 (BIA 1995).
18. UNHCR, *Handbook on Procedures and Criteria for Determining Refugee Status Under the 1951 Convention and the 1967 Protocol Relating to the Status of Refugees*, UN Doc. HCR/PRO/4 (1979), revised 1992, paragraph 136.
19. *Skalak v. INS*, 944 F.2d 364, 365 (7th Cir. 1991). See also *Baka v. INS*, 963 F.2d 1376, 1379 (10th Cir. 1992).
20. See Daniel Jonah Goldhagen, *Hitler's Willing Executioners: Ordinary Germans and the Holocaust* (New York: Knopf, 1996).
21. Andrew Shacknove, "Who is a Refugee?," *Ethics*, 95 (1985), pp. 277–8.
22. Ibid., p. 281 n. 18.
23. Shacknove is careful to note that his argument only pertains to the "concept" of the refugee, and stops short of arguing that other states have any particular obligation to refugees. But if Shacknove is right that the persecuted are similarly situated to other refugees, there is no justification for treating them differently for purposes of asylum law. It follows from Shacknove's argument that if we offer asylum to persecuted people, then we should offer it to other refugees as well.
24. Shacknove resists this conclusion, distinguishing between a threat to basic needs caused by human malice or negligence, on the one hand, and by nature, on the other hand: "to the extent that a life-threatening situation occurs *because of human actions rather than natural causes*, the state has left unfulfilled its basic duty to protect the citizen from the actions of others. All other human rights are meaningless when starvation results *from the neglect or malice* of the local regime." Shacknove, "Who Is a Refugee?," p. 280 (emphasis added). But a less faint-hearted humanitarian may be unwilling to make Shacknove's concession.
25. Ibid., p. 277.
26. Quoted in David Rieff, *A Bed for the Night: Humanitarianism in Crisis* (New York: Simon & Schuster, 2002), p. 75.
27. John Rawls, *Law of Peoples* (Cambridge, MA: Harvard University Press, 1999), p. 65.
28. On this account, there is nothing that *conceptually* links the right to have rights with a right to membership. The link is made as a matter of

practical judgment: "*it is much wiser* to rely on an 'entailed inheritance' of rights which one transmits to one's children like life itself, and to claim one's rights to be the 'rights of an Englishman' rather than the inalienable rights of man." Hannah Arendt, *Origins of Totalitarianism* (San Diego, CA: Harcourt, Brace, 1973), p. 299 (emphasis added).

29. Ibid., pp. 291–2. See also Michael Ignatieff, *Human Rights as Politics and Idolatry* (Princeton University Press, 2001), p. 80, arguing that "we do not build foundations on human nature but on human history, on what we know is likely to happen when human beings do not have the protection of rights." Thanks to Dana Villa for drawing this connection.

30. Examples include prolonged administrative detention of immigrants, special registration of immigrants from designated countries, and the criminalization of "material support" – which may include membership – of foreign terrorist organizations. See David Cole, *Enemy Aliens* (New York: Free Press, 2003), and Karen C. Tumlin, "Suspect First: How Terrorism Policy is Reshaping Immigration Policy," *California Law Review*, 92 (2004), p. 1173.

31. See Nancy Morawetz, "Understanding the Impact of the 1996 Deportation Laws and the Limited Scope of Proposed Reforms," *Harvard Law Review*, 113 (2000), p. 1936.

32. See Peter Schuck, "The Devaluation of American Citizenship" in Schuck (ed.), *Citizens, Strangers, and In-Betweens* (Boulder, CO: Westview Press, 1998), pp. 163–75; David Jacobson, *Rights Across Borders* (Baltimore, MD: Johns Hopkins Press, 1996).

33. On guest workers in Europe generally, see Jacobson, *Rights Across Borders*, and Yasemin Soysal, *Limits of Citizenship* (University of Chicago Press, 1994).

34. Immigration and Refugee Protection Act (2001 ch. 27) section 97(1).

35. Nina Bernstein, "U.S. is Ending Haven for Those Fleeing a Volcano," *New York Times*, August 9, 2004, p. A-1.

36. 8 U.S.C. section 1229b(b)(1)(A)–(D).

37. 8 U.S.C. section 1254a(h).

38. Citizens of Montserrat were first designated as eligible for TPS on August 28, 1997. Designation of Montserrat Under Temporary Protected Status, 62 Fed. Reg. 45,685 (August 28, 1997).

39. Termination of the Designation of Montserrat Under the Temporary Protected Status Program, 69 Fed. Reg. 40,642 (July 6, 2004) (effective February 27, 2005).

40. Bernstein, "U.S. is Ending Haven," p. A-1.

41. The US contended that the Montserratians could have gone somewhere else: Britain. Montserrat is a British overseas territory. Indeed, Britain did resettle many Montserratians; and, as sovereign over the island, it had

primary responsibility for their well-being. But, counterfactually, if Britain had refused to discharge its responsibility, the United States would have been wrong to force the islanders to leave.

42. Extension of the Designation of Temporary Protected Status for Somalia; Automatic Extension of Employment Authorization Documentation for Somalia TPS Beneficiaries, 71 Fed. Reg. 42,653 (July 27, 2006).

43. EU Qualifications Directive, art. 15.

44. UK Immigration Rules, section 339C.

45. Home Office, "Humanitarian Protection and Discretionary Leave," APU notice issued April 1, 2003, www.bia.homeoffice.gov.uk/sitecontent/ documents/policyandlaw/asylumpolicyinstructions/ (last visited April 3, 2008).

46. 8 U.S.C. section 1254a(b).

47. See EU Temporary Protection Directive.

48. See Michael Walzer, "The Distribution of Membership" in Peter G. Brown and Henry Shue (eds.), *Boundaries: National Autonomy and its Limits* (Totowa, NJ: Rowman & Littlefield, 1981); Joseph H. Carens, "The Philosopher and the Policymaker: Two Perspectives on the Ethics of Immigration with Special Attention to the Problem of Restricting Asylum" in Kay Hailbronner *et al.* (eds.), *Immigration Admissions: The Search for Workable Policies in Germany and the United States* (Providence, RI: Berghahn Books, 1997), p. 14; Aristide R. Zolberg, Astri Suhrke, and Sergio Aguayo, *Escape From Violence* (New York: Oxford University Press, 1989), pp. 33, 289.

49. For a discussion, see Hathaway, *Law of Refugee Status*, p. 133.

50. Joseph H. Carens, "States and Refugees: A Normative Analysis" in Howard Adelman (ed.), *Refugee Policy: Canada and the United States* (Toronto: York Lanes Press, 1991), pp. 18–29.

51. See Judith N. Shklar, *American Citizenship* (Cambridge, MA: Harvard University Press, 1991), arguing that the right to earn is at the core of what it means to be an American citizen.

52. Carens, "The Philosopher," p. 19.

53. Ibid.

54. James C. Hathaway, *The Rights of Refugees Under International Law* (Cambridge University Press, 2005), p. 805.

55. EU Temporary Protection Directive, art. 13.

56. EU Qualifications Directive, arts. 28–9.

57. The Welfare Reform Act of 1996 exempted asylees and certain others from the five-year bar on federal means-tested public benefits that applies to immigrants generally. 8 U.S.C. section 1613(b).

58. Hathaway, *The Rights of Refugees*, p. 805.

59. Matthew J. Gibney, "Between Control and Humanitarianism: Temporary Protection in Contemporary Europe," *Georgetown Immigration Law Journal*, 14 (2000), p. 698. The policy was changed in 2002 because it had the effect of encouraging litigation by recipients of temporary protection who wished to upgrade their status to asylum recipient, in order to receive greater benefits. See US Committee for Refugees, "Country Report – The Netherlands," *World Refugee Survey 2002* (Washington, DC: US Committee for Refugees, 2002).

60. *Johnson* v. *Eisentrager*, 339 U.S. 763, 770 (1950); *Mathews* v. *Diaz*, 426 U.S. 67, 80 (1976).

61. Zolberg *et al.* admit as much when they answer the objection that "resource-rich countries of the North would not want to relieve famine or massive poverty in the South by means of a large-scale relocation of people." The North need not worry, they say, because "the most needy victims of economic violence usually do not become intercontinental refugees ..." Zolberg *et al.*, *Escape From Violence*, pp. 270–1.

62. Together, these three countries represent 86 percent of overseas resettlement. Small numbers of refugees were resettled by New Zealand, Norway, Sweden, Denmark, Finland, the Netherlands, Ireland and the UK. US Department of State, "Proposed Refugee Admissions for FY 2008 – Report to the Congress" (2007), p. 3, www.state.gov/documents/organization/91978.pdf (last visited March 2, 2008).

63. 8 U.S.C. section 1101(a)(42)(A).

64. For fiscal year 2008, these groups included Jews, evangelical Christians, and Ukrainian Catholic and Orthodox religious activists in the former Soviet Union, certain Cubans and Vietnamese, Burmese in Thailand and Malaysia, Bhutanese in Nepal, Sudanese Darfurians living in Iraq, Iranian religious minorities, and Burundians in Tanzania. US Department of State, "Proposed Refugee Admissions for FY 2008," pp. 10–11.

65. These were, as of fiscal year 2008, Afghanistan, Burma, Burundi, Colombia, Congo-Brazzaville, Cuba, Democratic Republic of the Congo, Ethiopia, Eritrea, Haiti, Iran, Iraq, North Korea, Rwanda, Somalia, Sudan, and Uzbekistan. Ibid., pp. 12–13.

66. Ibid., p. 56, table VIII.

67. Alan Travis, "Asylum Service Criticised," *The Guardian* (UK), July 16, 2003.

68. Hathaway and Neve, "Making International Refugee Law Relevant Again," p. 115; Schuck, "Refugee Burden-Sharing," pp. 285, 297.

69. Quoted in Catherine Skulan, "Australia's Mandatory Detention of 'Unauthorized' Asylum Seekers: History, Politics and Analysis Under International Law," *Georgetown Immigration Law Journal*, 21 (2006), p. 82.

70. Australian Government, "Refugee and Humanitarian Issues: Australia's Response" (2005), p. 10, www.immi.gov.au/refugee/_pdf/refhumiss-fullv2.pdf (last visited April 3, 2008).

71. See, e.g., Skulan, "Australia's Mandatory Detention"; Human Rights Watch, "Human Rights Watch Commentary on Australia's Temporary Protection Visas for Refugees," www.hrw.org/backgrounder/refugees/australia051303.htm (last visited April 8, 2008).

72. Walzer, *Spheres of Justice*, p. 51. See also Peter Singer and Renata Singer, "The Ethics of Refugee Policy" in Mark Gibney (ed.), *Open Borders? Closed Societies? The Ethical and Political Issues* (New York: Greenwood Press, 1988), p. 119.

73. Matthew J. Gibney, "Asylum and the Principle of Proximity," *Ethics, Place, and Environment*, 3 (2000), p. 314.

74. See: John Morrison and Beth Crosland, "The Trafficking and Smuggling of Refugees: the End Game in European Asylum Policy?" (UNCHR New Issues in Refugee Research Working Paper No. 39, 2001), p. 29. Most inhabitants of refugee camps are women and children, but most asylum seekers are men. For a discussion, see Patricia Tuitt, "Rethinking the Refugee Concept" in Frances Nicholson and Patrick Twomey (eds.), *Refugee Rights and Realities* (Cambridge University Press, 1999), p. 106.

75. Walzer, *Spheres of Justice*, p. 51. See also Matthew J. Gibney, "Liberal Democratic States and Responsibilities to Refugees," *American Political Science Review*, 93 (1999), p. 176, referring to the existence of "a connection between the needy claimant and the state" in cases where "the person in desperate need is inside or at the borders of the state"; and Joseph H. Carens, "Who Should Get In? The Ethics of Immigration Admissions," *Ethics and International Affairs*, 17 (2003), p. 101, arguing that "[w]hat gives asylum seekers a vital moral claim ... is the fact that their arrival involves the state directly and immediately in their fate ... Those seeking to harm them could not do so if the destination state did not return them. That means that the moral responsibility for what happens to them is greater."

76. For a good collection on the act/omission distinction, see Bonnie Steinbock and Alastair Norcross (eds.), *Killing and Letting Die*, 2nd edn. (New York: Fordham University Press, 1994).

77. Carens, "Who Should Get In?," p. 101.

78. Singer and Singer, "The Ethics of Refugee Policy," p. 120.

79. UNHCR, *State of the World's Refugees 2006: Human Displacement in the New Millennium* (New York: Oxford University Press, 2006), p. 10.

80. T. Alexander Aleinikoff, David A. Martin, and Hiroshi Motomura, *Immigration and Citizenship: Process and Policy*, 4th edn. (St. Paul, MN: West Group, 1998), p. 1003.

81. Pub. L. 101-167 section 599D(b)(2)(A), 103 Stat. 1195, 1261 (1989), as amended.

82. Norman Zucker and Naomi Flink Zucker, *Desperate Crossings* (Armonk, NY: M. E. Sharpe, 1996), p. 38. See also Kathleen Newland, "The Impact of U.S. Refugee Policies on U.S. Foreign Policy: A Case of the Tail Wagging the Dog?" in Michael S. Teitelbaum and Myron Weiner (eds.), *Threatened Peoples, Threatened Borders* (New York: W. W. Norton, 1995), p. 207.

83. Aleinikoff *et al.*, *Immigration and Citizenship*, p. 1010.

84. US Department of State, "Proposed Refugee Admissions for FY 2005: Report to the Congress" (2004), p. 26, www.state.gov/documents/organization/36228.pdf.

85. US Department of State, "Proposed Refugee Admissions for FY 2008," p. 36.

86. Aleinikoff *et al.*, *Immigration and Citizenship*, p. 1005.

87. US Department of State, "Proposed Refugee Admissions for FY 2005," p. 5.

88. US Department of State, "Proposed Refugee Admissions for FY 2008," p. 4.

89. A cap on asylum was proposed by British Tory leader Michael Howard. See "Q & A: Tory Immigration Plans," *BBC News*, January 24, 2005, www.news.bbc.co.uk/1/hi/uk_politics/4199993.stm (last visited April 8, 2008).

90. See UN Convention Relating to the Status of Refugees, July 28, 1951, 19 U.S.T. 6259, 189 U.N.T.S. 137, at art. 33.

91. Skulan, "Australia's Mandatory Detention," p. 79. Australia's linkage between overseas resettlement slots and asylum grants is problematic in at least one way: Australia sets an overall cap for total refugee admissions, so that asylum – as a subset of this total – is also capped. If states are to link these two programs, the better approach is to leave asylum open-ended, and to adjust the cap for refugee resettlement in light of the expected asylum admissions. This would ensure that asylum would remain available to all those who could claim it, in accordance with states' non-refoulement obligations under art. 33 of the UN Refugee Convention and Protocol.

92. For a discussion of some of these factors, see Gibney, "Liberal Democratic States," pp. 176–7.

93. Matthew J. Gibney, "The State of Asylum: Democratization, Judicialization and Evolution of Refugee Policy in Europe" (UNHCR New Issues in Refugee Research Working Paper No. 50, October 2001), p. 8; Matthew J. Gibney, "Kosovo and Beyond: Popular and Unpopular Refugees," *Forced Migration Review*, 5 (September 1999), pp. 28–30.

94. Gibney, "Liberal Democratic States," p. 175.
95. UNHCR, *The State of the World's Refugees 2006: Human Displacement in the New Millennium* (New York: Oxford University Press, 2006), Annex 2; Central Intelligence Agency, *CIA World Factbook* (2005) (for populations).
96. "A Strange Sort of Sanctuary," *Economist*, March 15, 2003, p. 50.
97. UNHCR, "UNHCR Global Report 2003," pp. 30, 33, www.unhcr.org/publ/PUBL/40c6d74f0.pdf (last visited March 1, 2008).
98. Hathaway and Neve, "Making International Refugee Law Relevant Again," p. 148; Schuck, "Refugee Burden-Sharing," p. 297.
99. Joseph H. Carens, "Refugees and the Limits of Obligation," *Public Affairs Quarterly*, 6 (1992), p. 38.

6 | Restrictions on Access to Asylum

The Introduction identified two trends that have marked asylum policy over the last fifteen years. The first is the broadening of the substantive grounds for asylum eligibility. Court decisions have granted asylum to many classes of applicants who historically have been excluded – including those fleeing ethnic conflict, domestic violence, and abusive cultural practices like female genital mutilation. Those in support of a humanitarian approach to asylum have advocated further extending the grounds for eligibility beyond those fleeing persecution, to encompass people in need of protection from other sorts of harms, like famine, environmental catastrophe, generalized violence, and even extreme poverty. The bulk of this book has argued that there are good reasons – both theoretical and practical – for preserving asylum's traditional focus on assisting persecuted people, as opposed to other needy people who can be assisted through other types of refugee policy.

The second trend of the last fifteen years has been increasingly draconian measures that have made it difficult for would-be asylum seekers to file their claims. These include, as we shall see, the erection of barriers designed to make it more difficult for asylum seekers to enter the territory of an asylum state; the imposition of a variety of procedural rules that make it more difficult for asylum seekers to apply for asylum if they are able to enter the territory of an asylum state; and the denial of benefits and the use of detention to further discourage would-be applicants from making claims.

It is possible that states adopted these policies out of hostility to refugees, in the face of a sharp increase in the total number of asylum applications filed in the West. Between 1978 and 1992, new applications for asylum in industrialized countries exploded nearly twenty-fold, from roughly 45,000 to over 850,000.[1] The surge in numbers led to the public perception that Western states had lost control of their borders, and, in reaction, states adopted policies that reasserted authority to regulate admission to their territories. Germany – faced with an influx of hundreds of thousands of refugees from the Balkan wars in the early 1990s – was among the first states to enact procedural barriers to filing an asylum application, amending its constitution in 1993 to exclude from asylum those entering Germany via a third country that would have provided asylum. In the United States, asylum applications grew from 16,622 in 1985 to a peak of 149,065 one decade later.[2] In 1996, the United States enacted legislation that contained a variety of mechanisms making it more difficult to file an asylum claim. In the United Kingdom, asylum applications continued to rise into the new millennium, from about 37,000 in 1996 to over 103,000 in 2002.[3] Shortly afterward, the UK, too, adopted a raft of measures designed to prevent and discourage asylum applications.

But the rising number of applicants does not alone tell the full story. Although Western publics are hostile to asylum seekers, there remains significant support for the principle of asylum for those facing political persecution. In Britain, for example, 77 percent of respondents in a 2006 poll thought the UK should accept fewer asylum seekers, and in a 2003 poll, 80 percent agreed that the "problem of asylum seekers is out of control."[4] Yet in 2003, 45 percent agreed with the statement that "[a]sylum seekers who are genuinely fleeing persecution should be made welcome in Britain, even if they have arrived here illegally." (The number dropped to 39 percent in 2004.)[5] And in 1997, just over half of Europeans thought that the "right to asylum because of political persecution" should be respected in "all circumstances."[6] Western publics may have wanted to reassert control over their borders, but many also wanted to respect the tradition of granting asylum to the persecuted.

The various restrictive measures enacted over the last fifteen years can thus be explained as a response to a genuine policy dilemma: how to remain open to persecuted people seeking asylum, while at the same time preventing that loophole from unraveling otherwise restrictive immigration policies. Asylum is one of the few ways that migrants from the developing world can establish a legal presence within the West. Unless such migrants possess special skills, have large sums of money to invest, or have close relatives already living in the West, the ordinary avenues of immigration are closed to them, and asylum is the only hope they have of gaining legal status. That creates very strong incentives for "economic migrants" to submit fraudulent or bad faith asylum applications. As one indication of this phenomenon, it is striking

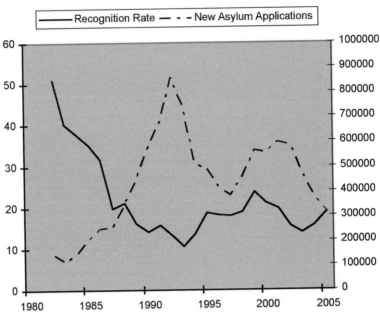

Figure 6.1. Convention recognition rates in the first instance vs. number of new asylum applications in industrialized countries, 1982–2005[7]

that, as the number of applications has risen, grant rates have declined – even though the substantive grounds for eligibility have widened. Merely filing an application gives the applicant a reprieve from deportation while the application is pending and, in many places, the right to work or collect welfare benefits. Also, there is always the possibility that a fraudulent claim will nonetheless be granted (see Figure 6.1, above).

While Western publics may remain committed to granting asylum to those fleeing persecution, they are unwilling to allow this exception to immigration controls to be exploited by those who simply wish to gain access to Western labor markets and welfare programs. The perception that the asylum system is rife with abuse has most recently become a political flashpoint in Britain, which received 103,000 asylum seekers in 2002, more than any other industrialized country and up over 50 percent from 1999.[8] In a 2004 poll, 85 percent of Britons thought that the government could "do more" to "to ensure Britain is not seen as a soft touch for bogus asylum seekers."[9] In 2003, 67 percent thought a "small minority" – less than a quarter – of asylum seekers were "genuinely fleeing persecution."[10] And in a 2002 poll, 43 percent of

Britons thought that asylum seekers sought refuge in Britain for economic reasons or to look for work, up from 11 percent in 1997.[11] In 2004, Britain granted asylum only to 4 percent of applicants; another 8 percent were given an alternative form of protection.[12] Of course, not all of the 88 percent of asylum seekers whose applications were rejected had filed in bad faith. But surely a good portion of those had, as tabloid headlines were keen to remind their readers (e.g., "Asylum seekers: 9 out of 10 are conmen").[13]

***

The policy dilemma faced by Western states is how to remain open to genuine refugees while at the same time preventing asylum from being exploited by those who are not entitled to it. In theory, bad faith and fraudulent claims should be easy to check. After all, the purpose of individually adjudicating asylum claims is to ensure that those eligible for asylum receive it, and that those who are ineligible do not. But in reality, matters are more complicated. A state must adopt procedural rules that strike a balance between two objectives: avoiding false positives (granting asylum to claimants who do not merit it); and avoiding false negatives (refusing asylum to those who have genuinely fled persecution). The difficulty is that many of the policies that successfully deter fraudulent applications also lead to the denial of meritorious claims. For example, requiring asylum seekers to corroborate their claims with documentary evidence helps to minimize asylum fraud, but also has the effect of denying asylum to persecuted people who are unable to provide any evidence beyond their own testimony.

Conversely, many procedural protections designed to ensure that meritorious claims are granted will also have the effect of attracting more claims made in bad faith, thereby undermining public support for asylum. For example, appellate review is an important safeguard against the erroneous denial of an asylum claim, especially given that the enormous workload of immigration courts raises doubts about their ability to adjudicate claims accurately in the first instance. But the more opportunities there are for appellate review and the wider the scope of that review, the longer it will take to process a claim. And delays in processing claims not only increase administrative costs, but also provide migrants with a strong incentive to file bad faith claims.

Consider the situation of an economic migrant who has managed to enter a country without documentation. Although applying for asylum requires that he make himself known to immigration officials, and therefore carries risk, he nonetheless has an incentive to do so. Not only is asylum his only hope for securing legal status, but also in many countries asylum applicants are eligible for work authorization or welfare benefits while their claims are being processed. In Canada, asylum seekers are eligible for work authorization upon filing and taking a medical exam; in the Netherlands, for thirteen weeks per year; in the U.S., six months after filing an application; and in the UK, one year after filing an application.[14]

In Europe, asylum seekers also have access to welfare benefits while their claims are being adjudicated; a recent EU Council Directive laying down minimum standards for the reception of asylum seekers requires member states to provide material assistance "to ensure a standard of living adequate for the health of applicants and capable of ensuring their subsistence."[15] In the UK, for example, asylum seekers are eligible to receive housing and approximately £40 a week if they would otherwise be destitute.[16] The longer it takes to process an asylum seeker's claim, the stronger is the incentive to apply and to avail oneself of these benefits. Destitute persons retain access to housing and vouchers even after their claims have been denied, until they are actually removed from the country.[17]

The incentive to file a bad faith application is even stronger for an economic migrant already in removal proceedings or with an expired (or soon-to-expire) non-immigrant visa. In 2003, it took an average of thirteen months to reach a first-instance asylum decision in the UK (though recent reforms look to shrink this time to sixty days for most applicants[18]), eleven months in Canada, and thirty-one weeks in the Netherlands.[19] But these numbers make the process appear deceptively quick. If a claim is denied, applicants may have access to several layers of appeal, and many take advantage of this opportunity. For instance, in the UK in 2003, 46,130 asylum seekers attempted to appeal their first-instance denial to the Immigration Appellate Authority. In 20 percent of appeals adjudicated, the asylum seeker prevailed.[20] Once appeals are factored in, an asylum claim in Canada or the UK can take as long as three years to move from initiation to the issuance of a removal order.[21]

In the United States, the immigration service is supposed to reach a first-instance judgment within sixty days of application and complete administrative adjudication within six months, though this deadline is often not met.[22] When an asylum application is denied in the first instance, and the applicant has no other legal basis for remaining in the country, she is referred to the immigration courts for removal proceedings. There, she can renew her asylum claim. Alternatively, an applicant can claim asylum for the first time once removal proceedings are already underway, as a defense to removal. In 2006, about 31 percent of asylum applications in the United States were lodged defensively, after removal proceedings had already begun. Those applications were granted 34 percent of the time, compared with a grant rate of 51 percent on applications filed "affirmatively," that is, absent any pending removal proceedings.[23] In either scenario, if asylum is denied by the immigration judge, the applicant can then petition for review before the Board of Immigration Appeals (BIA).

If one's application is denied by the BIA, one can further prolong the adjudication process by petitioning for review before the federal courts of appeal. The number of these petitions has soared in recent years, and in the government's view, that is because new, streamlined administrative review procedures have shrunk the time it takes for the BIA to adjudicate a case, making a petition to the federal courts of appeals a relatively more attractive option for aliens who wish to postpone deportation.[24] A petition for appellate review made in 2003 in the Second Circuit, which covers New York, took an average of 14.6 months to complete; in the Ninth Circuit, which covers California, the figure was 11.7 months.[25] Merely filing an asylum application and appealing a denial can extend one's legal presence, and thereby postpone one's departure, by years.

In responding to the policy dilemma posed by asylum – the need to prevent abuse of asylum while at the same time remaining open to those who genuinely qualify – states have emphasized the former goal at the expense of the latter. They have enacted barriers to entry (such as visa requirements and high-seas interdiction) that exclude good faith and bad faith claimants alike. They have also enacted deterrence measures (such as detention and benefits cuts) designed to discourage bad faith applications, but that impose unreasonable burdens on those who genuinely have claims. Finally, they have adopted procedural rules (such as filing deadlines and corroboration requirements) that may eliminate some fraudulent applications, but at the expense of many applicants who genuinely have fled persecution.

It is easy for advocates to condemn the hostility with which Western publics have greeted asylum seekers over the last fifteen years as cold-hearted, nativist, or both. And there is no doubt that concerns about asylum fraud have to some extent been exaggerated by right-wing tabloids and nativist politicians. At the same time, however, the policy dilemma is a real one, and advocates must come to grips with it. Bad faith and fraudulent asylum claims have significant costs – economic, political, and moral – that ultimately undermine the asylum system as a whole.

First, there is a marginal administrative cost to every additional application. Every asylum seeker receives a personal interview with an adjudicator, and failed claims (in the United States) are referred to already clogged immigration courts. The more applications that are filed, the more judicial resources are needed if backlogs are to be kept to a minimum. And for those states that commit themselves to providing economic assistance to asylum seekers while their cases are being adjudicated – in the form of welfare payments, housing vouchers, education, and health care – the economic cost of bad faith claims is even higher. These expenses add up. According to one estimate, in 2003, the West spent about $10 billion on the maintenance of asylum seekers and the adjudication of their claims.[26] In 2003, Britain alone spent about £1 billion to support 93,000 asylum seekers.[27]

Second, there are political costs to the exploitation of the asylum system by bad faith claimants. It lends to public perceptions that governments have "lost control of the borders," and fosters resentment against immigrants who are thought to take advantage of their hosts' generosity. It casts suspicion even on good faith asylum seekers and legal immigrants, and undermines political support for continuing to welcome them.

As a practical matter, asylum is a "scarce resource," politically speaking.[28] Western publics support granting asylum to persecuted people, but only if they feel that control over the borders more generally is being maintained. An influx of asylum seekers invites a backlash because it raises doubts about the effectiveness of border control, unless there is evidence that the sudden spike in demand can be attributed to "a real outbreak of implacable persecution." If the public perceives that the asylum system is being exploited by "ordinary" immigrants who have no claim to admission, support for asylum will quickly be eroded.[29]

The racial tensions that now periodically bubble over in Britain should serve as a caution: in June 2003, riots involving several hundred youths followed an altercation between an Iraqi Kurdish refugee and a local man. In Plymouth, where around 1,000 refugees live amidst a population of roughly 350,000 Britons, around twenty to thirty racist incidents were reported each month of 2003.[30] In Germany as well, the dramatic increase in asylum seekers in the early 1990s was met with a surge of skinhead violence against *auslander*.

Finally, there are moral costs when economic migrants are able to facilitate entry into the receiving country or prolong their stay by filing an asylum claim in bad faith. It is unfair to reward scofflaws with a free pass on immigration restrictions, while forcing law-abiding foreigners to spend years – sometimes more than a decade – in queues awaiting an immigration visa. For example, in August 2007, the backlog for Indians applying for an immigration visa to reunite with a brother or sister in the United States was eleven years; for Filipinos, the wait was twenty-two years. Permanent residents who had immigrated from China, India, and the Philippines faced a five-year wait to reunite with spouses and minor children; for those from Mexico, the wait was six years.[31]

So, states need to police the asylum process to ensure that it is not abused by those who have no genuine claim to asylum. But any burdens imposed on asylum applicants should satisfy three principles. The first is *selectivity*: policies should be designed, so far as is reasonable, to eliminate bad faith applications rather than the total number of applications. The second principle is *hospitality*: host states should resist deterrence policies that require asylum seekers to undergo serious hardship in order to prove their bona fides. The third principle is one of *caution*: given the high stakes for applicants, procedural rules should be designed, to the greatest extent possible given fragile public support, to minimize mistaken denials of asylum rather than mistaken grants of asylum. As we shall see, many current policies fail miserably when measured against these three principles.

Methods of restriction

Barriers to entry

One main method adopted by the West in order to control asylum abuse is to create barriers to entry. These make it more difficult for asylum seekers to reach territory from which they would be able to file an asylum claim. Examples of barriers to entry include the following.

Visa requirements and carrier sanctions

Western states routinely require that citizens of refugee-producing states possess visas in order to be admitted to their territory, and they impose penalties on transportation companies such as airlines and ship lines for bringing into their territory passengers lacking proper documentation.[32] States have also begun to post immigration officers abroad to to screen passengers at points of departure and to train airline employees to carry out document checks.[33] In addition, some states require that, in order to change planes in their airports, nationals of specified countries must possess "transit visas." For example, a Pakistani flying through London Heathrow must possess a valid visa for the time spent waiting in the departure lounge for his or her connecting flight.[34]

States have been candid in acknowledging that one main purpose of visa requirements is to reduce the number of asylum applications. In 1998, the New Zealand Minister for Immigration explained that a new visa requirement for Indonesian nationals would better enable New Zealand "to manage the risk of people seeking refugee status once they arrive here."[35] And a British official explained its visa requirement for Zimbabwean nationals, introduced in 2003, in similar terms: it was "intended to reduce the rising number of Zimbabweans seeking asylum in the UK."[36] These policies have their intended effect. The number of asylum applications received from Zimbabweans by the UK plummeted from over 7,600 in 2002 to about 3,300 in 2003 and just over 2,000 in 2004.[37] When Sweden imposed a visa requirement on Bosnians in 1992, the number of Bosnian asylum seekers dropped from 2,000 per week to less than 200.[38]

Because, for many asylum seekers, visa requirements and carrier sanctions have the effect of barring their lawful entrance into countries of asylum, they increasingly need to enlist the help of smugglers – who charge thousands, and sometimes tens of thousands, of dollars – to enter unlawfully. The German government estimated in 1997 that about half of Germany's asylum seekers were smuggled in; the current figure is likely to be higher. Recent Dutch estimates are as high as 60 to 70 percent.[39]

Internationalization of territory

The internationalization of ports creates the legal fiction that asylum seekers have not actually entered the national territory. Their removal thus does not constitute a denial of the right to apply for asylum.[40]

France has designated areas of its airports to be "international zones" where asylum seekers can be detained without the protections normally given under French law.[41] Denmark and the Netherlands have similar laws. Germany tried to implement one as well, but in 1996 the Federal Constitutional Court ruled that it was unconstitutional.[42]

In 2001, Australia determined that its offshore possessions along its northern coast – from which asylum seekers arriving by boat had frequently claimed asylum – were no long part of its "migration zone." Undocumented persons who arrived at these islands were subject to mandatory detention, and could apply for asylum only with the permission of the Minister of Immigration. In 2006, Australia announced that such persons would be detained offshore, in Nauru, and would remain there until accepted for resettlement in a third country.[43] (In 2008, the Rudd government ended Australia's mandatory detention policy and closed the detention facility in Nauru.)

Off-Shore Interdiction

In 1981, the US Coast Guard began to intercept and board Haitian fishing boats before they could reach US territory. Passengers were interrogated to ascertain whether they genuinely feared persecution in Haiti. Those who passed this cursory screening were brought to the United States where they could file an asylum application, and those that did not were directly repatriated. By late 1991, the Haitian influx had become so large – between November 1991 and April 1992, the Coast Guard intercepted more than 34,000 Haitians – that the Coast Guard could no longer perform a preliminary screening on its ships. At first, it transported Haitian asylum seekers to the naval base at Guantanamo Bay for screening, but facilities there were soon overcrowded. President Bush responded to the crisis in May 1992 by issuing an Executive Order that directed the Coast Guard to interdict Haitians on the high seas and repatriate them directly, without any preliminary screening.[44] Despite protests that the policy was "a textbook case of *refoulement*,"[45] the Supreme Court upheld its legality.[46]

Australian authorities have also employed off-shore interdiction, most notoriously in the case of the MV *Tampa* in August 2001. The *Tampa* had rescued 439 Afghan asylum seekers whose fishing vessel had foundered in international waters north of Christmas Island, an Australian possession. When the *Tampa*'s crew sought permission to dock at Christmas Island so that the asylum seekers could receive medical treatment, the Australian authorities refused, and eventually troops were deployed to prevent the ship from landing without permission. The asylum seekers were redirected to detention facilities on the island of Nauru, from which some were resettled in New Zealand and others were eventually accepted by Australia.

Europeans have also begun to interdict migrants off-shore. Spain is currently erecting an electronic barrier along the part of its coast closest to Morocco, and has been investing in patrol boats and night-vision and heat-seeking equipment.[47] And Italy has returned to Libya over 1,000 migrants who have landed by sea at Lampedusa, an island that lies closer to Tunisia than it does to the Italian mainland.[48] Some of those returned to Libya were subsequently sent home to Eritrea, where they may have faced persecution.[49]

Procedural restrictions

In addition to erecting barriers to entry, states have also introduced procedural requirements that make it more difficult to file an application even after one has already arrived in a country of asylum.

Safe countries of origin

Many states adopt presumptions against claims filed by individuals from what are deemed to be "safe" countries of origin. In 2004, twenty-five countries were on Britain's "safe" list. Countries added that year included Bangladesh, Bolivia, Brazil, Ecuador, South Africa, Sri Lanka and Ukraine,[50] from which Britain together received more than 4,500 asylum seekers in 2002 (3,130 were from Sri Lanka).[51] As of 2006, the British safe list included countries such as Albania and Nigeria (for males only).[52] France's list included countries like Benin, Georgia, India, Senegal, and Ukraine.[53] All of these countries were described by the US State Department's Human Rights Reports as having experienced human rights problems in 2006. These abuses included, depending on the country, arbitrary detention; torture; the use of excessive force by security forces; ethnic or religious violence; and female genital mutilation.[54] Rejected applicants from countries of origin deemed "safe" are subjected to an expedited adjudication process and have access only to non-suspensive appeals – that is, they may appeal, but the appeal does not suspend their deportation.[55]

Safe third country rules

These stipulate that if asylum seekers pass through a safe country in transit to the country in which they claim asylum, they can be returned to the safe country for processing there. Safe third country rules have become very popular in the EU. Germany, for example, revised its constitution in 1993 to exclude from its constitutional right to asylum anyone "who enters the federal territory from a member state of the European Communities or from another third state" that honors its Convention obligation of non-refoulement.[56] The first concern of German immigration officials is now to ascertain asylum seekers' travel itineraries in order to determine their eligibility to file an application.[57] In the year following this change, the number of new asylum applications filed in Germany dropped from 322,614 to 127,210.[58]

The Dublin Convention,[59] designed to combat forum-shopping by requiring asylum seekers to present their claim in the first signatory state they enter, effectively treats all EU members as safe third countries, including the transit states of Eastern Europe. Because the core asylum countries of Northern and Western Europe are surrounded by "safe" countries, it is very difficult for an asylum seeker to initiate an asylum claim at a land border in any of these states.

The results of safe third country rules have been two-fold: first, growing refugee populations in Eastern Europe, and second, the destruction of documents by asylum seekers who manage to enter the core asylum states in order to cover their tracks. If asylum seekers enter Germany through Poland, but have no travel documents connecting them to Poland, the Polish government will not take them back; Germany will have to hear their asylum claims itself. Most asylum seekers who arrive in Eastern Europe attempt to continue on: for example, in Slovakia, 83 percent of asylum applications initiated in 2000 were stopped due to asylum seekers' illegal departure, presumably for more attractive places of refuge further west;[60] and more than half of asylum seekers in Germany destroyed their documents to conceal their point of entry.[61] To combat this trend, Denmark has denied monthly cash allowances and limited food provision to asylum seekers who refuse to disclose their travel routes.[62]

Filing deadlines

In the United States, the Illegal Immigration Reform and Immigrant Responsibility Act 1996 provided that, absent a change in home country conditions or exceptional circumstances, such as serious illness or incompetent counsel, asylum seekers must file their claim within one year of arriving in the country.[63] In fiscal year 2003, 28 percent of affirmative asylum applicants failed to meet this filing deadline and were referred to an immigration judge for removal proceedings.[64]

While a one-year deadline may not seem too onerous, other states – in particular those in Eastern Europe – have imposed much stricter rules. For example, until 2000, Slovakia had a twenty-four-hour deadline, and Bulgaria had a seventy-two-hour deadline. In Slovakia, the clock began ticking when asylum seekers first entered the country, even if only to pass through en route to a destination further west. If they were returned from their destination in accordance with that state's safe-third-country rules, they would discover that they had already missed the filing deadline.[65]

Corroboration requirements

Asylum fraud can be very difficult to detect. Frequently, the only evidence presented in an asylum hearing is the testimony of the applicant; witnesses or documents that could corroborate the applicant's story are often unavailable. And the task of determining whether an applicant is telling the truth is even harder in the asylum context than in other adjudicatory contexts. The cues on which one ordinarily relies to detect dissembling – whether the witness makes eye contact, shifts nervously, testifies consistently, and so on – can be dangerously misleading when dealing with applicants who fear authority figures, suffer from post-traumatic stress disorder at very high rates, may testify through translators who fail faithfully to render subtle details in testimony, and come from cultures where body language (like eye contact) may carry a different significance. The problem of fraud is compounded further by the fact that well over half of the asylum seekers in Europe do not possess valid documentation.[66] It can, therefore, sometimes be difficult even to determine what country an applicant comes from, let alone whether he or she was persecuted there.

One response to the problem of fraud is simply to require applicants to present documentary corroboration of their claims or otherwise to increase the applicant's burden of proof. The original US House version of the Intelligence Reform and Terrorism Act of 2004 would have done exactly that: adjudicators would have been authorized to deny an application on the ground of incredibility if the applicant were unable to offer corroborating evidence of his story or if the persecution he feared were not mentioned in the State Department's annual human rights country reports. Applicants would also have faced a higher burden of proof to establish persecution.[67] Although these provisions were stripped from the final bill, current US law permits the adjudicator to reject an asylum application if the applicant fails to present corroborating evidence that, in the adjudicator's view, should be provided; the burden is placed on the applicant to show that such evidence is not reasonably available.[68]

Expedited removal

Almost every major country of asylum now has an accelerated decision-making and removal process for "manifestly unfounded" claims.[69] These include fraudulent claims and claims manifestly lacking in credibility, those unrelated to the criteria for asylum, and those that fail to meet eligibility limitations imposed by safe state of origin rules, safe third country rules, or filing deadlines. Claimants whose applications have been determined to be "manifestly unfounded" have limited access to appeal. While non-accelerated applicants are typically permitted two levels of appeal,[70] those subject to expedited removal are permitted only one.[71] Rejected applicants further have only a very brief window within which appeals can be filed – as of at least 2000, in Germany, manifestly unfounded applicants had three days to appeal; in Belgium, such port-of-entry applicants detained close to the port had only one day to appeal.[72] And in many countries, such as France and the United States, an appeal does not automatically suspend deportation; instead, a court must issue a stay.[73]

In the United States, expedited removal was until recently applied only to inadmissible aliens arriving at ports of entry, though the Department of Homeland Security recently decided to apply it as well to inadmissible aliens arrested within 100 miles of the Canadian or Mexican border who had been present in the United States for fewer than fourteen days.[74] An alien arriving at a port of entry whose admissibility is in question is given a "secondary inspection" by an immigration officer. During secondary inspection, the alien is asked if she fears persecution in her homeland. If she indicates that she does, then she is referred to an asylum officer for a "credible fear interview," which typically takes place within a few weeks. If she indicates that she does not, and she otherwise is inadmissible, then she is issued a removal order that bars reentry to the United States for five years and is immediately removed.

The alien is kept in detention until the credible fear interview. At that point, if the asylum officer finds that there is a "significant possibility" that the alien would qualify for asylum,[75] she enters the normal asylum system and is eligible to be released from detention pending a full-blown asylum hearing in immigration court (though, as discussed below, the Department of Homeland Security often continues to detain even those asylum seekers who have shown a credible fear of persecution). Between 1997 and 1999, 88 percent of persons given a credible fear interview passed on to the normal asylum system.[76] Aliens who fail the credible fear interview are issued an expedited removal order, which is reviewed by an immigration judge within seven days. Immigration judges affirmed negative credible fear determinations in 88 percent of the cases they reviewed.[77]

Deterrence

In addition to policies designed to make it more *difficult* for would-be asylum seekers to arrive and to have their applications heard, states have also adopted policies that make it less *desirable* for would-be asylum seekers to apply.

Benefits cuts

In 1993, Germany administratively separated benefits for asylum seekers from welfare in order to reduce benefits to 80 percent of the level given to citizens, and replaced cash transfers with in-kind benefits.[78] In 1998, it passed an amendment that restricted welfare support for failed asylum seekers to what is "absolutely necessary considering the circumstances of the individual case."[79] In 2003 in France, asylum seekers received only a one-time waiting allowance of €305 per adult upon arrival. Those who lived outside reception centers were also given a monthly allowance of about €23.[80]

In January 2003, the British government attempted to offer welfare assistance only to those asylum seekers who applied at a port of entry and who requested support within three days of entering the country. Otherwise, applicants would have needed to fend for themselves while their claims were being processed. A subsequent court decision, however, held that the state could not withdraw basic support unless it was assured that the individual had an alternative source of support.[81] Parliament also passed the Asylum and Immigration Act of 2004, which removed public support from certain failed asylum seekers with families.[82]

In the United States, prior to 1995, any asylum seeker whose application was not frivolous was eligible for work authorization. Regulatory and statutory reforms that year changed the law to require that asylum seekers wait six months after filing an application before receiving work authorization.[83] In the meantime, they must rely for their subsistence on help from family members or charities.

Detention and deportation

Those favoring restriction have also sought to deter asylum seekers by detaining them while their claims are being processed. As noted above, applicants subjected to expedited removal are frequently detained while their claims are pending. Australia had such a policy until 2008: its law provided for the mandatory and unreviewable detention of any asylum seeker who arrived in Australia without a valid visa, until either temporary protection was granted or the asylum seeker was deported.[84] William Hague, the Conservative candidate for British prime minister in 2001, advocated a similar approach.[85]

Prime Minister Blair instead proposed establishing "transit processing centres" located on prominent smuggling routes into Europe, such as in Croatia, Romania, or Albania. Asylum applicants would be removed from Britain to these centers, where their claims would be adjudicated. Those accepted would be brought back to Britain; those whose claims failed would be sent back to their countries of origin.[86] Blair was forced to drop the plan after objections from Germany, Sweden, and Greece, among others. The Greek government spokesman contended that the plan smacked of "concentration camps."[87] A revised version that would require asylum seekers to apply in Africa – potentially in Morocco, Tunisia, Algeria, or Libya – was subsequently studied by the EU, over the objections of France, Sweden, and Spain.[88] These plans are appealing from the standpoint of restriction because they create strong disincentives to making a claim in bad faith. The motivation for filing such a claim – namely, to gain access to employment markets – is stymied if asylum seekers are detained for the length of their claim or removed to an off-shore adjudication facility.

These plans also make it substantially easier to deport failed asylum seekers, an issue of prime importance for the Western states. Figures on the proportion of failed asylum seekers who actually depart are hard to come by, but a 1996 US Department of Justice Inspector General report found that only 11 percent of non-detained aliens under order to "voluntarily" depart actually left. By contrast, 94 percent of aliens in detention were actually removed following a removal order.[89] According to Matthew Gibney and Randall Hansen, the Greater London Authority estimated in 2002 that 100,000 failed asylum seekers were resident there.[90] Despite Prime Minister Blair's goal to remove 30,000 per year, his government was only able to remove about 13,000 per year in 2003–5 and 16,330 in 2006.[91] Gibney and Hansen further reported that, according to German Interior Minister Otto Schilly, over 400,000 failed asylum seekers resided illegally in Germany. Many of these individuals remained eligible for public assistance, even though their claims had been rejected.[92] The ineffectiveness of deportation encourages bad faith asylum claims, since one has nothing to lose by filing.

Assessing restrictive policies

Measured against the three principles of selectivity, hospitality, and caution, many of the restrictive policies adopted by Western states are deeply flawed.

Barriers to entry

Barriers to entry are deeply troubling from the perspective of selectivity: they exclude asylum seekers regardless of the strength of their claims. Their goal is simply to reduce the total number of applications, even if many of those excluded could file successful claims. The problem, however, is not too many genuine refugees; it is one of too many *asylum seekers*, many of whom apply in bad faith.[93] Policies should aim specifically at providing disincentives for asylum *abuse*, rather than simply at reducing the total number of applicants.

Deterrence measures

Deterrence measures, such as benefit cuts and detention, are objectionable from the standpoint of hospitality. There is no doubt that cutting benefits reduces one incentive for filing a claim in bad faith, and claimants who are detained while their claims are pending cannot use asylum to gain access to the host state's labor market. However, these policies are problematic because their method of deterring bad faith applicants is to impose hardship on good faith applicants. Such an approach makes the asylum process too closely resemble medieval trial by ordeal: claimants' bona fides are established by their willingness to rely on charity for their subsistence or to submit themselves to weeks, months, or even years of detention.

Limited detention might be justified for two small groups of asylum seekers: those who arrive at ports of entry without a valid visa and must present themselves for inspection; and those who are apprehended by border patrol while attempting to cross into a country illegally. These two groups have an incentive to file for asylum because doing so is the only way to gain entry. If they are released from detention pending their hearing, they can abscond and live illegally. Border applications are a minority of the total number of applications filed. In 2006 in Britain, they were only about 15 percent of total asylum claims;[94] in 2003 in the United States, about 12.5 percent;[95] in 2000 in Germany, they were fewer than 10 percent.[96] But detention should be used for border applicants as part of expedited removal proceedings only, and applicants determined to have a "credible fear" of persecution should generally be released pending full-blown asylum hearings (absent national security concerns in a particular case).

And, if detention is a regular feature of the asylum procedure, applicants should be given comfortable accommodations – something more akin to a reception center than a jail, particularly for families traveling with children. Perhaps decommissioned military bases could serve as detention space. Currently, the US Department of Homeland Security (DHS) places asylum seekers in cells with non-asylum-seeking immigration violators, and also rents space in penitentiaries.[97]

Unfortunately, in the United States, even asylum seekers who have shown a credible fear of persecution are regularly detained until their asylum hearings. DHS policy guidelines direct that parole "is a viable option and should be considered" for those asylum seekers "who meet the credible fear standard, can establish identity and community ties, and are not subject to any possible bars to asylum involving violence or misconduct."[98] But the ultimate decision to grant or refuse parole rests with district directors,[99] who, as Michele Pistone and Philip Schrag argue, have "powerful incentives" due to "career and budgetary considerations" to opt for detention over release even of these qualified asylum seekers.[100] In 2000, such asylum seekers were detained for an average of fifty-seven days.[101] However, the average length varied widely among ports of entry. In New York, for example, the average length of detention was 124 days.[102] That is far too long.

One objection to releasing point-of-entry asylum applicants prior to having their claims finally determined is that it is very easy for bad faith applicants to show a "credible fear" of persecution – as noted above, almost nine in ten people given a credible fear interview are deemed to have a "credible fear" – and that, once released from detention, they will abscond. It is true that detention ensures a 100 percent appearance rate, but it does so at significant cost – not only human, but also economic, about $7,300 per person detained.[103] Recent studies have shown that very high appearance rates can be achieved with substantially more humane and less costly policies.

For example, the Vera Institute's Appearance Assistance Program demonstrated that community-based supervised release offers a workable alternative to detention. The US immigration service agreed to parole asylum seekers, as well as other aliens, on condition that they enroll in one of two Vera Institute supervision programs. The more intensive version required asylum seekers to report regularly in person and by telephone to program workers. The less intensive program required them to attend an orientation program about the asylum process and put them in contact with social service providers. The former boosted court appearance rates from 78 percent for those paroled without supervision to 93 percent, while the latter increased appearance rates from 62 percent to 84 percent.[104] The cost of the intensive program is less than half the cost of detention: $3,300 per person.[105] In 2004, DHS began a pilot supervision program for 200 aliens in each of eight cities: Baltimore, Philadelphia, Miami, St. Paul, Denver, Kansas City, San Francisco, and Portland, Oregon.[106] DHS has also implemented nationwide use of electronic monitoring bracelets, which alert authorities when asylum seekers leave their homes for longer than authorized.[107] While electronic monitoring is still troubling from a civil liberties standpoint, it is certainly preferable to detention.

Blair's off-shore processing centers might seem to be another solution to the problem of selectively deterring bad faith claimants without forcing good faith applicants to undergo a trial by ordeal. Relocating the entire asylum adjudication process to another country – for point-of-entry applicants as well as those who raise asylum as a defense to deportation – would ensure that economic migrants could not use the asylum application process as a way to circumvent immigration restrictions. After all, bad faith claimants have little to gain from spending a few months in Romania; their goal is to access the employment market of London, not Bucharest. At the same time, the British government can provide asylum seekers with food, shelter, and pocket money much more cheaply in Romania than it can in the UK. And because there is no need to prevent asylum seekers housed in Romania from interacting with the local population – there is no risk that they will abscond, since their goal is to make it to England, not Romania – there is no need for detention. Those housed in processing centers could be free to come and go as they wish. If many states relocate their asylum seekers to the same processing centers, the plan could also facilitate burden-sharing among receiving states.

The proposal has, however, proved to be a political non-starter. Moreover, it may end up deterring bona fide refugees as well as fraudulent claimants. The proposal would effectuate deportation of all failed asylum seekers, while doing nothing to increase the deportation of other undocumented immigrants present within Britain. Even claimants applying for asylum in good faith may prefer to take their chances as undocumented immigrants in Britain itself than as asylum seekers applying for admission to Britain from Romania. An applicant's chance of succeeding at the latter will depend on the vagaries of an adjudication system that is hardly error-free, and the outcome may be difficult for asylum seekers to predict. Finally, some observers have expressed concern that the processing centers would ultimately become permanent detention centers even for those who are recognized as Convention refugees, displacing the institution of asylum.[108]

Procedural restrictions

This leaves us with procedural restrictions, some of which are more defensible than others. Filing deadlines may seem to make good sense: they prevent undocumented economic migrants who have resided in a country for many years from using asylum as a tactic to delay deportation proceedings. But filing deadlines burden good faith claimants also – even America's seemingly generous one-year rule. Many asylum seekers fail to apply within the deadline because they genuinely wish to return home and hope conditions will improve enough to allow them to do so. Although a grant of asylum does not, of course, commit the asylum seeker to permanent exile, for many people forced to flee their home-lands, claiming asylum is psychologically tantamount to giving up hope for return. Refugees may, therefore, be reluctant to apply until they feel they have no choice.

Moreover, many good faith asylum seekers may not know where to file for asylum, how to do so, or even that such an option exists. They may be unable to acquire such information quickly due to linguistic difficulties, trauma, or the sheer need to provide for their immediate subsistence, since they often arrive without any money and without any support network in place. They may also need significant time to gather documents that corroborate their claim, many of which may have been left behind in their home country. Pistone and Schrag note that, prior to 1995, when the filing deadline was introduced, "fewer than half of the successful asylum applicants represented by volunteers from the Lawyers Committee for Human Rights applied for asylum within their first year in the United States."[109] Filing deadlines might even impose greater burdens on good faith applicants than on bad faith applicants, since the latter are less likely to be suffering from crippling post-traumatic stress disorder or depression.

"Safe country of origin" rules, meanwhile, are acceptable in theory – so long as they create only a rebuttable presumption against asylum seekers from those countries, and not a blanket exclusion. In practice, however, the lists have been overinclusive. Britain's decision in 2003 to include Sri Lanka on its "white list" is a case in point. In that year, 715 Sri Lankans successfully appealed the rejection of their respective claims (13 per cent of total appeals by Sri Lankans) – appeals which, due to the white list, would no longer suspend deportation.[110] A "safe country" designation is more appropriate for countries like Mexico, which sent 8,977 asylum seekers to the United States in 2002, of which only 31 (0.35 percent) were recognized as eligible.[111]

"Safe third country" rules are also acceptable in theory, but have been implemented in problematic ways. The danger is that genuine asylum seekers will be deported to a "safe" third country that is not, in fact, safe. For example, while the transit states of Eastern Europe are deemed "safe," refugee advocates have alleged that some fail to provide asylum seekers with adequate procedural safeguards. For example, in 2006, Slovakia granted asylum to only a handful of the nearly 1,100 applications it received from ethnic Chechens from Russia, while other EU states granted asylum to such applicants at substantially higher rates.[112] In total, Slovakia's grant rate in 2005 was only 3 percent (25 grants compared with 812 rejections); the same year, Greece granted relief to only 88 applicants in the more than 4,500 cases it decided.[113] And, according to Sabine Weidlich, Polish officials at the Department for Migration and Refugee Affairs have "reportedly deterred asylum seekers from lodging applications by telling them to come back in several weeks."[114] Adequate translation is also often difficult to find.

Furthermore, these countries also have safe third country rules themselves, but there is no guarantee that those "safe" countries are actually safe. The danger is that people who qualify for asylum will nonetheless undergo a "chain deportation"[115] all the way back to their country of origin. For example, at least as recently as 2003, Germany regarded the Czech Republic as safe, the Czech Republic regarded Slovakia as safe, and Slovakia regarded Zimbabwe as safe![116] Slovakia has also returned Chechen asylum seekers to Ukraine, which in turn has deported them back to the Russian Federation.[117]

Corroboration requirements are also problematic. Without doubt, fraud is a major problem, and it is important to protect the integrity of asylum programs by giving adjudicators the tools they need to separate true stories from tall tales. But at the same time, policymakers must exercise caution. It would be possible, of course, to require such extensive documentation in support of an asylum application that no one could possibly make a fraudulent claim. However, the consequence would be that many eligible asylum seekers, who lack such documentation, would be rejected. For many applicants, forced to flee quickly and covertly, there may be little opportunity to gather files and collect affidavits. Nor can one realistically expect third party monitoring groups, like the State Department, Human Rights Watch, or Amnesty International, to record every variety or instance of persecution that occurs. Indeed, at the margin, requiring corroborating documentation may have the perverse effect of favoring fraudulent applicants, who will design their stories around the available evidence. Granting asylum to a certain number of fraudulent applicants is an inevitable cost of remaining open to those who genuinely fear persecution but may have little evidence other than their own testimony. With so much at stake in these cases – they are literally a matter of life and death – policy should be guided by a spirit of generosity rather than by distrust and skepticism. One should not impose corroboration requirements that are unrealistic for most good faith applicants, even if some amount of fraud is the inevitable consequence.

Rather than creating procedural rules that make large numbers of applicants ineligible, states should remain committed to adjudicating asylum applications on their merits. However, they should devote the resources needed to speed up substantially the time it takes to process an application. Length of processing time directly affects the incentives to file a bad faith application. For those facing removal – either at a port of entry or in deportation proceedings after having gained entry (either illegally or by overstaying a visa) – filing for asylum is a very effective dilatory tactic. Not only does it delay removal by months or years, but it also makes the applicant eligible for benefits such as work authorization or welfare (depending on the country) in the interim. Reducing the time it takes to process an asylum application correspondingly reduces the incentives to file in bad faith.

One can go about reducing processing times in several ways. First, one could conduct a very fast initial review to screen out applicants whose claims are assured of failure, while moving other applicants on to a more full-blown adjudication. Second, one could devote the resources needed to ensure that the full-blown adjudication can be carried out in a timely fashion. Third, one could limit access to appellate review. All three policies should be employed, but with caution. The danger of speeding up processing times is that applicants will receive a more cursory – and, inevitably, a more grudging – review of their applications. While mistakes can never be entirely eliminated, neither should processing be expedited at the expense of reasonable accuracy.

Expedited removal policies implement the first approach. Expedited removal at the border allows the immigration service selectively to deter bad faith claimants by ensuring that only those with credible claims for asylum have access to full-blown asylum proceedings. Claiming asylum at the border, therefore, no longer permits an end run around entry requirements. One could also imagine an expedited review system for applications filed by asylum seekers already present within a country: an initial layer of review would determine whether an in-country applicant's claim is manifestly unfounded; if so, the applicant would not enter the normal asylum determination system, and, if unlawfully present, the applicant would be referred to removal proceedings. Otherwise, the applicant would continue on to a full-scale adjudication. A system similar to this has been used in Belgium.[118]

Critics have put forward a number of objections to the way expedited proceedings have so far functioned in the United States.[119] In general, these objections counsel reform of the expedited removal process, not its elimination.

A number of objections concern the manner in which "secondary inspections" are conducted at ports of entry. A secondary inspection, which lasts about an hour, is conducted by a customs officer when a primary customs inspector believes that an alien seeking entry is not admissible. If the alien indicates a fear of persecution or states the intent to apply for asylum, she is removed from secondary inspection and is transferred to a detention center to await a "credible fear determination" made by an asylum officer. Otherwise, if the alien lacks valid travel documents, she is ordered to be removed, and that order is not subject to review by the courts.

Governing regulations require secondary inspectors to inform a person subject to expedited removal that US law provides protection to people who fear persecution, that if the person fears persecution she should tell the inspector because she "may not have another chance," and that if she communicates such a fear, she will be able to speak to another officer "privately and confidentially" about that fear. Inspectors are also required to ask three questions designed to elicit information relating to a fear of persecution: "Why did you leave your home country or country of last residence? Do you have any fear or concern about being returned to your home country or being removed from the United States? Would you be harmed if you are returned to your home country or country of last residence?"[120]

However, studies of the expedited removal process in the United States have revealed that inspectors communicated the required information in only about half of cases, and that, in such cases, aliens were "seven times more likely to be referred for a credible fear determination."[121] Inspectors also failed to ask the mandatory three questions in between 5 percent and 15 percent of cases.[122] Moreover, studies have shown that many aliens who do express a fear of return are nonetheless returned. A General Accounting Office study found that in seven of the 365 case files it examined, aliens were removed in violation of the regulations; and a more recent report by the US Commission of International Religious Freedom (USCIRF) concluded that "[o]ne in six aliens who expressed a fear of return during the Secondary Inspection interview were placed in Expedited Removal or allowed to withdraw their application for admission," at least in some cases under pressure by the inspector.[123]

Secondary inspectors are also required to make a written record of the interview and to have the alien read and sign that record to verify its accuracy. The USCIRF study found that in 72 percent of cases, aliens signed the record of their interview without reading it or having it read to them; and, since 80 percent of interviews were conducted through interpreters, in a large number of those cases, aliens could have no way of knowing what the inspector had recorded.[124] The resulting danger is two-fold: first, an inspector might mistakenly order an alien removed based upon a misunderstanding; and second, even if an alien eventually receives an asylum hearing, the inspector's record will form part of the alien's file, and misunderstandings may later appear to be inconsistencies in the alien's story that undermine his credibility.[125]

All of these errors are compounded by deficient supervision. Supervisors are supposed to approve all expedited removal orders, and they often approve such orders even when the interview record shows that mandatory questions have not been asked. Moreover, supervisors often conduct review telephonically. As Michele Pistone and John Hoeffner point out, this practice encourages secondary inspectors to "briefly and contemporaneously summarize their interviews," at the risk of "omit[ting] or mischaracteriz[ing] important facts that a verbatim reading of the record would reveal."[126]

Another problem with secondary inspection noted by critics of expedited removal is a provision of the US Customs and Border Protection Inspectors' Field Manual, which permits inspectors to remove even persons who have expressed a fear of return when the fear "would clearly not qualify that individual for asylum."[127] But customs inspectors and supervisors are not trained in asylum law, and they may not recognize that a fear which at first glance appears unrelated to the grounds for asylum – for example, a fear of domestic violence – may nonetheless qualify the alien for asylum. When an alien in secondary inspection expresses a fear of return, the alien should be referred to a credible fear interview with an asylum officer, even if it appears to the customs officer that the nature of the fear will not qualify the alien for asylum.[128]

Pistone and Hoeffner suggest a number of sensible regulatory changes to solve these problems with secondary inspection, including prohibiting telephonic supervisory review and changing the Field Manual to make clear that aliens should be referred to a credible fear interview with an asylum officer if they express any fear of return. At the same time, however, they rightly note that many problems stem from an enforcement culture that fails to penalize customs officers for flouting already existent regulations designed to prevent the return of refugees. In an attempt to promote accountability, they advocate using testers to assess customs officials' compliance with regulations, videotaping secondary inspection interviews, and requiring immediate supervisors to re-interview aliens when the secondary inspection interview is facially incomplete (for example, when the mandatory three questions concerning fear of return have not been asked).[129] There should also be a strict policy against shackling or handcuffing people awaiting secondary inspection, unless there is some reason for an inspector to believe that an alien seeking admission is violent or a flight risk.[130] Such a practice can dissolve the trust needed for traumatized asylum seekers to be willing to identify themselves as fleeing persecution.

Asylum seekers who express a fear of persecution during their secondary inspection are placed in detention, pending a credible fear interview with an asylum officer. Critics raise several objections to this stage of expedited removal as well.

First, they note that the intimidating atmosphere of a detention center makes it difficult for trauma survivors to feel comfortable opening up to authority figures and that too many people are detained for too long.[131] Unfortunately, limited detention is a necessary part of expedited removal at ports of entry. If otherwise inadmissible port-of-entry applicants could automatically gain entry simply by uttering the word "asylum," border controls would be easily circumvented. But the initial screening should not take longer than a few days, and detention facilities should be more like reception centers than jails. The principle of hospitality should be flexible enough to permit limitations on liberty that are so limited in scope.

Second, critics allege that expedited proceedings give asylum seekers insufficient time to prepare their stories or find counsel.[132] This objection could be met, first, by distributing to all asylum seekers written information about the asylum process in their native languages, and second, by ensuring that non-governmental organizations have access to asylum seekers in detention to provide expert advice, and at least in some cases, representation.[133]

Finally, critics object that expedited procedures provide good faith asylum seekers with too few procedural protections, resulting in the removal and return of individuals who have a solid claim for refuge. Of course, any determination system will make errors. Some persecuted people will be denied asylum, and some economic migrants – with a good story to tell and a convincing demeanor – will be granted it. A system should be set up to minimize the former type of mistake, even at the expense of increasing the latter type – just as the criminal justice system is willing to tolerate the acquittal of many guilty people to avoid the mistaken conviction of innocent people. However, only so many mistaken grants can be made before a skeptical public loses faith in the system, and withdraws its support altogether. That is precisely the dynamic underway in Europe, most acutely in the UK.

Expedited review squarely addresses the issue of public faith; but if carried out properly, it does so in a way that preserves procedural protections for those most likely to be genuine refugees. Only those with "manifestly unfounded" claims are subject to expedited proceedings. Ideally, the very existence of such proceedings will deter those with manifestly unfounded claims from applying in the first place. Those applicants with material claims receive the same protections they have always had. Will the authorities on occasion fail to recognize some genuine refugees as having material claims? Yes, undoubtedly. The imprecision of translation, the debilitating effect of post-traumatic stress disorder on refugees' ability to tell their stories with detail, and the unavoidable subjectivity of credibility determinations all contribute to errors of judgment. The policymaker's goal cannot realistically be to eliminate entirely the risk of such errors. Rather, the goal must be to eliminate as many mistakes as possible, while still preserving public faith in the determination system. Expedited removal procedures aim toward this goal.

At the same time, expedited removal is hardly a silver bullet that will solve the problem of asylum claims made in bad faith. Most asylum seekers file their applications once they are within a country, not at a port of entry. Also, in the United States, almost nine out of ten persons who claim asylum at a port of entry succeed in demonstrating a "credible fear" of persecution and thus are moved along to the regular asylum adjudication process. So, for someone who has knowledge of the asylum system and is prepared to lie, expedited removal hardly serves as a deterrent. For these reasons, much greater emphasis needs to be placed on substantially speeding up regular asylum adjudications. Although in the United States, the Department of Homeland Security aims to render first-instance asylum decisions within six months of the filing date of an application, delays are common. It can occasionally even take years for a first-instance decision to be made.

Applicants then have access to several layers of appeal. For those applicants who initiate the asylum process by filing an "affirmative" application (rather than claim asylum in the course of removal proceedings), an adverse determination by an asylum adjudicator will result in a "referral" to an immigration judge (IJ), before whom they will have the chance to make their claim a second time. If an application is denied by an IJ, the asylum seeker can seek review by the Board of Immigration Appeals, and then ultimately by a federal court of appeals. Followed through to the end, this process can stretch on for many years – even if the denial is affirmed at each level with a summary disposition.

There are two ways of speeding up this process. The first is to increase resources in order to eliminate backlogs. The second is to limit access to appeals or, alternatively, to limit the scope of appellate review, permitting a more straightforward and faster resolution of a case. Unfortunately, the United States has chosen to limit the scope of appellate review while failing to devote the resources needed to ensure that the initial adjudication was conducted fairly and properly.

A statutory amendment in 1996 emphasized that federal courts of appeal cannot overturn findings of fact – which include the determination that an asylum seeker is not credible – made by the immigration agency "unless any reasonable adjudicator would be compelled to conclude to the contrary."[134] And an amendment in 2005 outlined the possible bases for finding an asylum seeker to be not credible. They include:

demeanor, candor, or responsiveness of the applicant or witness, the inherent plausibility of the applicant's or witness's account, the consistency between the applicant's or witness's written and oral statements (whenever made and whether or not made under oath, and considering the circumstances under which the statements were made), the internal consistency of each such statement, the consistency of such statements with other evidence of record (including the reports of the Department of State on country conditions), and any inaccuracies or falsehoods in such statements, without regard to whether an inconsistency, inaccuracy, or falsehood goes to the heart of the applicant's claim, or any other relevant factor.[135]

A finding that an asylum seeker is not credible due to his or her demeanor, explains the committee report accompanying this legislation, can be based upon "the expression of [the applicant's] countenance, how he sits or stands, whether he is inordinately nervous, his coloration during critical examination, the modulation or pace of his speech and other non-verbal communication."[136]

Moreover, the 2005 legislation states that "[w]here the trier of fact determines that the applicant should provide evidence that corroborates otherwise credible testimony, such evidence must be provided unless the applicant does not have the evidence and cannot reasonably obtain the evidence."[137] It further provides that "[n]o court [of appeals] shall reverse a determination made by a trier of fact with respect to the availability of corroborating evidence ... unless the court finds ... that a reasonable trier of fact is compelled to conclude that such corroborating evidence is unavailable."[138]

Certainly, credibility determinations are an unavoidable part of asylum adjudication. Applicants frequently have little corroborating evidence, and their claims will stand or fall on whether they are able to tell their stories specifically and convincingly. And there are good reasons for reviewing courts to defer to a fact-finder's credibility determination: testimony that may look convincing on paper may have been utterly unconvincing when delivered in person.

At the same time, however, determining credibility is especially difficult in the asylum context for numerous reasons. First, different cultures communicate differently. For example, Westerners may regard witnesses as shifty or untrustworthy if they fail to look their questioner in the eye; in other cultures, a failure to make eye contact may be a sign of respect. Second, asylum seekers often suffer from post-traumatic stress disorder that can make it difficult for them to remember specific details of the persecution they have suffered; insensitivity to that fact may lead an IJ to conclude mistakenly that an applicant is lying. Third, in a large majority of asylum hearings, a translator is used. Translators may fail to render nuances in an asylum seeker's testimony; worse, they may fail to translate the testimony accurately, introducing inconsistencies into an asylum seeker's recorded testimony that can become the basis for rejecting an application.[139] Attempts to clarify such inconsistencies often lead to further confusion – since the asylum seeker was unaware of the translation error – that can be mistaken by an IJ for evasion or non-responsiveness. These risks are compounded, first, by the fact that translators are often translating telephonically, and second, by the prerogative of the IJ to find an applicant not credible based on inconsistencies in testimony that are tangential or unrelated to the applicant's basis for claiming asylum. Finally, in demanding corroborating evidence, an IJ may fail to take account of the fact that the kinds of documents easily available to people in the United States may not be available to people in other countries.[140]

Perhaps one could sleep easily, despite the deference that appellate courts are required to show to the credibility determinations of IJs, if the latter could be counted on to do their jobs professionally and fairly. Unfortunately, that assumption is doubtful. Judge Richard Posner has noted that IJs commonly succumb to the pitfalls outlined above when assessing the credibility of applicants' testimony. They show (1) a "lack of familiarity with the relevant foreign cultures"; (2) an "exaggerated notion of how much religious people know about their religion"; (3) an "exaggerated notion of the availability, especially in poor nations, of documentary evidence of religious membership"; (4) "[i]nsensitivity to the possibility of misunderstandings caused by the use of translators of difficult languages such as Chinese, and relatedly, insensitivity to basing a determination of credibility on the demeanor of a person from a culture remote from the American, such as the Chinese"; and (5) "[r]eluctance to make clean determinations of credibility," making it difficult for an appellate court to decide whether a claim was rejected because the IJ found the alien to be not credible or for some other reason.[141]

Wide disparities in asylum grant rates among IJs in the same district – who should see roughly equivalent pools of applicants, since case assignments are based only on the judge's availability and the date an application was filed – are further evidence that asylum applications are adjudicated in an arbitrary manner. In New York, between 2000 and 2005, IJs' grant rates ranged from 4 percent to 90 percent (the standard deviation in grant rates was 25 percent). In San Francisco, grant rates ranged from 13 percent to 76 percent (with a standard deviation of 18 percent); in Miami, the low end was 3 percent and the high end 78 percent (with a standard deviation of 17 percent). Moreover, grant rates also vary widely across districts – ranging from 15 percent in Atlanta and 26 percent in Houston to 56 percent in Orlando and 75 percent in Phoenix.[142] As one observer notes, one might well conclude from these figures that "the most important factor determining whether [an applicant] received asylum was which judge heard her case."[143] A more recent study has shown that inconsistency also reigns at the level of asylum officers, who hear affirmative asylum applications in the first instance.[144]

The problems of error and inconsistency are compounded by an administrative review process that is broken. Beginning in 2002, the Board of Immigration Appeals (BIA) – tasked with reviewing the decisions of IJs prior to any appeal to the federal courts of appeal – was reduced in size from twenty-three members to eleven, and instead of hearing cases in three member panels and issuing written opinions, the BIA began to issue large numbers of summary orders by single board members. The purpose of this reform was to reduce backlogs and streamline administrative appeals: in 2001, the BIA had over 57,000 pending cases.[145]

That objective, however, has been achieved at the cost of basic fairness. Following the reform, orders summarily affirming the decision of an IJ increased from 3 percent to 60 percent;[146] between 2000 and 2005, the percentage of BIA decisions in favor of asylum seekers decreased from roughly 30 percent to less than 15 percent.[147] In fiscal year 2006, the eleven BIA members resolved 41,479 matters – about fifteen per working day per BIA member.[148] Such a staggering workload makes it impossible for BIA members even to familiarize themselves with the record when reviewing asylum decisions, let alone carefully consider the rationale of the IJ. The errors repeatedly made by IJs when determining applicants' credibility, together with the BIA's failure to ensure meaningful administrative review, led Judge Posner to conclude that "the adjudication of [immigration] cases at the administrative level has fallen below the minimum standards of legal justice."[149] The President of the National Association of Immigration Judges, Dana Leigh Marks, described the situation in these words:

> We were encouraged to do things in a short-and-dirty manner, knowing the BIA would return them if we went too far ... Now, the BIA is using all of these affirmances without opinion and we have no resources to do a top-notch job from the beginning ... We're like the guy behind the curtain in "The Wizard of Oz," for God's sake.[150]

One consequence, perhaps not surprisingly, has been a surge in the number of immigration appeals from the BIA to the federal courts of appeals. In the Second Circuit, which covers New York, immigration appeals mushroomed from 168 in 2001 to more than 2,000 in 2003. In the Ninth Circuit, which covers California, they more than quadrupled from roughly 900 in 2001 to about 4,000 in 2003. Immigration cases now account for roughly 18 percent of the federal appellate docket; historically, they constituted between 2 and 3 percent.[151] The rate at which federal courts of appeals reverse the BIA is similarly shocking: according to Judge Posner, in 2005, the Seventh Circuit (which includes Chicago) reversed the BIA "in a staggering 40 percent of the 136 petitions ... that were reviewed on the merits."[152] Nationwide that year, the federal courts of appeal reversed the BIA in asylum cases at a rate of 16.4 percent.[153] Lest this latter, comparatively low number provide comfort, recall that credibility determinations and fact-finding are largely insulated from review by the federal courts of appeals. Such determinations must be upheld "unless any reasonable adjudicator would be compelled to conclude to the contrary."[154]

Speeding up the asylum adjudication process is an important policy objective. But, in the United States, it has been advanced at the expense of too much fairness and accuracy. If the scope of appellate review is to be limited – either by summary affirmance or by rules binding appellate courts to administrative fact-finding – then more resources, training, and staff must be given to IJs, along with better legal and policy guidance, so that they can decide cases with greater consistency and accuracy in the first instance.[155] It is hardly surprising that unfairness results when roughly 210 immigration judges are asked to dispose of nearly 366,000 matters per year – nearly seven matters per judge per working day.[156] Even more important is making counsel more widely available. Unrepresented affirmative asylum applicants win at a rate of 16 percent in immigration court, compared with 46 percent for applicants with counsel.[157]

Detention and the war on terror

Since September 11, 2001, asylum has come under fire as a backdoor through which terrorists can enter the West without being subject to ordinary immigration controls. The war on terror has been used as a justification for, among other things, detaining port-of-entry asylum seekers even after they have established a "credible fear" of persecution. The worry is that a credible fear can be easily established; that, by asserting such a fear, terrorists could gain admittance into the United States pending full-scale asylum adjudication; and that they could then abscond and disappear. The response has been to tighten up the conditions under which a port-of-entry applicant will be released from detention pending a full-scale asylum adjudication.

In March 2003, the Department of Homeland Security (DHS) announced a plan – called Operation Liberty Shield – to institute mandatory detention for all asylum seekers arriving at ports of entry from thirty-three countries with large Muslim or Arab populations.[158] Although the program was discontinued one month later, the Lawyers' Committee on Human Rights reported that the mandatory detention of these asylum seekers continued as an unofficial policy.[159] In some cases, asylum seekers have been detained even *after* they have been *granted asylum*, while the government appeals the decision.[160]

It is obvious why detention is desirable to the government: it is rightly concerned that terrorists will seek to use the asylum process to gain access to the United States. Indeed, one of the 1993 World Trade Center bombers was on parole while waiting for a decision on his asylum application, as was Mir Aimal Kasi, who killed two in a shooting rampage at CIA Headquarters in 1993. Mohammed Hadayet, who strafed the El Al counter at Los Angeles International Airport with machine-gun fire in 2001, had been granted asylum. In other countries as well, terrorists gained entry by claiming asylum. For example, Ahmed Ressam, who was caught entering the United States with explosives in his vehicle on his way to attack Los Angeles airport, had received refugee status in Canada.

Nonetheless, these mandatory detention policies are misguided and unfair. Security goals can be accomplished through individualized dangerousness determinations. The Immigration and Nationality Act already requires DHS to check an applicant's identity against FBI and State Department watchlists before granting asylum,[161] and it prohibits granting asylum to any alien whom "there are reasonable grounds for regarding ... as a danger to the security of the United States."[162] Regulations furthermore prohibit the parole of anyone judged to "present ... a security risk."[163] Background checks and an individualized dangerousness determination can be made at the time parole is requested, so that individuals who pose no security threat could be released. Operation Liberty Shield was especially troubling insofar as it mandated the detention of asylum seekers for no reason other than their nationality – the very kind of reason for detention that asylum condemns when carried out by a foreign government.

Refusals to grant parole should also be reviewable by an IJ.[164] Currently, parole decisions are left to the discretion of DHS administrators subject only to *habeas corpus* review by federal courts for abuse of discretion.[165] The courts have been clear that such review is "narrow" in scope:

[T]he [district director's] exercise of his broad discretionary power must be viewed at the outset as presumptively legitimate and bona fide in the absence of strong proof to the contrary. The burden of proving that discretion was not exercised or was exercised irrationally or in bad faith is a heavy one and rests at all times on the unadmitted alien challenging denial of parole.[166]

Immigration judges should be empowered to grant parole despite a district director's denial when the director is unable to provide an individualized reason to believe that an asylum seeker is a security threat, so long as the asylum seeker has established his identity and has ties to the United States.

Finally, it is important to remember that, from a security standpoint, illegal migration is a much more pressing concern than port-of-entry asylum applicants. The 5,500 or so people who claimed asylum at American ports of entry in 2003 represent just a fraction of the hundreds of thousands who crossed illegally over the Canadian and Mexican borders. And most of the thousands who cross the Mediterranean or Adriatic to enter Spain and Italy have no intention of applying for asylum. If controlling labor market access and stopping terrorists are important policy goals, then regulatory resources should be directed primarily to this much larger problem, not to ensuring that the asylum process is as airtight as possible. This is especially so when clamping down on port-of-entry applicants disadvantages persecuted people who choose to utilize legal channels in search of a refuge, rather than simply entering as undocumented migrants.

Conclusion

The world's asylum system is in crisis. In recent years, asylum seekers have come under attack as fraudsters, leeches, terrorists, and worse. States have responded by erecting barriers to entry to keep asylum seekers out; by enacting burdensome procedural requirements that make it more difficult for asylum seekers to have their claims heard on the merits; by detaining asylum seekers and reducing the public support available to them while their applications are pending; and by offering less to those who are granted asylum.

While it is tempting to criticize states without qualification for these practices, in fact, states have responded to a genuine dilemma with which advocates must come to grips. Any adjudication system must balance the need to avoid false positives (here, mistaken grants of asylum) with the need to avoid false negatives (mistaken denials of asylum). When an asylum system is tilted too far in the direction of avoiding mistaken denials – by, for example, setting a low evidentiary bar, or by making available several layers of appeal that have the consequence of extending the adjudication process by months or years – and when public support or work authorization is given to those whose cases are pending, there are strong incentives for unqualified applicants to submit fraudulent or bad faith claims. By doing so, such applicants can legally extend their presence in Western states for quite a long time while gaining the benefits of public support or work authorization.

Ultimately, genuine refugees bear the brunt of that kind of abuse. Political support for asylum is limited. When asylum is exploited as a loophole that enables ordinary migrants to circumvent immigration restrictions, public disaffection and backlash is likely to follow. The last fifteen years demonstrate that dynamic. In short, advocates have an interest in ensuring that genuine refugees are not wrongfully denied asylum; but they also have an interest in ensuring that the adjudication process has enough bite to distinguish meaningfully between applicants who qualify and those who do not. False negatives must be avoided, but so too must false positives.

The pendulum has swung too far in the latter direction, however. States have responded to public outrage by enacting a raft of policies that impose significant burdens on genuine refugees and that violate the traditional principle of sheltering the persecuted (not to mention the international law obligation of non-refoulement). I have argued that restrictive policies should reflect three principles: selective deterrence, hospitality, and caution. That is, they should be designed to reduce the number of fraudulent applications, not the number of applications overall; they should not transform the asylum application process into a medieval trial by ordeal; and they should be designed, to the greatest extent possible given the fragility of public support for asylum, to minimize mistaken denials rather than mistaken grants. The stakes for a refugee who is wrongly returned are too great to do otherwise.

Notes

1. UNHCR, "Asylum Applications in Industrialized Countries, 1980–1999" (November 2001), tables III.1, VI.4, www.unchr.org/statistics/STATISTICS/3c3eb40f4.pdf.
2. UNHCR, *Statistical Yearbook 2001* (October 2002), tables C.1, C.2.
3. UNHCR, *Statistical Yearbook 2005* (April 2007), table C.1.
4. YouGov poll, April 25, 2006; YouGov poll, August 14, 2003, both at Polling the Nations, www.poll.orspub.com.
5. YouGov poll, April 2–3, 2004; YouGov poll, August 11–14, 2003, both at Polling the Nations, www.poll.orspub.com.
6. Eurobarometer, Spring 1997, at Polling the Nations, www.poll.orspub.com.
7. Data from UNHCR, *Statistical Yearbook 2005* (April 2007), tables C.1, C.13 (for years 1996–2005); UNHCR, *Statistical Yearbook 2001* (October 2002), tables C.1, C.2, C.26, C.27 (for years 1982–95).
8. Due to serious efforts taken by the government to reduce the number of asylum seekers, the number of new applications in the UK fell to 60,050 in 2003 and 27,850 in 2006. UNHCR, "Asylum Levels and Trends in Industrialized Countries, 2006" (March 23, 2007), table 1, www.unchr.org/statistics/STATISTICS/460150272.pdf. For a list of the steps taken by the UK, see Home Office, "Home Office Statistical Bulletin: Asylum Statistics: United Kingdom 2003" (August 24, 2004), p. 10, www.homeoffice.gov.uk/rds/pdfs04/hosb1104.pdf (last visited February 24, 2008). Although numbers have declined, asylum remains politically salient in the UK. In other EU countries, the number of new applicants has also leveled off over the last few years, at least in large part due to the erection of successful barriers to entry like those described below.
9. ICM/*News of the World*, February 16, 2004, at Polling the Nations, www.poll.orspub.com.
10. YouGov, August 14, 2003, at Polling the Nations, www.poll.orspub.com.
11. The Refugee Council, "Attitudes Toward Refugees and Asylum Seekers: A Survey of Public Opinion" (May 2002), p. 4, www.refugeecouncil.org.uk/downloads/mori_report.pdf (last visited February 24, 2008).
12. The UK's recognition rates reached a nadir in 2004; the figures are for first-instance decisions. First-instance asylum grant rates were 6 percent in 2003, 7 percent in 2005, and 11 percent in 2006. See Home Office, "Asylum Statistics: United Kingdom 2006" (August 21, 2007), table 1.1, www.homeoffice.gov.uk/rds/pdfs07/hosb1407.pdf (last visited February 26, 2008).
13. *Daily Star* (UK), May 22, 2002. Other examples include: "One in five flock here; asylum: we're too damn soft," *Daily Star* (UK), January 23,

2004; "'Asylum rejects' scandal: 90 per cent stay anyway," *Daily Star* (UK), September 16, 2002; "Bogus asylum seekers are draining millions from the NHS," *Daily Express* (UK), November 26, 2002.

14. US Committee for Refugees and Immigrants, "Country Report: Canada," *World Refugee Survey 2007* (New York: US Committee for Refugees, 2007), p. 40 (Canada), p. 62 (the Netherlands); 8 C.F.R. section 208.7(a)(1) (US); Immigration Rules section 360 (UK).

15. EU Reception Directive, Council Directive 2003/9/EC of January 27, 2003, laying down minimum standards for the reception of asylum seekers, art. 13.

16. Home Office, "Asylum Support," www.bia.homeoffice.gov.uk/asylum/support (last visited February 26, 2008).

17. Immigration and Asylum Act of 1999 (c. 33), section 4; Home Office, "Section 4 Support," www.bia.homeoffice.gov.uk/asylum/support/apply/section4 (last visited February 26, 2008).

18. Indeed, in 2003, 82 percent of new applicants in Britain had received a first-instance decision within two months, and 63 percent had received a final decision, including appeal, within six months. Home Office, "Home Office Statistical Bulletin: Asylum Statistics: United Kingdom 2003," p. 23.

19. "A strange sort of sanctuary," *Economist*, March 15, 2003, p. 51.

20. Home Office, "Asylum Statistics: United Kingdom 2003," table 1.1.

21. Matthew J. Gibney and Randall Hansen, "Deportation and the Liberal State: the Forcible Return of Asylum Seekers and Unlawful Migrants in Canada, Germany, and the United Kingdom" (UNHCR New Issues in Refugee Research, Working Paper No. 77, February 2003), p. 13.

22. For example, the immigration service only places about 60 percent of applications into "expedited review," designed to conclude within 180 days of filing. US Department of Justice, Executive Office of Immigration Review, *FY 2006 Statistical Year Book* (February 2007), p. L1, www.usdoj.gov/eoir/statspub/fy06syb.pdf (last visited February 26, 2008).

23. Ibid., pp. I1, K3.

24. US Department of Justice, Executive Office of Immigration Review, "Fact Sheet – BIA Streamlining" (September 15, 2004), www.usdoj.gov/eoir/press/04/BIAStreamlining2004.pdf (last visited February 26, 2008). Some observers have disagreed with the government's explanation, and have argued that the rise in petitions for federal court review is due to the inadequacy of the BIA's streamlined procedures. John R. B. Palmer, Stephen W. Yale-Loehr, and Elizabeth Cronin, "Why Are So Many People Challenging Board of Immigration Appeals Decisions in Federal Court? An Empirical Analysis of the Recent Surge in Petitions for Review," *Georgetown Immigration Law Journal*, 20 (2005), pp. 1–99.

25. Ibid., table 12.
26. "A Strange Sort of Sanctuary," p. 50.
27. Alan Travis, "Asylum Service Criticised," *The Guardian* (UK), July 16, 2003.
28. David A. Martin, "The Refugee Concept: On Definitions, Politics, and the Careful Use of a Scarce Resource" in Howard Adelman (ed.), *Refugee Policy: Canada and the United States* (Toronto: York Lanes Press, 1991), p. 34.
29. Ibid., p. 35.
30. Martin Bright, "Refugees Find No Welcome in City of Hate," *Observer* (UK), July 6, 2003.
31. US Department of State, "Visa Bulletin" (August 2007), www.travel.state. gov/visa/frvi/bulletin/bulletin_3269.html (last visited February 26, 2008).
32. Randall Hansen, "Asylum Policy in the European Union," *Georgetown Immigration Law Journal*, 14 (2000), p. 786; James C. Hathaway and R. Alexander Neve, "Making International Refugee Law Relevant Again: A Proposal for Collectivized and Solution-Oriented Protection," *Harvard Human Rights Journal*, 10 (1997), p. 120.
33. Jens Velsted-Hansen, "Europe's Response to the Arrival of Asylum Seekers: Refugee Protection and Immigration Control" (UNHCR New Issues in Refugee Research, Working Paper No. 6, May 1999), p. 21.
34. Among the forty-nine countries covered by the British transit visa program are: Burma, China, Democratic Republic of Congo, Eritrea, Iran, Kenya, Nigeria, Pakistan, Somalia, and Zimbabwe.
35. James C. Hathaway, *The Rights of Refugees Under International Law* (Cambridge University Press, 2005), p. 292.
36. Ibid.
37. Home Office, "Asylum Statistics: United Kingdom, 2004" (August 23, 2005), table 2.1, www.homeoffice.gov.uk/rds/pdfs05/hosb1305.pdf (last visited February 27, 2008).
38. Hathaway, *Rights of Refugees*, p. 293.
39. John Morrison and Beth Crosland, "The Trafficking and Smuggling of Refugees: the End Game in European Asylum Policy?" (UNCHR New Issues in Refugee Research Working Paper No. 39, 2001), p. 17.
40. Hansen, "Europe's Response," p. 784.
41. Hathaway and Neve, "Making International Refugee Law Relevant," p. 122.
42. Wolfgang Bosswick, "Development of Asylum Policy in Germany," *Journal of Refugee Studies*, 13 (2000), p. 51.
43. US Committee for Refugees and Immigrants, "Country Report – Australia," in *World Refugee Survey 2006* (Washington, DC: US Committee for Refugees and Immigrants, 2006), www.refugees.org/ worldmap.aspx (last visited March 1, 2008).
44. Exec. Order 12,807, 57 Fed. Reg. 23,133 (1992).

45. Harold Hongju Koh, "Reflections on Refoulement and *Haitian Centers Council*," *Harvard International Law Journal*, 35 (1994), p. 9.
46. *Sale* v. *Haitian Centers Council*, 509 U.S. 155 (1993).
47. Marlise Simons, "Under Pressure, Spain Tries to Close an Open Door," *New York Times*, October 10, 2004.
48. Ian Fisher and Richard Bernstein, "On Italian Isle, Migrant Plight Draws Scrutiny," *New York Times*, October 5, 2004.
49. US Committee for Refugees and Immigrants, "Country Update – European Union," *World Refugee Survey 2005* (Washington, DC: US Committee for Refugees and Immigrants, 2005), www.refugees.org/worldmap.aspx (last visited March 1, 2008).
50. Home Office, "Asylum Statistics: United Kingdom 2003" (August 24, 2004), p. 10, www.homeoffice.gov.uk/rds/pdfs04/hosb1104.pdf (last visited February 27, 2008).
51. Ibid., p. 29 and table 2.
52. Home Office, "Asylum Statistics: United Kingdom 2006," p. 9.
53. US Committee for Refugees and Immigrants, "Country Report – European Union," in *World Refugee Survey 2006*.
54. US Department of State, *2006 Country Reports on Human Rights Practices* (March 6, 2007), www.state.gov/g/drl/rls/hrrpt/2006/ (last visited February 28, 2008).
55. Home Office, "Asylum Statistics: United Kingdom 2003," p. 10.
56. Grundgesetz, art. 16a(2).
57. Sabine Weidlich, "First Instance Asylum Proceedings in Europe: Do Bona Fide Refugees Find Protection?," *Georgetown Immigration Law Journal*, 14 (2000), p. 660.
58. There is debate, however, about whether this decline was due to the amendment or to improving conditions in the Balkans, from where the overwhelming majority of asylum seekers had fled. Bosswick, "Development of Asylum Policy," p. 50.
59. Convention determining the State responsible for examining applications for asylum lodged in one of the Member States of the European Communities, August 19, 1997, EU Doc. No. 97/C 254/01, available at www.aei.pitt.edu/archive/00001736/ (last visited February 28, 2008).
60. European Council on Refugees and Exiles, "ECRE Country Report 2000: Slovak Republic," www.ecre.org/country00/slovak%20republic.pdf (last visited February 28, 2008).
61. Weidlich, "First Instance Asylum Proceedings," p. 652.
62. US Committee for Refugees, "Country Report – Denmark," *World Refugee Survey 2003* (Washington, DC: US Committee for Refugees, 2003), www.refugees.org/worldmap.aspx (last visited March 1, 2008).
63. 8 U.S.C. section 1158(a)(2)(B)–(D).

64. Department of Homeland Security, Office of Immigration Statistics, *2003 Yearbook of Immigration Statistics* (September 2004), table 18 (cases referred to immigration judge past filing deadline / (cases granted + cases denied + cases referred to immigration judge past filing deadline + cases referred to immigration judge following interview). The percentage of defensive applications which failed the one-year filing deadline is not available, but is likely to be higher, since defensive applicants wait to apply for asylum until they have been placed in removal proceedings, rather than initiating the claim themselves.

65. Weidlich, "First Instance Asylum Proceedings," p. 658.

66. Morrison and Crosland, "The Trafficking and Smuggling of Refugees," p. 17.

67. 9/11 Recommendations Implementation Act, H.R.10.IH (as introduced in the House), 108th Cong., section 3007(a)(2) (2004).

68. 8 U.S.C. section 1158(b)(1)(B)(ii).

69. States differ as to whether expedited procedures apply to all applicants, or only to those who file at a port of entry.

70. Exceptions include Denmark and Sweden, which allow only one level of appeal. Karen Musalo, Jennifer Moore, and Richard A. Boswell (eds.), *Refugee Law and Policy: A Comparative and International Approach*, 2nd edn. (Durham, NC: Carolina Academic Press, 2002), p. 138.

71. Denmark allows appeals only in expedited procedures when the non-governmental Refugee Council objects to a decision to deny. Velsted-Hansen, "Europe's Response," p. 11.

72. Weidlich, "First Instance Asylum Proceedings," p. 666.

73. US Committee for Refugees, "Country Report – France," *World Refugee Survey 2002* (Washington, DC: US Committee for Refugees, 2002), www.refugees.org/worldmap.aspx (last visited March 1, 2008); 8 U.S.C. section 1252(b)(3)(B).

74. This change was adopted in August 2004. DHS emphasized, "The expanded use of expedited removal is primarily directed at those illegal aliens who are not citizens of Mexico or Canada." US Department of Homeland Security, "Press Release, DHS Announces Expanded Border Control Plans" (August 10, 2004). The expedited removal law authorizes the executive branch to apply expedited removal to any inadmissible alien arrested anywhere in the United States who has been continuously present for less than two years. 8 U.S.C. section 1225(b)(1)(A)(ii)(II).

75. 8 U.S.C. section 1225(b)(1)(B)(v).

76. "The Expedited Removal Study: Report on the First Three Years of Implementation of Expedited Removal," *Notre Dame Journal of Law, Ethics, and Public Policy*, 15 (2001), p. 44.

77. Ibid., p. 60.

78. Bosswick, "Development of Asylum Policy," pp. 51–2; US Committee for Refugees, "Country Report – Germany," *World Refugee Survey 2003*.

79. US Committee for Refugees and Immigrants, "Country Report – Germany," *World Refugee Survey 2003*.

80. US Committee for Refugees and Immigrants, "Country Report – France," *World Refugee Survey 2003*.

81. *R (Limbuela)* v. *Secretary of State for the Home Department*, [2004] Q.B. 1440.

82. Asylum and Immigration (Treatment of Claimants, etc.) Act of 2004 (ch. 19), section 9 (July 22, 2004).

83. 8 U.S.C. section 1158(d)(2).

84. Migration Act of 1958, sections 189, 196(1). For a discussion, see Catherine Skulan, "Australia's Mandatory Detention of 'Unauthorized' Asylum Seekers: History, Politics and Analysis Under International Law," *Georgetown Immigration Law Journal*, 21 (2006), pp. 84–94.

85. "Hague Sparks Asylum Anger," *BBC News*, May 18, 2001, www.news.bbc.co.uk/vote2001/hi/english/newsid_1338000/1338363.stm (last visited March 1, 2008).

86. Home Office, "New International Approaches to Asylum Processing and Protection" (March 27, 2003).

87. "Setback for UK at EU Summit," *BBC News*, June 19, 2003, www.news.bbc.co.uk/1/hi/world/europe/3002390.stm (last visited March 1, 2008).

88. Simons, "Under Pressure."

89. US Department of Justice, Office of the Inspector General, "Immigration and Naturalization Service Deportation of Aliens after Final Orders Have Been Issued" (1996), p. 1.

90. Gibney and Hansen, "Deportation and the Liberal State," p. 6.

91. "Blair Sets Asylum Removal Target," *BBC News*, September 16, 2004, www.news.bbc.co.uk/1/hi/uk_politics/3661178.stm (last visited March 1, 2008); Home Office, "Asylum Statistics: United Kingdom 2006," table 1.1.

92. Gibney and Hansen, "Deportation and the Liberal State," p. 6.

93. See Joseph H. Carens, "The Philosopher and the Policymaker: Two Perspectives on the Ethics of Immigration with Special Attention to the Problem of Restricting Asylum," in Kay Heilbronner *et al.* (eds.), *Immigration Admissions: The Search for Workable Policies in Germany and the United States* (Providence, RI: Berghahn Books, 1997), pp. 8–9.

94. Home Office, "Asylum Statistics: United Kingdom 2006," table 1.1.

95. In 2003, 5,367 applicants claimed asylum at a US port of entry. US Department of Homeland Security, Office of Immigration Statistics,

Yearbook of Immigration Statistics: 2003 (2004), p. 48, www.dhs.gov/xlibrary/assets/statistics/yearbook/2003/2003Yearbook.pdf (last visited March 1, 2008).

96. Morrison and Crosland, "The Trafficking and Smuggling of Refugees," p. 17.

97. Michele R. Pistone and Philip G. Schrag, "The New Asylum: Improved But Still Unfair," *Georgetown Immigration Law Journal*, 16 (2001), pp. 40–1 and n. 225.

98. Human Rights First, "In Liberty's Shadow: U.S. Detention of Asylum Seekers in the Era of Homeland Security" (2004), p. 8, www.humanrightsfirst.org/asylum/libertys_shadow/Libertys_Shadow.pdf (last visited March 1, 2008).

99. 8 C.F.R. section 212.5(a)–(c).

100. Pistone and Schrag, "The New Asylum," p. 71.

101. "The Expedited Removal Study," p. 68.

102. Ibid., p. 69.

103. Eileen Sullivan *et al.*, "Testing Community Supervision for the INS: An Evaluation of the Appearance Assistance Program" (Vera Institute of Justice, 2000), p. 8, www.vera.org/publication_pdf/aapfinal.pdf (last visited March 1, 2008).

104. Ibid, p. 27.

105. Ibid., p. 8.

106. US Immigration and Customs Enforcement, "Fact Sheet, Detention and Removal Operations: Alternatives to Detention" (July 14, 2004), www.ice.gov/pi/news/factsheets/061704detFS2.htm (last visited March 1, 2008).

107. Ibid.; Human Rights First, "In Liberty's Shadow," p. 43.

108. For criticism, see UNHCR, *State of the World's Refugees 2006: Human Displacement in the New Millennium* (New York: Oxford University Press, 2006), pp. 38–9.

109. Pistone and Schrag, "The New Asylum," p. 9. As originally proposed, the filing deadline was thirty days. Ibid., p. 10.

110. Home Office, "Asylum Statistics: United Kingdom 2003," table 7.4.

111. US Department of Homeland Security, *2002 Yearbook of Immigration Statistics* (2003), table 20, www.dhs.gov/xlibrary/assets/statistics/yearbook/2002/Yearbook2002.pdf (last visited March 1, 2008).

112. US Committee for Refugees and Immigrants, "Country Report – European Union," *World Refugee Survey 2005*.

113. UNHCR, *Statistical Yearbook 2005* (April 2007), table III.1, www.unhcr.org/statistics/STATISTICS/464478a72.html (last visited March 1, 2008).

114. Weidlich, "First Instance Asylum Proceedings," p. 658.

115. Ibid.
116. US Committee for Refugees, "Country Report – Slovak Republic," *World Refugee Survey 2003*, p. 220.
117. US Committee for Refugees and Immigrants, "Country Report – Europe," *World Refugee Survey 2007*, p. 60.
118. US Committee for Refugees, "Country Report – Belgium," *World Refugee Survey 2003*.
119. The following discussion draws heavily on Michele R. Pistone and John J. Hoeffner, "Rules Are Made to Be Broken: How the Process of Expedited Removal Fails Asylum Seekers," *Georgetown Immigration Law Journal*, 20 (2006), p. 167.
120. Pistone and Hoeffner, "Rules Are Made to Be Broken," pp. 176, 178.
121. United States Commission on International Religious Freedom, "Report on Asylum Seekers in Expedited Removal," vol. 1 (February 2005), p. 6, cited in Pistone and Hoeffner, "Rules Are Made to Be Broken," pp. 177–8.
122. Ibid. vol. 2, table 2.1, cited in Pistone and Hoeffner, "Rules Are Made to Be Broken," pp. 178–9.
123. Ibid., vol. 2, p. 29; US General Accounting Office, "Opportunities Exist to Improve the Expedited Removal Process," Publication No. GAO/GGD-00-176 (September 2000), p. 40, both cited in Pistone and Hoeffner, "Rules Are Made to Be Broken," p. 180.
124. United States Commission on International Religious Freedom, "Report on Asylum Seekers," vol. 2, table 1.4, cited in Pistone and Hoeffner, "Rules Are Made to Be Broken," pp. 181–2.
125. Pistone and Hoeffner, "Rules Are Made to Be Broken," p. 182.
126. Ibid., p. 187.
127. US Customs and Border Protection Inspector's Manual section 17.15 (2003), cited in Pistone and Hoeffner, "Rules Are Made to Be Broken," p. 188.
128. Pistone and Hoeffner, "Rules Are Made to Be Broken," pp. 190–1.
129. Ibid., pp. 196–210.
130. Pistone and Schrag, "The New Asylum," pp. 59–63.
131. Ibid., pp. 49–50; Sharon A. Healey, "The Trend Toward the Criminalization and Detention of Asylum Seekers," *Human Rights Brief*, 12.1 (2004), p. 14; Lory Diana Rosenberg, "The Courts and Interception: The United States' Interdiction Experience and its Impact on Refugees and Asylum Seekers," *Georgetown Immigration Law Journal*, 17 (2003), pp. 216–17.
132. Pistone and Schrag, "The New Asylum," p. 52.
133. Ibid., pp. 53–7, 66–70.
134. 8 U.S.C. section 1252(b)(4)(B).

135. 8 U.S.C. section 1158(b)(1)(B)(iii).
136. H.R. Rep. No. 109–13 (109th Cong. 1st Sess., May 13, 2005), p. 168.
137. 8 U.S.C. section 1158(b)(1)(B)(ii).
138. 8 U.S.C. section 1252(b)(4).
139. For a discussion of translation difficulties in relation to credibility determinations, see Neal P. Pfeiffer, Note, "Credibility Findings in INS Asylum Adjudications: A Realistic Assessment," *Texas Journal of International Law*, 23 (1988), pp. 139–51.
140. For an example of these problems, see *Castaneda-Castillo v. Gonzales*, 488 F.3d 17, 26–32 (1st Cir. 2007) (en banc).
141. *Iao v. Gonzales*, 400 F.3d 530, 533–5 (7th Cir. 2005) (Posner J.). See also *Benslimane v. Gonzales*, 430 F.3d 828 (7th Cir. 2005) (Posner J.), and *Wang v. Attorney General*, 423 F.3d 260 (3d Cir. 2005) (Fuentes J.).
142. Sydenham B. Alexander III, "A Political Response to Crisis in the Immigration Courts," *Georgetown Immigration Law Journal*, 21 (2006), p. 28, table 4.
143. Ibid., p. 23.
144. Jaya Ramji-Nogales, Andrew I. Schoenholtz, and Philip G. Schrag, "Refugee Roulette: Disparities in Asylum Adjudication," *Stanford Law Review*, 60 (2007), pp. 295–411.
145. Procedural Reforms to Improve Case Management, 67 Fed. Reg. 54,878 (August 26, 2002).
146. Alexander, "A Political Response," p. 12.
147. Ramji-Nogales *et al.*, "Refugee Roulette," p. 358.
148. US Department of Justice, Executive Office for Immigration Review, *FY 2006 Statistical Year Book* (February 2007), p. S2, www.usdoj.gov/eoir/statspub/fy06syb.pdf (last visited March 2, 2008).
149. *Benslimane*, 430 F.3d at 830.
150. Solomon Moore and Ann M. Simmons, "Immigrant Pleas Crushing Federal Appellate Courts: As Caseloads Skyrocket, Judges Blame the Work Done by the Board of Immigration Appeals," *Los Angeles Times*, May 2, 2005, p. 1, quoted in Alexander, "A Political Response," pp. 12–13.
151. Alexander, "A Political Response," p. 10.
152. *Benslimane*, 430 F.3d at 829.
153. Ramji-Nogales *et al.*, "Refugee Roulette," p. 362.
154. 8 U.S.C. section 1252(b)(4)(B).
155. For suggestions on reform, see Stephen H. Legomsky, "Learning to Live With Unequal Justice: Asylum and the Limits to Consistency," *Stanford Law Review*, 60 (2007), pp. 444–57, and Ramji-Nogales *et al.*, "Refugee Roulette," pp. 378–89.

156. US Department of Justice, *FY 2006 Statistical Year Book*, p. B2.

157. Ramji-Nogales *et al.*, "Refugee Roulette," p. 384; see also Donald Kerwin, "Revisiting the Need for Appointed Counsel," *mpi Insight* (Migration Policy Institute, April 2005), pp. 12–16, www.migrationpolicy.org/insight/Insight_Kerwin.pdf (last visited March 1, 2008).

158. Philip Shenon, "Administration's New Asylum Policy Comes Under Fire," *New York Times*, March 19, 2003. DHS declined to identify which countries had been selected for security reasons, but anecdotal evidence presented by the Lawyer's Committee for Human Rights indicated that the list included Afghanistan, Algeria, Bahrain, Bangladesh, Djibouti, Egypt, Eritrea, Indonesia, Iran, Iraq, Jordan, Kazakhstan, Kuwait, Lebanon, Libya, Malaysia, Morocco, Oman, Pakistan, Philippines, Qatar, Saudi Arabia, Somalia, Sudan, Syria, Tajikistan, Thailand, Tunisia, Turkey, Turkmenistan, the United Arab Emirates, Uzbekistan, Yemen, and the Gaza Strip and West Bank. Human Rights First, "In Liberty's Shadow," p. 24.

159. Human Rights First, "In Liberty's Shadow," pp. 28–9.

160. Ibid., p. 29. However, a recent DHS memo makes clear that, absent exceptional security concerns, it is Department policy to release aliens who have been granted asylum by an IJ, even when the Department has an appeal pending before the BIA. See "Memorandum from Michael Garcia, Detention Policy Where an Immigration Judge Has Granted Asylum and ICE Has Appealed" (February 9, 2004), www.humanrightsfirst.org/asylum/Garcia_memo_detn_duringappeal.pdf (last visited March 2, 2008).

161. 8 U.S.C. section 1158(d)(5)(A)(i).

162. 8 U.S.C. section 1158(b)(2)(A)(iv).

163. 8 C.F.R. section 212.5(b).

164. Human Rights First, "In Liberty's Shadow," p. 46.

165. 8 C.F.R. section 212.5(a); 8 U.S.C. section 1182(d)(5)(A).

166. *Schoenmetz* v. *Ingham*, 949 F. Supp. 152 (W.D.N.Y. 1996) (alterations in original) (quoting *Bertrand* v. *Sava*, 684 F.2d 204, 212–13 (2d Cir. 1982)).

Conclusion

For billions of people, existence is precarious. The World Bank estimates that 985 million people live on less than one dollar a day and 2.6 billion live on less than two dollars a day.[1] Scores of millions more live amidst civil war or in failed states unable to ensure their physical security from criminal gangs, ethnic militias, or religious extremists. Each year, multitudes of such people traverse vast deserts and dangerous seas in search of a better life in the West. They arrive to the realization that they are unwanted and that their mere presence makes them criminals. By and large, the West's migration policy is indifferent to the reality of a brutal, dangerous, and grossly unequal world. Asylum, the main safety valve in a system of closed borders, is available to persecuted people; but most of the huddled masses who seek a new life in the West are not persecuted. Any humane sensibility must recognize the appeal of a more inclusive approach to asylum. In the face of extreme need, it seems perverse to single out one particular group – persecuted people – for special treatment.

In the last fifteen years, refugee advocates have succeeded in winning important court victories that have widened the scope of asylum. Courts have stretched their interpretation of the term "persecution" in order to encompass domestic violence, civil conflict, female genital mutilation, and other harm inflicted by non-state actors. In these respects, legal developments over the last fifteen years have marked a major departure from the traditional focus of asylum on sheltering people subjected to persecution carried out by official agents. Many observers have argued that eligibility for asylum should be expanded further still, to encompass non-persecuted people who are exposed to violence or serious harm. In sum, asylum has increasingly taken on a "palliative," humanitarian orientation focused on protecting people from serious harm of all kinds.

Even as the substantive grounds for eligibility have widened, however, states have adopted numerous procedural measures that have made it more difficult for asylum seekers to have their claims heard on the merits. The dizzying array of these measures has led to a dramatic decline in the number of new asylum applications filed. It seems clear that, despite the legal victories that have expanded the substantive grounds for asylum, refugees seeking asylum are far worse off today than they were fifteen years ago.

These two trends – an expansive view of the purpose of asylum and the adoption of barriers to limit the number of applications – are conceptually connected. If need for protection is the yardstick by which an asylum claim is measured, many people usually regarded as ordinary immigrants or "economic migrants" are not so different after all from those who have traditionally benefited from asylum. As one observer argues:

I cannot see why the moral importance of admitting political refugees should be any greater than that of admitting so-called economic migrants. For one thing, the politically persecuted are not, in general, worse off than the desperately poor. Being imprisoned for one's beliefs is not, in general, worse than working 16-hour days while being permanently hungry ... [Additionally,] the desperately poor are *also* the victims of political oppression, for they are excluded from all better economic opportunities through the coercive power of governments. Their plight is produced by the present national and international economic order which is coercively upheld by their governments and ours.[2]

Many economic migrants are driven by grinding poverty and insecurity to search for a better life elsewhere. Consider, for example, the resident of a Brazilian favello who lives in shocking poverty and who regularly experiences insecurity due to the struggle for power between the state and criminal gangs. Or recall from the Introduction the example of Alain Baptiste, an HIV-positive Haitian unable to obtain antiretroviral drugs in Haiti, or Angela, the Jamaican woman who feared she would be killed because she provided police with the name of the gang member who had killed her daughter. Their need for resettlement abroad may be as great as, or greater than, the need of (for example) dissidents who have been detained by the state for their political views.

But as the rationale for asylum expands to include more and more of the people traditionally regarded as ordinary migrants, its status as a narrow exception to immigration controls is undermined. From the viewpoint of a skeptical Western public, ordinary migrants are increasingly gaining admission using a loophole that was never intended for them. The exception threatens to swallow the rule. The solution: close the loophole.

States have attempted exactly that, enacting the various restrictive policies outlined in Chapter 6. If need alone creates an entitlement to asylum, then states must find some means of limiting the number of potential claimants. A humanitarian approach to asylum lacks any clear limiting principle. Asylum policy, driven by the fear of open floodgates, becomes focused on limiting the number of applicants, just as immigration policy has generally come to emphasize protecting borders and limiting numbers.

Moreover, asylum is an extremely inefficient way to pursue humanitarian goals. The resources spent adjudicating asylum seekers' applications, and supporting and integrating those whose applications are accepted, could instead be allocated to relief aid to be distributed to the millions of refugees unable to travel far from their states of origin; to foreign assistance to solve the root causes of refugee flows; or, along the lines suggested by James Hathaway, Alexander Neve, and Peter Schuck, to provide temporary protection in refugees' regions of origin.[3] If asylum policy is animated by the larger humanitarian goal of protecting refugees from insecurity, then it is difficult indeed to see why a state should bother with an asylum program at all. Generosity to those in need is a virtue, indeed, a moral duty. But surely it makes more sense to meet that duty by exporting aid abroad than by importing the recipients.

That logic poses a practical danger. We should be cautious before tampering with long-established institutions and practices, such as granting asylum to persecuted people, even when they are incomplete solutions. Perfection can be the enemy of the good. Even from a humanitarian perspective, refugees as a whole may be better served by a targeted asylum policy, with eligibility limited to persecuted people, than by a broader approach to asylum that contains the seeds of its own destruction.

***

The preceding pages have presented a theory of asylum that offers a rationale for its continued vitality and a principled basis for its traditional focus on sheltering persecuted people. Asylum effectuates core

Western political values by condemning states that flout them, and, in tandem with other instruments of foreign policy, by aiming at the reformation of persecutory regimes. For example, asylum can be linked to international benefits, such as membership in international organizations or conditional aid; it can also be linked to more forceful sanctions, such as trade restrictions, asset control, and in extreme cases, military intervention. Asylum can also act as a kind of "peer pressure" that might, at the margin, induce states highly sensitive to international opinion to reform their practices. Sheltering persecuted people, therefore, continues to have ideological value even in a post-Cold War world, because it expresses and acts upon a commitment to promoting human rights and to ensuring that states adhere to the basic conditions for international legitimacy.

To retain this expressive, political significance, however, asylum must be limited to persecuted people. Expanding eligibility beyond the persecuted, for example, to those fleeing private violence that the state has attempted in good faith to punish and prevent, or to those fleeing extreme poverty or natural disaster, would obscure asylum's political meaning. Asylum's purpose – to shelter refugees in a way that expresses and promotes political values – dictates its limits.

Additionally, according to the political approach, asylum should give persecuted people not only protection abroad, but also membership abroad. When people are persecuted, that is, targeted by the state for violence for illegitimate reasons, they not only face a threat to their bodily integrity or liberty; they are also effectively expelled from their political communities. They are not only victims, but also exiles. Asylum responds not only to victims' need for protection, but also to their need for political standing, by extending membership in a new political community.

The hope is that if asylum is limited in scope to a defined class of applicants who flee a distinctive kind of harm, and if asylum is reconnected to the West's fundamental political values, Western policymakers and the public will be less inclined to view asylum seekers as "conmen" to be excluded and will be more committed to ensuring that asylum remains available for those who genuinely fear persecution.

Of course, an asylum policy aimed at helping persecuted people would exclude from asylum many people who are in urgent need of protection from other sorts of harm. That humanitarian critique, however, misses the distinction between persecution and other types of harm. It also misunderstands the unique role of asylum vis-à-vis other refugee policy tools. Persecution calls for a distinctive response: not simply to shelter the victims, but also to condemn the perpetrators and to take action to prevent further victimization. Asylum performs that role; it is not merely palliative. But asylum is only one of several refugee policy tools. While states should continue to grant asylum to persecuted people who manage to seek shelter abroad, they should also redouble their commitments to other refugee policy tools. States have a humanitarian duty to assist people exposed to insecurity of all kinds.* Policy tools such as humanitarian aid, development assistance, regional temporary protection, and humanitarian protection abroad should be employed to assist those in urgent need of protection who are excluded from asylum. A targeted asylum policy is consistent with a generous refugee policy.

***

The arguments advanced in this book are directed mainly at policy-makers and the public. The goal has been to explain why the restrictive measures adopted over the last fifteen years are a mistake – beyond a generalized appeal to compassion and empathy, and taking as a premise a public desire to limit immigration. The political approach to asylum that I have outlined recognizes persecuted people as having suffered a distinctive kind of harm, one that sets them apart from those who generally seek a better life abroad. Additionally, it sees asylum as intertwined with, and expressive of, the core political values shared by the West. The tradition of granting asylum to persecuted people is one worth preserving and protecting.

But the arguments I have advanced have implications for asylum advocates, political theorists, and judges as well. Asylum advocates are often lawyers, and lawyers are trained – and ethically bound – to achieve the maximum for their clients in specific cases. But sometimes success in particular cases can result in legislative changes that leave

---

* The UNHCR's formal mandate should thus encompass not only Convention refugees, but others exposed to insecurity. Already the UNHCR deploys its resources to help people who would fall under this wider category, but under its "good offices." A formal expansion of the UNHCR's mandate would signal the international community's recognition of a humanitarian obligation to assist all persons whose basic needs are unmet. At the same time, however, eligibility for asylum should remain firmly linked to persecution.

others similarly situated much worse off. "International refugee law is finally coming of age," one prominent lawyer and advocate has written, reporting on a series of court decisions that have granted asylum to classes of applicants previously excluded.[4] But in the same period, unprecedented legislative and regulatory restrictions have made asylum a mirage for countless others. Expansion in one part of the system has been met with contraction in another – and the contraction has been far more damaging to refugees on the whole than the expansion has been beneficial. When an advocacy strategy focuses narrowly on achieving success for particular clients, it tends to overlook the potentially perverse system-wide consequences of victory.

Another lesson is for political theorists. Debate among political theorists on the subject of immigration typically takes place among "liberal nationalists" who think that states can justifiably impose restrictions on migration, and "cosmopolitans" who view such restrictions as enforcing an unjust international economic order. For liberal nationalists, asylum policy has typically been an afterthought, treated as a narrow humanitarian exception to the general principle that states may control immigration.[5] They have failed to recognize that asylum policy expresses and advances national political values, and reflects the political narratives of receiving states. Indeed, much more could be said about the way in which many national narratives have been built (at least in part) around the provision of refuge to the persecuted.

As for cosmopolitans, such a down-in-the-weeds analysis as I've offered here may seem to miss large structural faults (for example, the connection between political persecution and economic inequality) and become bogged down in insignificant details. But the methodology of this book demonstrates the payoff to using the tools of political theory to perform a fine-grained, differentiated analysis of actual legal institutions that can be leveraged to advance global justice within realistic constraints. Such institutions often are premised on implicit theoretical assumptions that can be exposed and scrutinized. And as a practical matter, the broad-barreled approach often espoused by cosmopolitans – for example, justice requires open borders or massive redistribution of global wealth – may do more harm than good. By directing criticism toward structures so fundamental to the world order, that approach invites inaction: the problem of global economic inequality can seem so large that little can be done to solve it. By contrast, a fine-grained approach as offered here focuses our theoretical attention on specific, distinctive problems that can be addressed within existing institutions.

Finally, the theory of asylum offered in the preceding pages has implications for the way in which "persecution" is interpreted by courts and immigration services. The recent trend among Commonwealth courts is to tie the definition of "persecution" to international human rights law, so that the deprivation of human rights – whether caused by a state official, a private person, or simply by circumstances or economic and political structures – constitutes persecution. This approach stretches the meaning of "persecution" too wide, effectively reading a humanitarian conception of asylum into the term "persecution." Instead, I have argued, "persecution" involves the toleration or infliction of harm by state officials for illegitimate reasons. The nexus clause, which requires that persecution be inflicted "for reasons of race, religion, nationality, membership of a particular social group, or political opinion," specifies the kind of reasons that are illegitimate by drawing on the liberal values of equality, religious toleration, and political accountability. It is inextricably intertwined with the concept of persecution itself, not (as the human rights approach makes it appear) an arbitrary limitation on asylum's scope.

With these principles in mind, we can return to the three stories presented at the beginning of the Introduction. First consider Alain Baptiste, the HIV-positive Haitian whose life depends on accessing anti-retroviral drugs. Compassion demands that he be helped; but asylum is not the proper tool. People like Alain can be more effectively aided by the distribution of such drugs in their countries of origin. Next consider Angela, the Jamaican woman who fears she will be killed because she provided the police with the name of the gang member who murdered her daughter. While she needs protection abroad, again asylum is not the right response. Victims of non-state, private violence should be eligible for asylum only if the state is somehow accountable for that violence by promoting it, condoning it, or refusing to protect against it for the kinds of reasons listed in the nexus clause. Instead, protection for a presumptively temporary period – combined with efforts to assist the Jamaican government in maintaining security for its citizens – is the better response to Angela's situation.

Finally, consider Rodi Alvarado Peña, the victim of brutal domestic violence whose state (Guatemala) refused to protect her. Rodi is differently situated than the other two. All face a threat of serious harm, but only Rodi faces harm because the state responsible for her security and protection has refused it to her on the basis of an immutable characteristic – her gender. In that sense, she is like the classic recipient of asylum: the member of a racial, national, or religious minority targeted for serious harm by the state on account of her race, nationality, or religion, or the political dissident targeted by the state on account of her political opinion. The bonds of political membership having been sundered, these victims of persecution need not only protection abroad, but also surrogate membership. And their states deserve not assistance, but condemnation. Asylum's purpose is to help people like them.

Notes

1. World Bank, "Poverty Drops Below 1 Billion, says World Bank," Press Release No. 2007/159/DEC, April 15, 2007, web.worldbank.org.
2. Thomas Pogge, "Migration and Poverty," in Veit Bader (ed.), *Citizenship and Exclusion* (New York: St. Martin's Press, 1997), p. 15 (Original emphasis).
3. James C. Hathaway and R. Alexander Neve, "Making International Refugee Law Relevant Again: A Proposal for Collectivized and Solution-Oriented Protection," *Harvard Human Rights Journal*, 10 (1997), pp. 115–211; Peter H. Schuck, "Refugee Burden-Sharing: A Modest Proposal," in Schuck (ed.), *Citizens, Strangers, and In-Betweens* (Boulder, CO: Westview Press, 1998), p. 297.
4. Deborah E. Anker, "Refugee Law, Gender, and the Human Rights Paradigm," *Harvard Human Rights Journal*, 15 (2002), p. 133.
5. See, for example, Michael Walzer, *Spheres of Justice* (New York: Basic Books, 1983), p. 50; Yael Tamir, *Liberal Nationalism* (Princeton University Press, 1993), p. 159.

Bibliography

Books and Articles

Ackerman, Bruce, *Social Justice in the Liberal State* (New Haven, CT: Yale University Press, 1980).

Adler, Matthew D., "Expressive Theories of Law: A Skeptical Overview," *University of Pennsylvania Law Review*, 148 (2000), pp. 1363–450.

Aeschylus, *The Suppliants*, trans. Peter Burian (Princeton University Press, 1991).

Aeschylus, *The Oresteia*, trans. Robert Fagles (Princeton University Press, 1984).

Aleinikoff, T. Alexander, "Safe Haven: Pragmatics and Prospects," *Virginia Journal of International Law*, 35 (1994), pp. 71–9.

Aleinikoff, T. Alexander, "The Meaning of 'Persecution' in U.S. Asylum Law" in Howard Adelman (ed.), *Refugee Policy: Canada and the United States* (Toronto: York Lanes Press, 1991), pp. 292–320.

Aleinikoff, T. Alexander, David A. Martin, and Hiroshi Motomura, *Immigration and Citizenship: Process and Policy*, 4th edn. (St. Paul, MN: West Group, 1998).

Alexander III, Sydenham B., "A Political Response to Crisis in the Immigration Courts," *Georgetown Immigration Law Journal*, 21 (2006), pp. 1–59.

American State Papers: Documents, Legislative and Executive, of the Congress of the United States, vol. 1 (1789–1815) (Washington, DC: Gales and Seaton, 1832).

Anderson, Elizabeth S., *Value in Ethics and Economics* (Cambridge, MA: Harvard University Press, 1993).

Anderson, Elizabeth S., and Richard H. Pildes, "Expressive Theories of Law: A General Restatement," *University of Pennsylvania Law Review*, 148 (2000), pp. 1503–72.

Anker, Deborah E., "Refugee Law, Gender, and the Human Rights Paradigm," *Harvard Human Rights Journal*, 15 (2002), pp. 133–54.

Anker, Deborah E., "Refugee Status and Violence Against Women in the 'Domestic' Sphere: The Non-State Actor Question," *Georgetown Immigration Law Journal*, 15 (2001), pp. 391–402.

Anker, Deborah E., and Michael H. Posner, "The Forty Year Crisis: A Legislative History of the Refugee Act of 1980," *San Diego Law Review*, 19 (1981), pp. 9–89.

Anker, Deborah E., Joan Fitzpatrick, and Andrew Shacknove, "Crisis and Cure: A Reply to Hathaway/Neve and Schuck," *Harvard Human Rights Journal*, 11 (1998), pp. 295–310.

Anker, Deborah E., Lauren Gilbert, and Nancy Kelly, "Women Whose Governments are Unable or Unwilling to Provide Reasonable Protection from Domestic Violence May Qualify as Refugees under United States Asylum Law," *Georgetown Immigration Law Journal*, 11 (1997), pp. 709–45.

Arendt, Hannah, *Origins of Totalitarianism* (San Diego, CA: Harcourt, Brace, 1973).

Bader-Zaar, Birgitta, "Foreigners and the Law in Austria" in Andreas Fahrmeir *et al.* (eds.), *Migration Control in the North Atlantic World* (New York: Berghahn Books, 2003), pp. 39–54.

Bailliet, Cecilia M., "Assessing Jus ad Bellum and Jus in Bello Within the Refugee Status Determination Process: Contemplations on Conscientious Objectors Seeking Asylum," *Georgetown Immigration Law Journal*, 20 (2006), pp. 337–84.

Barry, Brian, and Robert Goodin, *Free Movement* (University Park, PA: Pennsylvania State University Press, 1992).

Bassiouni, M. Cherif, *International Extradition: United States Law and Practice*, 3rd edn. (Dobbs Ferry, NY: Oceana Publications, 1996).

Bau, Ignatius, *This Ground is Holy: Church Sanctuary and Central American Refugees* (New York: Paulist Press, 1985).

Beccaria, Cesare, *On Crimes and Punishments*, trans. Henry Paolucci (Indianapolis, IN: Bobbs-Merrill, 1963).

Beerbühl, Margrit Schulte, "British Nationality Policy as a Counter-Revolutionary Strategy During the Napoleonic Wars: The Emergence of Modern Naturalization Regulations" in Andreas Fahrmeir *et al.* (eds.), *Migration Control in the North Atlantic World* (New York: Berghahn Books, 2003), pp. 55–72.

Benhabib, Seyla, *Transformations of Citizenship* (Amsterdam: Koninklijke Van Gorcum, 2001).

Bhabha, Jacqueline, "Embodied Rights: Gender Persecution, State Sovereignty, and Refugees," *Public Culture*, 9 (1996), pp. 3–32.

Blake, Michael, "Immigration" in R. G. Frey and Christopher Heath Wellman (eds.), *A Companion to Applied Ethics* (Malden, MA: Blackwell Publishing, 2003), pp. 224–37.

Blakesley, Christopher L., "The Practice of Extradition from Antiquity to Modern France and the United States: A Brief History," *Boston College International and Comparative Law Review*, 4 (1981), pp. 39–60.

Blay, Sam, and Andreas Zimmermann, "Recent Changes in German Refugee Law: A Critical Assessment," *American Journal of International Law*, 88 (1994), pp. 361–78.

Blum, Carolyn Patty, "License to Kill: Asylum Law and the Principle of Legitimate Governmental Authority to 'Investigate its Enemies,'" *Willamette Law Review*, 28 (1992), pp. 719–50.

Blum, Carolyn Patty, "Political Assumptions in Asylum Decision-Making: The Example of Refugees from Armed Conflict" in Howard Adelman (ed.), *Refugee Policy: Canada and the United States* (Toronto: York Lanes Press, 1991), pp. 282–91.

Bosswick, Wolfgang, "Development of Asylum Policy in Germany," *Journal of Refugee Studies*, 13 (2000), pp. 43–60.

Boyle, Elizabeth Heger, and Sharon E. Preves, "National Politics as International Process: The Case of Anti-Female-Genital-Cutting Laws," *Law and Society Review*, 34 (2000), pp. 703–32.

Bull, Hedley, "The Importance of Grotius in the Study of International Relations" in Hedley Bull *et al.* (eds.), *Hugo Grotius and International Relations* (New York: Oxford University Press, 1990).

Butler, A. Hays, "The Growing Support for Universal Jurisdiction" in Stephen Macedo (ed.), *Universal Jurisdiction: National Courts and the Prosecution of Serious Crimes Under International Law* (Philadelphia, PA: University of Pennsylvania Press, 2004), pp. 67–76.

Caestecker, Frank, "The Transformation of Nineteenth-Century West European Expulsion Policy, 1880–1914" in Andreas Fahrmeir *et al.* (eds.), *Migration Control in the North Atlantic World* (New York: Berghahn Books, 2003), pp. 120–37.

Carens, Joseph H., "Who Should Get In? The Ethics of Immigration Admissions," *Ethics and International Affairs*, 17 (2003), pp. 95–110.

Carens, Joseph H., "The Philosopher and the Policymaker: Two Perspectives on the Ethics of Immigration with Special Attention to the Problem of Restricting Asylum" in Kay Hailbronner, David A. Martin, and Hiroshi Motomura (eds.), *Immigration Admissions: The Search for Workable Policies in Germany and the United States* (Providence, RI: Berghahn Books, 1997), pp. 3–50.

Carens, Joseph H., "Aliens and Citizens: The Case for Open Borders," in Ronald Beiner (ed.), *Theorizing Citizenship* (Albany, NY: SUNY Press, 1995), pp. 229–53.

Carens, Joseph H., "Refugees and the Limits of Obligation," *Public Affairs Quarterly*, 6 (1992), pp. 31–44.

Carens, Joseph H., "States and Refugees: A Normative Analysis" in Howard Adelman (ed.), *Refugee Policy: Canada and the United States* (Toronto: York Lanes Press, 1991), pp. 18–29.

Carlier, Jean-Yves, *et al.* (eds.), *Who is a Refugee?* (The Hague: Kluwer Law International, 1997).

Chimni, B. S., "Globalization, Humanitarianism and the Erosion of Refugee Protection," *Journal of Refugee Studies*, 13 (2000), pp. 243–63.

Chimni, B. S., "The Geopolitics of Refugee Studies: A View from the South," *Journal of Refugee Studies*, 11 (1998), pp. 350–74.

Cleveland, Sarah H., "Norm Internalization and U.S. Economic Sanctions," *Yale Journal of International Law*, 26 (2001), pp. 1–92.

Coke, Sir Edward, *The Second Part of the Institutes of the Laws of England*, 5th edn. (London: Streater *et al.*, 1671).

Coke, Sir Edward, *The Third Part of the Institutes of the Laws of England*, (London: Flesher, 1644).

Cole, David, *Enemy Aliens* (New York: Free Press, 2003).

Coles, Gervase, "Approaching the Refugee Problem Today" in Gil Loescher and Laila Monahan, *Refugees and International Relations* (New York: Oxford University Press, 1989), pp. 373–410.

Coles, Gervase, "The Human Rights Approach to the Solution of the Refugee Problem: A Theoretical and Practical Enquiry" in Alan E. Nash (ed.), *Human Rights and the Protection of Refugees under International Law* (Halifax: Institute for Research on Public Policy, 1988), pp. 195–222.

"Constitutional Watch: A Country-by-Country Update on Constitutional Politics in Eastern Europe and the ex-USSR – Hungary," *East European Constitutional Review*, 10 (Spring/Summer 2001).

Copelon, Rhonda, "Recognizing the Egregious in the Everyday: Domestic Violence as Torture," *Columbia Human Rights Law Review*, 25 (1994), pp. 291–367.

Coutin, Susan Bibler, *The Culture of Protest: Religious Activism and the U.S. Sanctuary Movement* (Boulder, CO: Westview Press, 1993).

Crittenden, Ann, *Sanctuary: A Story of American Conscience and the Law in Collision* (New York: Weidenfeld & Nicolson, 1988).

Davidson, Miriam, *Convictions of the Heart: Jim Corbett and the Sanctuary Movement* (Tucson, AZ: University of Arizona Press, 1988).

Edminster, Steven, "Recklessly Risking Lives: Restrictive Interpretations of 'Agents of Persecution' in Germany and France" in US Committee for Refugees, *World Refugee Survey, 1999* (Washington, DC: US Committee for Refugees, 1999).

Euripides, *Four Tragedies*, trans. and eds. David Grene and Richard Lattimore (University of Chicago Press, 1955).

Fahrmeir, Andreas, *Citizens and Aliens: Foreigners and the Law in Britain and the German States 1789–1870* (New York: Berghahn Books, 2000).

Faron, Olivier, and Cyril Grange, "Paris and its Foreigners in the Late Eighteenth Century" in Andreas Fahrmeir *et al.* (eds.), *Migration*

Control in the North Atlantic World (New York: Berghahn Books, 2003), pp. 39–54.

Feinberg, Joel, "The Expressive Function of Punishment" in Feinberg (ed.), *Doing and Deserving: Essays in the Theory of Responsibility* (Princeton University Press, 1970), pp. 95–118.

Feldman, David, "Changes in Nineteenth-Century Immigration Controls" in Andreas Fahrmeir *et al.* (eds.), *Migration Control in the North Atlantic World* (New York: Berghahn Books, 2003).

Finnemore, Martha, and Kathryn Sikkink, "International Norm Dynamics and Political Change," *International Organization*, 52 (1998), pp. 887–917.

Fitzpatrick, Joan, "Temporary Protection of Refugees: Elements of a Formalized Regime," *American Journal of International Law*, 94 (2000), pp. 279–306.

Fitzpatrick, Joan, "Flight from Asylum: Trends Toward Temporary 'Refuge' and Local Responses to Forced Migrations," *Virginia Journal of International Law*, 35 (1994), pp. 13–70.

Foster, Michelle, "Causation in Context: Interpreting the Nexus Clause in the Refugee Convention," *Michigan Journal of International Law*, 23 (2002), pp. 265–340.

Fraher, Richard M., "The Theoretical Justification for the New Criminal Law of the High Middle Ages: 'Rei Publicae Interest, Ne Crimina Remaneant Impunita,'" *University of Illinois Law Review*, 1984 (1984), pp. 577–95.

Gaius, *The Institutes of Gaius*, trans. Francis de Zulueta (Oxford: Clarendon Press, 1946).

Gibney, Mark, "The Divorce Between Refugee Determinations and Pursuit of Human Rights Objectives Through U.S. Foreign Policy: The Case of Female Genital Mutilation" in Lydio F. Tomasi (ed.), *In Defense of the Alien*, vol. XVIII (New York: Center for Migration Studies, 1996), pp. 170–81.

Gibney, Mark and Michael Stohl, "Human Rights and U.S. Refugee Policy" in Mark Gibney (ed.), *Open Borders? Closed Societies? The Ethical and Political Issues* (New York: Greenwood Press, 1988), pp. 151–83.

Gibney, Matthew J., *The Ethics and Politics of Asylum* (Cambridge University Press, 2004).

Gibney, Matthew J., "The State of Asylum: Democratization, Judicialization and Evolution of Refugee Policy in Europe," UNHCR New Issues in Refugee Research, Working Paper No. 50, October 2001.

Gibney, Matthew J., "Asylum and the Principle of Proximity," *Ethics, Place, and Environment*, 3 (2000), p. 313.

Gibney, Matthew J., "Between Control and Humanitarianism: Temporary Protection in Contemporary Europe," *Georgetown Immigration Law Journal* 14 (Spring 2000), pp. 689–707.

Gibney, Matthew J., "Kosovo and Beyond: Popular and Unpopular Refugees," *Forced Migration Review*, 5 (September 1999), pp. 28–30.

Gibney, Matthew J., "Liberal Democratic States and Responsibilities to Refugees," *American Political Science Review*, 93 (1999), pp. 169–81.

Gibney, Matthew J., and Randall Hansen, "Deportation and the Liberal State: the Forcible Return of Asylum Seekers and Unlawful Migrants in Canada, Germany and the United Kingdom," UNHCR New Issues in Refugee Research, Working Paper No. 77, February 2003.

Gilbert, Geoff, "Rights, Legitimate Expectations, Needs and Responsibilities," *International Journal of Refugee Law*, 10 (1998), pp. 349–88.

Goldberg, Pamela, "Anyplace but Home," *Cornell International Law Journal*, 26 (1993), pp. 565–604.

Goldhagen, Daniel Jonah, *Hitler's Willing Executioners: Ordinary Germans and the Holocaust* (New York: Knopf, 1996).

Goodman, Ryan, and Derek Jinks, "How to Influence States: Socialization and International Human Rights Law," *Duke Law Journal*, 54 (2004), pp. 621–703.

Goodwin-Gill, Guy, *The Refugee in International Law*, 2nd edn. (New York: Oxford University Press, 1996).

Grahl-Madsen, Atle, *The Status of Refugees in International Law*, 2 vols. (Leiden: A. W. Sijthoff, 1966, 1972).

Grotius, Hugo, *Rights of War and Peace*, trans. A. C. Campbell (Westport, CT: Hyperion Press, 1979).

Grotius, Hugo, *De Jure Belli Ac Pacis Libri Tres*, trans. Francis W. Kelsey (Oxford: Clarendon Press, 1925).

Hansen, Randall, "Asylum Policy in the European Union," *Georgetown Immigration Law Journal*, 14 (2000), pp. 779–800.

Hathaway, James C., *The Rights of Refugees Under International Law* (Cambridge University Press, 2005).

Hathaway, James C., "Can International Refugee Law Be Made Relevant Again?" in US Committee on Refugees, *World Refugee Survey 1996* (Washington, DC: US Committee on Refugees, 1996), pp. 14–19.

Hathaway, James C., "New Directions to Avoid Hard Problems: The Distortion of the Palliative Role of Refugee Protection," *Journal of Refugee Studies*, 8 (1995), pp. 288–94.

Hathaway, James C., "Reconceiving Refugee Law as Human Rights Protection," *Journal of Refugee Studies*, 4 (1991), pp. 113–31.

Hathaway, James C., *Law of Refugee Status* (Toronto: Butterworths, 1991).

Hathaway, James C. and R. Alexander Neve, "Making International Refugee Law Relevant Again: A Proposal for Collectivized and Solution-Oriented Protection," *Harvard Human Rights Journal*, 10 (1997), pp. 115–211.

Healey, Sharon A., "The Trend Toward the Criminalization and Detention of Asylum Seekers," *Human Rights Brief*, 12.1 (2004), p. 14.

Held, David, *et al.*, *Global Transformations* (Stanford University Press, 1999).

Helton, Arthur C., *The Price of Indifference* (New York: Oxford University Press, 2002).

Helton, Arthur C., "Political Asylum Under the 1980 Refugee Act: An Unfulfilled Promise," *University of Michigan Journal of Law Reform*, 17 (1984), pp. 243–64.

Herodotus, *The History*, trans. David Grene (University of Chicago Press, 1987).

Heyman, Michael G., "Redefining Refugee: A Proposal for Relief for the Victims of Civil Strife," *San Diego Law Review*, 24 (1987), p. 449.

Hobbes, Thomas, *Leviathan* (New York: Penguin, 1977).

Hufbauer, Gary Clyde, *et al.*, *Economic Sanctions Reconsidered: Supplemental Case Histories*, 2nd edn., vol. 2 (Washington, DC: Institute for International Economics, 1990).

Human Rights First, "Abandoning the Persecuted: Victims of Terrorism and Oppression Barred From Asylum" (New York: Human Rights First, 2006).

Human Rights First, "In Liberty's Shadow: U.S. Detention of Asylum Seekers in the Era of Homeland Security" (New York: Human Rights First, 2004).

Ignatieff, Michael, *Human Rights as Politics and Idolatry* (Princeton University Press, 2001).

International Commission on Intervention and State Sovereignty, *Responsibility to Protect* (Ottawa: International Development Research Center, 2001).

International Federation of Red Cross and Red Crescent Societies, *World Disasters Report 1996* (Dordrecht : Martinus Nijhoff, 1996).

Jacobson, David, *Rights Across Borders* (Baltimore, MD: Johns Hopkins Press, 1996).

Jaeger, Gilbert, "A Comment on the Distortion of the Palliative Role of Refugee Protection," *Journal of Refugee Studies*, 8 (1995), pp. 300–2.

Johnson, Kevin R., "A 'Hard Look' at the Executive Branch's Asylum Decisions," *Utah Law Review*, 1991 (1991), p. 289.

Joly, Daniele, "A New Asylum Regime in Europe" in Frances Nicholson and Patrick Twomey (eds.), *Refugee Rights and Realities* (Cambridge University Press, 1999), pp. 336–56.

Justinian, *Digest of Justinian*, vol. 1, trans. Alan Watson (Philadelphia, PA: University of Pennsylvania Press, 1998).

Justinian, "Code of Justinian" in *The Civil Law*, trans. S. P. Scott (Cincinnati, OH: Central Trust Co., 1932).

Kälin, Walter, "Non-State Agents of Persecution and the Inability of the State to Protect," *Georgetown Immigration Law Journal*, 15 (2001), pp. 415–31.

Kant, Immanuel, *Political Writings*, trans. and ed. Hans Reiss (Cambridge University Press, 1991).

Katzenstein, Peter J., "Introduction: Alternative Perspectives on National Security" in Katzenstein (ed.), *The Culture of National Security: Norms and Identity in World Politics* (New York: Columbia University Press, 1996), pp. 1–32.

Kelly, Nancy, "Gender-Related Persecution: Assessing the Asylum Claims of Women," *Cornell International Law Journal*, 26 (1993), pp. 625–74.

Kerwin, Donald, "Revisiting the Need for Appointed Counsel," *mpi Insight* (Washington, DC: Migration Policy Institute, April 2005), pp. 12–16.

Khan, Rex D., "Why Refugee Status Should Be Beyond Judicial Review," *University of San Francisco Law Review*, 35 (2000), pp. 57–81.

Kirchheimer, Otto, *Political Justice: The Use of Legal Procedure for Political Ends* (Princeton University Press, 1961).

Knight, W. S. M., *The Life and Works of Hugo Grotius* (London: Sweet and Maxwell, 1925).

Koh, Harold Hongju, "Reflections on Refoulement and *Haitian Centers Council*," *Harvard International Law Journal*, 35 (1994), pp. 1–20.

Krasner, Stephen D., "Sovereignty, Regimes, and Human Rights" in Volker Rittberger (ed.), *Regime Theory and International Relations* (New York: Oxford University Press, 1993).

Lambert, Helene, "The Conceptualisation of 'Persecution' by the House of Lords: *Horvath v. Secretary of State for the Home Department*," *International Journal of Refugee Law*, 13 (2001), pp. 16–31.

Legomsky, Stephen H., "Learning to Live With Unequal Justice: Asylum and the Limits to Consistency," *Stanford Law Review*, 60 (2007), pp. 444–57.

Legomsky, Stephen H., "Political Asylum and the Theory of Judicial Review," *Minnesota Law Review*, 73 (1989), pp. 1205–16.

Loescher, Gil, *Beyond Charity* (New York: Oxford University Press, 1993).

Loescher, Gil and John A. Scanlan, *Calculated Kindness* (New York: Free Press, 1986).

Macklin, Audrey, "Cross-Border Shopping for Ideas: A Critical Review of United States, Canadian, and Australian Approaches to Gender-Related Asylum Claims," *Georgetown Immigration Law Journal*, 13 (1998), pp. 25–71.

Marrus, Michael, *The Unwanted* (New York: Oxford University Press, 2002).

Martin, David A., "Two Cheers for Expedited Removal in the New Immigration Laws," *Virginia Journal of International Law*, 40 (2000), pp. 673–704.

Martin, David A., "The Refugee Concept: On Definitions, Politics, and the Careful Use of a Scarce Resource" in Howard Adelman (ed.), *Refugee Policy: Canada and the United States* (Toronto: York Lanes Press, 1991), pp. 30–51.

Martin, David A., "Reforming Asylum Adjudication: On Navigating the Coast of Bohemia," *University of Pennsylvania Law Review*, 138 (1990), pp. 1247–378.

Martin, Susan, Andy Schoenholtz, and Deborah Waller Meyers, "Temporary Protection: Towards a New Regional and Domestic Framework," *Georgetown Immigration Law Journal*, 12 (1998), pp. 543–87.

Marx, Reinhard, "The Notion of Persecution by Non-State Agents in German Jurisprudence," *Georgetown Immigration Law Journal*, 15 (2001), pp. 447–61.

Meissner, Doris, "Reflections on the U.S. Refugee Act of 1980" in David A. Martin (ed.), *The New Asylum Seekers: Refugee Law in the 1980s* (Norwell, MA: Kluwer Academic, 1988).

Michelman, Frank I., "Parsing 'A Right to Have Rights,'" *Constellations*, 3 (1996), pp. 200–7.

Miller, David, *On Nationality* (New York: Oxford University Press, 1995).

Moore, Jennifer, "Whither the Accountability Theory," *International Journal of Refugee Law*, 13 (2001), pp. 32–50.

Moore, Jennifer, "From Nation State to Failed State: International Protection from Human Rights Abuses by Non-State Agents," *Columbia Human Rights Law Review*, 31 (1999), pp. 81–121.

Morawetz, Nancy, "Understanding the Impact of the 1996 Deportation Laws and the Limited Scope of Proposed Reforms," *Harvard Law Review*, 113 (2000), pp. 1936–62.

Morrison, John, and Beth Crosland, "The Trafficking and Smuggling of Refugees: the End Game in European Asylum Policy?," UNCHR New Issues in Refugee Research, Working Paper No. 39, 2001.

Musalo, Karen, Jennifer Moore, and Richard A. Boswell (eds.), *Refugee Law and Policy: A Comparative and International Approach*, 2nd edn. (Durham, NC: Carolina Academic Press, 2002).

Musalo, Karen and Stephen Knight, "Steps Forward and Steps Back: Uneven Progress in the Law of Social Group and Gender-Based Claims in the United States," *International Journal of Refugee Law*, 13 (2001), pp. 51–70.

National Commission on Terrorist Attacks Upon the United States, *The 9/11 Commission Report* (July 2004).

Newland, Kathleen, "The Impact of U.S. Refugee Policies on U.S. Foreign Policy: A Case of the Tail Wagging the Dog?" in Michael S. Teitelbaum and Myron Weiner (eds.), *Threatened Peoples, Threatened Borders* (New York: W.W. Norton, 1995), pp. 190–214.

Noll, Gregor, "Rejected asylum seekers: the problem of return," UNHCR New Issues in Refugee Research, Working Paper No. 4, May 1999.

Note, "Political Legitimacy in the Law of Political Asylum," *Harvard Law Review*, 99 (1985), pp. 450–70.

Ogletree, Jr., Charles J., "America's Schizophrenic Immigration Policy: Race, Class, and Reason," *Boston College Law Review*, 41 (2000), pp. 755–70.

O'Higgins, Paul, "The History of Extradition in British Practice, 1174–1794," *Indian Year Book of International Affairs*, Part II (1964), pp. 78–115.

Palmer, John R. B., Stephen W. Yale-Loehr, and Elizabeth Cronin, "Why Are So Many People Challenging Board of Immigration Appeals Decisions in Federal Court? An Empirical Analysis of the Recent Surge in Petitions for Review," *Georgetown Immigration Law Journal*, 20 (2005), pp. 1–99.

Parry, Clive (ed.), *British Digest of International Law*, Part VI (London: Stevens and Sons, 1965).

Pfeiffer, Neal P., Note, "Credibility Findings in INS Asylum Adjudications: A Realistic Assessment," *Texas Journal of International Law*, 23 (1988), pp. 139–151.

Phillipson, Coleman, *The International Law and Custom of Ancient Greece and Rome*, vol. 1 [1911], reprint (Buffalo, NY: William S. Hein, 2001).

Pistone, Michele R., and John J. Hoeffner, "Rules Are Made to Be Broken: How the Process of Expedited Removal Fails Asylum Seekers," *Georgetown Immigration Law Journal*, 20 (2006), pp. 167–211.

Pistone, Michele R., and Philip G. Schrag, "The New Asylum: Improved But Still Unfair," *Georgetown Immigration Law Journal*, 16 (2001), pp. 1–79.

Pogge, Thomas, "Migration and Poverty," in Veit Bader (ed.), *Citizenship and Exclusion* (New York: St. Martin's Press, 1997), pp. 12–27.

Porter, Bernard, *The Refugee Question in Mid-Victorian Politics* (Cambridge University Press, 1979).

Preston, Richard K., "Asylum Adjudications: Do State Department Advisory Opinions Violate Refugees' Rights and U.S. International Obligations?," *Maryland Law Review*, 45 (1986), pp. 91–140.

Pufendorf, Samuel, *De Jure Naturae et Gentium Libri Octo*, trans. C. H. Oldfather and W. A. Oldfather (Oxford: Clarendon Press, 1934).

Pyle, Christopher H., *Extradition, Politics, and Human Rights* (Philadelphia, PA: Temple University Press, 2001).

Ramanthan, Erik D., "Queer Cases: A Comparative Analysis of Global Sexual Orientation-Based Asylum Jurisprudence," *Georgetown Immigration Law Journal*, 11 (1996), pp. 1–44.

Ramji-Nogales, Jaya, Andrew I. Schoenholtz, and Philip G. Schrag, "Refugee Roulette: Disparities in Asylum Adjudication," *Stanford Law Review*, 60 (2007), pp. 295–411.

Randolph, Thomas Jefferson (ed.), *Memoir, Correspondence, and Miscellanies from the Papers of Thomas Jefferson*, 2nd edn., vol. 3 (Boston, MA: Gray and Bowen, 1830).

Rawls, John, *Law of Peoples* (Cambridge, MA: Harvard University Press, 1999).

Rieff, David, *A Bed for the Night: Humanitarianism in Crisis* (New York: Simon & Schuster, 2002).

Rigsby, Kent J., *Asylia: Territorial Inviolability in the Hellenistic World* (Berkeley, CA: University of California Press, 1996).

Risse, Thomas P., Steven C. Ropp, and Kathryn Sikkink, *The Power of Human Rights: International Norms and Domestic Change* (Cambridge University Press, 1999).

Roberts, Adam, "More Refugees, Less Asylum," *Journal of Refugee Studies*, 11 (1998), pp. 375–95.

Rosenberg, Lory Diana, "The Courts and Interception: The United States' Interdiction Experience and its Impact on Refugees and Asylum Seekers," *Georgetown Immigration Law Journal*, 17 (2003), pp. 199–219.

Schuck, Peter H., "Refugee Burden-Sharing: A Modest Proposal" in Schuck (ed.), *Citizens, Strangers, and In-Betweens* (Boulder, CO: Westview Press, 1998), pp. 282–325.

Schuck, Peter H., "The Devaluation of American Citizenship" in Schuck (ed.), *Citizens, Strangers, and In-Betweens* (Boulder, CO: Westview Press, 1998), pp. 163–75.

Schumacher, Rob W. M., "Three Related Sanctuaries of Poseidon: Geraistos, Kalaureia and Tainaron" in Nanno Marinatos and Robin Hägg (eds.), *Greek Sanctuaries: New Approaches* (London: Routledge, 1993), pp. 62–87.

Sen, Amartya, *Poverty and Famines: An Essay on Entitlement and Deprivation* (Oxford: Clarendon Press, 1981).

Shacknove, Andrew, "From Asylum to Containment," *International Journal of Refugee Law*, 5 (1993), pp. 516–33.

Shacknove, Andrew, "Who is a Refugee?," *Ethics*, 95 (1985), pp. 274–84.

Shklar, Judith N., *American Citizenship* (Cambridge, MA: Harvard University Press, 1991).

Shoemaker, Karl Blaine, "Sanctuary Law: Changing Conceptions of Wrongdoing and Punishment in Medieval European Law," Ph.D. dissertation, University of California-Berkeley, 2001.

Sibley, N. W., and Alfred Elias, *The Aliens Act and the Right of Asylum* (London: Williams Clowes, 1906).

Singer, Peter, and Renata Singer, "The Ethics of Refugee Policy" in Mark Gibney (ed.), *Open Borders? Closed Societies? The Ethical and Political Issues* (New York: Greenwood Press, 1988), pp. 111–30.

Sinha, S. Prakash, *Asylum and International Law* (The Hague: Martinus Nijhoff, 1971).

Sinn, Ulrich, "Greek Sanctuaries as Places of Refuge" in Nanno Marinatos and Robin Hägg (eds.), *Greek Sanctuaries: New Approaches* (London: Routledge, 1993), pp. 88–109.

Skran, Claudena M., *Refugees in Inter-War Europe: The Emergence of a Regime* (New York: Oxford University Press, 1995).

Skulan, Catherine, "Australia's Mandatory Detention of 'Unauthorized' Asylum Seekers: History, Politics and Analysis Under International Law," *Georgetown Immigration Law Journal*, 21 (2006), pp. 61–110.

Slaughter, Anne-Marie, "Defining the Limits: Universal Jurisdiction and National Courts" in Stephen Macedo (ed.), *Universal Jurisdiction: National Courts and the Prosecution of Serious Crimes Under International Law* (Philadelphia, PA: University of Pennsylvania Press, 2004), pp. 168–90.

Sophocles, *Three Theban Plays*, trans. Robert Fagles (New York: Penguin Books, 1982).

Soysal, Yasemin, *Limits of Citizenship* (University of Chicago Press, 1994).

State Papers and Publick Documents of the United States: 1789–96, vol. 1 (Boston: T. B. Wait, 1815).

Steinbock, Bonnie, and Alastair Norcross (eds.), *Killing and Letting Die*, 2nd edn. (New York: Fordham University Press, 1994).

Steinbock, Daniel J., "Interpreting the Refugee Definition," *UCLA Law Review*, 45 (1998), p. 794.

Stephens, Sir James Fitzjames, *History of the Criminal Law of England*, vol. 2 (London: Macmillan, 1883).

Storey, Hugo, and Rebecca Wallace, "War and Peace in Refugee Law Jurisprudence," *American Journal of International Law*, 95 (2001), pp. 349–66.

Suhrke, Astri, "Global Refugee Movements and Strategies of Response" in Mary M. Kritz (ed.), *U.S. Immigration and Refugee Policy: Global and Domestic Issues* (Lexington, MA: Lexington Books, 1983), pp. 157–73.

Sunstein, Cass R., "On the Expressive Function of Law," *University of Pennsylvania Law Review*, 144 (1996), pp. 2021–53.

Sztucki, Jerzy, "Who is a Refugee? The Convention Definition: Universal or Obsolete?" in Frances Nicholson and Patrick Twomey (eds.), *Refugee Rights and Realities* (Cambridge University Press, 1999), pp. 44–80.

Tacitus, *Historical Works, Vol. 1: The Annals*, trans. Arthur Murphy (London: J. M. Dent, 1908).

Tacitus, *The Annals*, trans. Henry G. Bohn as *The Works of Tacitus: The Annals*, vol. 1, Oxford, 1854.

Tamir, Yael, *Liberal Nationalism* (Princeton University Press, 1993).

"The Expedited Removal Study: Report on the First Three Years of Implementation of Expedited Removal," *Notre Dame Journal of Law, Ethics and Public Policy*, 15 (2001), pp. 1–155.

Thucydides, *History of the Peloponnesian War*, trans. Rex Warner (New York: Penguin Books, 1972).

Tomsho, Robert, *The American Sanctuary Movement* (Austin, TX: Texas Monthly Press, 1987).

Tuck, Richard, *Rights of War and Peace* (New York: Oxford University Press, 1999).

Tuitt, Patricia, "Rethinking the Refugee Concept" in Frances Nicholson and Patrick Twomey (eds.), *Refugee Rights and Realities* (Cambridge University Press, 1999), pp. 106–17.

Tumlin, Karen C., "Suspect First: How Terrorism Policy is Reshaping Immigration Policy," *California Law Review*, 92 (2000), pp. 1173–239.

Twomey, Patrick, "Europe's Other Market: Trafficking in People," *European Journal of Migration and Law*, 2 (2000), pp. 1–36.

United Nations High Commissioner for Refugees, *UNHCR Statistical Yearbook 2005* (Geneva: UNHCR, April 2007).

United Nations High Commissioner for Refugees, *State of the World's Refugees 2006: Human Displacement in the New Millennium* (New York: Oxford University Press, 2006).

United Nations High Commissioner for Refugees, *UNHCR Statistical Yearbook 2001* (Geneva: UNHCR, 2002).

United Nations High Commissioner for Refugees, *The State of the World's Refugees: Fifty Years of Humanitarian Action* (New York: Oxford University Press, 2000).

United Nations High Commissioner for Refugees, *The State of the World's Refugees 1997–8: A Humanitarian Agenda* (New York: Oxford University Press, 1997).

United Nations High Commissioner for Refugees, "Note on International Protection," A/AC/96/830 (September 7, 1994).

United Nations High Commissioner for Refugees, *Handbook on Procedures and Criteria for Determining Refugee Status under the 1951 Convention and the 1967 Protocol relating to the Status of Refugees*, HCR/IP/4/Eng/REV.1, Geneva, 1992.

US Committee for Refugees and Immigrants, *World Refugee Survey 2007* (Washington, DC: US Committee for Refugees and Immigrants, 2007).

US Committee for Refugees and Immigrants, *World Refugee Survey 2005* (Washington, DC: US Committee for Refugees and Immigrants, 2005).

US Committee for Refugees, *World Refugee Survey 2003* (Washington, DC: US Committee for Refugees, 2003).

US Committee for Refugees, *World Refugee Survey 2002* (Washington, DC: US Committee for Refugees, 2002).

US Committee for Refugees, *World Refugee Survey 2001* (Washington, DC: US Committee for Refugees, 2001).

US Department of Justice, Executive Office of Immigration Review, *FY 2006 Statistical Year Book* (February 2007).

US Immigration and Naturalization Service, *Asylum Adjudications: An Evolving Concept and Responsibility for the Immigration and Naturalization Service* (June and December, 1982).

Vattel, Emer de, *The Law of Nations or the Principles of Natural Law*, trans. Charles G. Fenwick (Geneva: Slatkine Reprints – Henry Dunant Institute, 1983).

Vedsted-Hansen, Jens, "Europe's Response to the Arrival of Asylum Seekers: Refugee Protection and Immigration Control," UNHCR New Issues in Refugee Research, Working Paper No. 6, May 1999.

Vermeulen, Ben, *et al.*, "Persecution by Third Parties," Research and Documentation Centre of the Ministry of Justice of the Netherlands, Nijmegen, May 1998.

"Veto Message, January 28, 1915," *Compilation of the Messages and Papers of the Presidents*, vol. 18 (New York: Bureau of National Literature, 1917), p. 8043.

Von Sternberg, Mark R., "The Plight of the Non-Combatant in Civil War and the New Criteria for Refugee Status," *International Journal of Refugee Law*, 9 (1997), pp. 169–95.

Walzer, Michael, *Spheres of Justice* (New York: Basic Books, 1983).

Walzer, Michael, "The Distribution of Membership" in Peter G. Brown and Henry Shue (eds.), *Boundaries: National Autonomy and Its Limits* (Totowa, NJ: Rowman & Littlefield, 1981).

Walzer, Michael, *Just and Unjust Wars* (New York: Basic Books, 1977).

Weidlich, Sabine, "First Instance Asylum Proceedings in Europe: Do Bona Fide Refugees Find Protection?," *Georgetown Immigration Law Journal*, 14 (2000), pp. 643–72.

Wendt, Alexander, *Social Theory of International Politics* (Cambridge University Press, 1999).

Wendt, Alexander, "Constructing International Politics," *International Security*, 20 (1995), pp. 71–81.

Wendt, Alexander, "Collective Identity Formation and the International State," *American Political Science Review*, 88 (1994), pp. 384–96.

Wijngaert, Christine Van den, *The Political Offence Exception to Extradition* (Boston, MA: Kluwer-Deventer, 1980).

Wolff, Christian, *Jus Gentium Methodo Scientifica Pertractatum*, trans. Joseph H. Drake (Oxford: Clarendon Press, 1934).

Yarnold, Barbara M., *Refugees Without Refuge: Formation and Failed Implementation of U.S. Political Asylum Policy in the 1980s* (Lanham, MD: University Press of America, 1990).

Zolberg, Aristide R., *A Nation By Design: Immigration Policy in the Fashioning of America* (Cambridge, MA: Harvard University Press, 2006).

Zolberg, Aristide R., Astri Suhrke, and Sergio Aguayo, *Escape From Violence* (New York: Oxford University Press, 1989).

Zucker, Norman and Naomi Flink Zucker, *Desperate Crossings* (Armonk, NY: M. E. Sharpe, 1996).

Court Cases

United States: Federal Courts

Aguilar-Solis v. *INS*, 168 F.3d 565 (1st Cir. 1999).

American Baptist Churches v. *Thornburgh*, 760 F. Supp. 796 (N.D. Cal. 1991).

Baballah v. *Ashcroft*, 367 F.3d 1067 (9th Cir. 2004).

Baballah v. *Ashcroft*, 335 F.3d 981 (9th Cir. 2003).

Baka v. *INS*, 963 F.2d 1376 (10th Cir. 1992).

Barrraza Rivera v. *INS*, 913 F.2d 1443 (9th Cir. 1990).

Begzatowski v. *INS*, 278 F.3d 665 (7th Cir. 2002).

Benslimane v. *Gonzales*, 430 F.3d 828 (7th Cir. 2005).

Canas-Segovia v. *INS*, 970 F.2d 599 (9th Cir. 1992).

Canas-Segovia v. *INS*, 902 F.2d 717 (9th Cir. 1990).

Castaneda-Castillo v. *Gonzales*, 488 F.3d 17 (1st Cir. 2007) (en banc).

Chanco v. *INS*, 82 F.3d 298 (9th Cir. 1996).

DeShaney v. *Winnebago County Department of Social Services*, 489 U.S. 189 (1989).

Desir v. *Ilchert*, 840 F.2d 723 (9th Cir. 1988).

Diallo v. *Ashcroft*, 381 F.3d 687 (7th Cir. 2004).

Dwomoh v. *Sava*, 696 F. Supp. 970 (S.D.N.Y. 1988).

Elias-Zacarias v. *INS*, 502 U.S. 478 (1992).

Elien v. *Ashcroft*, 364 F.3d 392 (1st Cir. 2004).

Escobar v. *Gonzales*, 417 F.3d 363 (3d Cir. 2005).

Fatin v. *INS*, 12 F.3d 1233 (3rd Cir. 1993).

Filartiga v. *Pena-Irala*, 630 F.2d 876 (2d Cir. 1980).

Fisher v. *INS*, 79 F.3d 955 (9th Cir. 1996) (en banc).

Foroglou v. *INS*, 170 F.3d 68 (1st Cir. 1999).

Ghaly v. *INS*, 58 F.3d 1425 (9th Cir. 1995).

Hernandez v. *Ashcroft*, 345 F.3d 824 (9th Cir. 2003).

Hernandez-Ortiz v. *INS*, 777 F.2d 509 (9th Cir. 1985).

Iao v. *Gonzales*, 400 F.3d 530 (7th Cir. 2005).

In re Estate of Marcos Human Rights Litig., 978 F.2d 493 (9th Cir. 1992).

INS v. *Aguirre-Aguirre*, 526 U.S. 415 (1999).

INS v. *Cardoza-Fonseca*, 480 U.S. 421 (1987).

INS v. *Doherty*, 502 U.S. 314 (1992).

Johnson v. *Eisentrager*, 339 U.S. 763 (1950).

Kadic v. *Karadzic*, 70 F.3d 232 (2d Cir. 1995).

Kaveh-Haghigy v. *INS*, 783 F.2d 1321 (9th Cir. 1986).

Kovac v. *INS*, 407 F.2d 102 (9th Cir. 1969).

Lazo-Majano v. *INS*, 813 F.2d 1432 (9th Cir. 1987).

Li v. *Ashcroft*, 356 F.3d 1153 (9th Cir. 2004) (en banc).

Li v. *Ashcroft*, 312 F.3d 1094 (9th Cir. 2002).

M.A. v. *INS*, 899 F.2d 304 (4th Cir. 1990).

Maldonado-Cruz v. *U.S. I.N.S.*, 883 F.2d 788 (9th Cir. 1989).

Mathews v. *Diaz*, 426 U.S. 67 (1976).

Matter of Doherty, 599 F. Supp. 270 (S.D.N.Y. 1984).

Mikhailevitch v. *INS*, 146 F.3d 384 (6th Cir. 1998).

Mitev v. *INS*, 67 F.3d 1325 (7th Cir. 1995).

Osaghae v. *INS*, 942 F.2d 1160 (7th Cir. 1991).

Perlera-Escobar v. *Executive Office for Immigration*, 894 F.2d 1292 (9th Cir. 1990).

Pitcherskaia v. *INS*, 118 F.3d 641 (9th Cir. 1997).

Prasad v. *INS*, 47 F.3d 336 (9th Cir. 1995).

Safaie v. *INS*, 25 F.3d 636 (8th Cir. 1994).

Sale v. *Haitian Centers Council*, 509 U.S. 155 (1993).

Schoenmetz v. *Ingham*, 949 F. Supp. 152 (W.D.N.Y. 1996).

Singh v. *Ilchert*, 801 F. Supp. 313 (N.D. Cal. 1992).

Skalak v. *INS*, 944 F.2d 364 (7th Cir. 1991).

Sosa v. *Alvarez-Machain*, 542 U.S. 692 (2004).

Tachiona v. *Mugabe*, 234 F. Supp. 2d 401 (S.D.N.Y. 2002).

Town of Castle Rock, Colo. v. *Gonzales*, 545 U.S. 748 (2005).

Ucelo-Gomez v. *Gonzales*, 464 F.3d 163 (2d Cir. 2006).

Valdiviezo-Galdamez v. *Attorney General*, 502 F.3d 285 (3d Cir. 2007).

Wang v. *Attorney General*, 423 F.3d 260 (3d Cir. 2005).

Xuncax v. *Gramajo*, 886 F. Supp. 162 (D. Mass. 1995).

Yadegar-Sargis v. *INS*, 297 F.3d 596 (7th Cir. 2002).

Zehatye v. *Gonzales*, 453 F.3d 1182 (9th Cir. 2006).

United States: Board of Immigration Appeals

In re H –, 21 I. & N. Dec. 337 (BIA 1996).

In re R – A –, 22 I. & N. Dec. 906 (BIA 1999).

In re S – P –, 21 I. & N. Dec. 486 (BIA 1996).

Matter of A – G –, 19 I. & N. Dec. 502 (BIA 1987).
Matter of Acosta, 19 I. & N. Dec. 211 (BIA 1985).
Matter of B –, 21 I. & N. Dec. 66 (BIA 1995).
Matter of Chang, 20 I. & N. Dec. 38 (BIA 1989).
Matter of Chen, 20 I. & N. Dec. 16 (BIA 1989).
Matter of Izatula, 20 I. & N. Dec. 149 (BIA 1990).
Matter of Kasinga, 21 I. & N. 357 (BIA 1996).
Matter of Maldonado-Cruz, 19 I. & N. Dec. 509 (BIA 1988).
Matter of R – , 20 I. & N. Dec. 621 (BIA 1992).
Matter of Rodriguez-Majano, 19 I & N Dec. 811 (BIA 1988).

Australia

Minister for Immigration and Multicultural Affairs v. *Abdi* [1999] 162 A.L.R.
    105 (Fed. Ct. Aust.).
Minister for Immigration and Multicultural Affairs v. *Khawar* [2002] H.C.A. 14.

Canada

Canada (Attorney General) v. *Ward* [1993] S.C.R. 689.
Cheung v. *Canada (Minister of Employment and Immigration)* [1993] 102
    D.L.R. (4th) 214 (Fed. Ct. App.).
Hinzman v. *Canada* [2007] F.C.A. 171.
Hinzman v. *Minister of Citizenship and Immigration* [2006] F.C. 420.
Isa v. *Secretary of State (Canada)* [1995] 28 Imm. L.R. (2d) 68 (Fed. Ct.).
MCI v. *Jessica Robyn Dolamore* [2001] F.T.C. 421.
Salibian v. *Canada* [1990] 3 F.C. 250.

United Kingdom

A v. *Secretary of State for the Home Department* [2003] EWCA Civ. 175 (CA).
Adan v. *Secretary of State for the Home Department* [1999] 1 A.C. 293.
Horvath v. *Secretary of State for the Home Department* [2001] 1 A.C. 489.
In re Meunier [1894] 2 Q.B. 415.
R. (Limbuela) v. *Secretary of State for the Home Department* [2004] Q.B. 1440.
R. v. *Immigration Appeal Tribunal and another, ex parte Shah* [1999] 2 A.C.
    629.

New Zealand

Refugee Appeal No. 71462/99 (September 27, 1999).
Refugee Appeal No. 71427/99, [2000] N.Z.A.R. 545 (August 16, 2000).
Refugee Appeal No. 74665/03 (July 7, 2004).

Index